MAKING THE VOID FRUITFUL

Making the Void Fruitful

Yeats as Spiritual Seeker and Petrarchan Lover

Patrick J. Keane

https://www.openbookpublishers.com

© 2021 Patrick J. Keane

ISBN Paperback: 9781800643208
ISBN Hardback: 9781800643215
ISBN Digital (PDF): 9781800643222
ISBN Digital ebook (epub): 9781800643239
ISBN Digital ebook (mobi): 9781800643246
ISBN XML: 9781800643253
DOI: 10.11647/OBP.0275

Cover image: William Blake, watercolor illustrations to Robert Blair's 'The Grave', object 15: 'The Reunion of the Soul & the Body' (1805), Wikimedia, https://commons.wikimedia.org/wiki/File:Illustrations_to_Robert_Blair%27s_The_Grave,_object_15_The_Reunion_of_the_Soul_%26_the_Body.jpg.

Cover design by Anna Gatti.

In Memoriam

Harold Bloom
(*1930–2019*)

I was the world in which I walked, and what I saw
And heard or felt came not but from myself;
And there I found myself more truly and more strange.

Wallace Stevens, 'Tea at the Palaz of Hoon'

Contents

Abbreviations

References to Yeats's work are abbreviated and parenthetically inserted. To avoid the clutter of citing page numbers for poems, all are referenced by title. However, to enable readers to date the versions quoted, the list in the Index of poems includes the page numbers in *The Variorum Edition of the Poems of W. B. Yeats*, ed. Peter Allt and Russell K. Alspach New York: Macmillan, 1957. For the convenience of most readers, I've cited the one-volume Allan Wade *Letters* rather than the definitive but less accessible multi-volume Oxford edition. In all quotes the italics are mine, unless otherwise stated.

Au	*Autobiographies*. London: Macmillan, 1955.
E&I	*Essays and Introductions*. London and New York: Macmillan, 1961.
Ex	*Explorations*. New York: Macmillan, 1963.
G-YL	*The Gonne-Yeats Letters 1893–1938: Always Your Friend*, ed. Anna MacBride White and A. Norman Jeffares. London: Norton, 1992.
L	*The Letters of W. B. Yeats*, ed. A. Wade. New York: Macmillan, 1955.
LDW	*Letters on Poetry from W. B. Yeats to Dorothy Wellesley*, intro. Kathleen Raine. New York and London: Oxford UP, 1964.
LTSM	*W. B. Yeats and T. Sturge Moore: Their Correspondence, 1901–1937*, ed. Ursula Bridge. New York: Oxford UP, 1953.
Mem	*Memoirs*, ed. Denis Donoghue. New York: Macmillan, 1972.
Myth	*Mythologies*. London and New York: Macmillan, 1959.
VP	*The Variorum Edition of the Poems of W. B. Yeats*, ed. Peter Allt and Russell K. Alspach New York: Macmillan, 1957.
Vis	(1925) *A Vision*. London: T. Werner Laurie, 1925
Vis	*A Vision* (1937 edition). London: Macmillan, 1962.

Acknowledgments

The first debt is to the legion of dedicated critics and scholars who have illuminated virtually every aspect of Yeats's life, thought, and poetry. I have more personal debts to friends: Gordon Boudreau, Barron Boyd, Warren and Susan Cheesman, John Cooke, Elizabeth Costello, Kate Costello-Sullivan, Dan Dowd, Helen Edelman, Laura Faul, Julie Grossman, Maureen Hanratty, Paul Johnston, David Lloyd, Roger Lund, Alicia Mathias, Don and Judy McCormack, Tracie Meisel, Julie Olin-Ammentorp, Tom Parker, John Rigney, Ann Ryan, Jonathan Schonsheck, Linda Schwartzberg, Bruce Shefrin, and Eleanor Souls.

The list of teachers and scholars who encouraged me along the way begins with Elizabeth Sewell, a visiting scholar from Oxford who praised an undergraduate essay on Keats I'd written at Fordham. W. Jackson Bate and John Unterecker both took the time to respond at length to letters and poems I inflicted on them back when I was in the army. At NYU, I found champions in Mack Rosenthal, David Erdman, and Conor Cruise O'Brien (then visiting Schweitzer Professor) who evolved from helpers to friends. Later, my work was amicably supported by transatlantic Romanticists Richard Gravil and Richard A. Brantley.

At the Yeats International Summer School, first as student, then as lecturer, I was encouraged by directors from T. R. Henn to John Kelly to Gus Martin (who once broke up a fist fight I was about to have with John Montague) to Ron Schuchard. During those years I was also helped by Northrop Frye, Erich Heller, M. H. Abrams, Richard Ellmann, and George Mills Harper. At Skidmore, I benefited from the friendship of Tom Lewis and the constant support of Bob Boyers, founder-editor of *Salmagundi*. Later friends and mentors have included three major critics, Harold Bloom (to whom the book is dedicated), Denis Donoghue, and Helen Vendler. My most recent debts are multiple. First, to Canadian novelist and critic Douglas Glover, who invited me to contribute to his splendid online magazine, *Numéro Cinc*, where some ideas presented here were test-run. Second and third, to Joe Hassett and Jay Rogoff, who kindly read portions of the manuscript; fourth to Warwick Gould, who corrected my initial confusion of the two figures who share the name Valentinus. Fifth, I'd like to thank the OBP team: Alison Gray, Anna Gatti, Melissa Purkiss and Alessandra Tosi. Sixth and finally, to Sandra Clarke, my cherished companion during the writing of this book and the ongoing COVID crisis.

This Muse-shadowed volume, dedicated to Harold Bloom, would have been, were it not for the discourtesy of death, dedicated to Helen Vendler, who read one entire version of the manuscript with her usual critical acumen and unrivaled love and knowledge of lyric poetry. Or to more intimate Muses in my life. I started to carry out the latter plan, a dedication prefaced by Yeats's 'Now must I these three praise—/ Three women that have wrought/ What joy is in my days,' only to realize that there were, inconveniently, four women.

But there is more than one way to be smitten. Along with many others of my generation, I have had a distant but cherished Muse for more than half a century: a woman whose face and eyes and incomparable voice I have long loved, and whose philosophy of life, political sanity, delight in books, sense of humor, and courageous equanimity in confronting a cruel disease, I have come to admire. So here's looking at you, Linda Ronstadt.

PART ONE

W. B. YEATS AS SPIRITUAL SEEKER

I shall find the dark grow luminous, the void fruitful, when I understand that I have nothing; that the ringers in the tower have appointed for the hymen of the soul a passing bell.

Yeats, *Per Amica Silentia Lunae*

The Soul. Seek out reality, leave things that seem.
The Heart. What, be a singer born and lack a theme?
The Soul. Isaiah's coal, what more can man desire?
The Heart. Struck dumb in the simplicity of fire!
The Soul. Look on that fire, salvation walks within.
The Heart. What theme had Homer but original sin?

Yeats, 'Vacillation,' VII

General Prologue:
The Thinking of the Body

Since the death of W. B. Yeats in 1939, something close to critical consensus has emerged. In W. H. Auden's image in his elegy, 'all' or at least most of the 'instruments agree' that Yeats was—as T. S. Eliot said in the first Yeats Memorial lecture, delivered a year after Auden's elegy—'the greatest poet of our time.' Attracted by the beauty and power of the poetry, readers have been seduced into engagement with the two subjects that, even more than aging and the Irish Troubles, dominate that poetry and most fascinated Yeats himself. First, his engagement, though it perplexed or repelled Eliot and Auden, with various forms of the occult; second, and more appealing to most readers, there is Yeats's fascination with his Muse, Maud Gonne, a romantic agony that resulted in the greatest body of love lyrics by a poet since the Laura-centered *Canzoniere* of Petrarch.

The older he got, the more Yeats revealed a mischievous sense of humor, a penchant for 'simplification through intensity,' and sexual candor, especially when it came to his most sacred subjects. In 1927, the sixty-two-year-old 'Mage' and Muse-poet announced in a letter, 'I am still of opinion that only two topics can be of the least interest to a serious and studious mind—sex and the dead' (L, 730). In thus reducing his very serious interest in the mingling of the erotic and occult, Yeats was exaggerating to amuse. He was writing, after all, to Olivia Shakespear, his first lover (half a lifetime ago, Yeats being then thirty-one), and later most intimate correspondent. But he was also serious. At the time he wrote this letter, his version of Sophocles' *Oedipus at Colonus* was being performed at the Abbey Theatre, and some inexplicable occurrences caused him to describe the play to Olivia as 'haunted.' He was also working, he told her, on new poems intended for the 1929 Fountain Press edition of *The Winding Stair*. He mentions specifically 'a new Tower poem "Sword and

 https://doi.org/10.11647/OBP.0275.18

Tower," which is a choice of rebirth rather than deliverance from birth,' a theme reflecting his interest in both reincarnation and the idea of Eternal Recurrence as presented by 'that strong enchanter, Nietzsche' (L, 379).

The eventual title of 'Sword and Tower' would be 'A Dialogue of Self and Soul,' for me not only the central poem in both editions of *The Winding Stair*, but, in many ways, the central poem in the Yeatsian canon, and one to which I devote considerable attention in the pages that follow. As he informed Olivia, 'I make my Japanese sword and its silk covering my symbol of life.' And he ended the letter, after referring to 'sex and the dead' as the 'only two topics' that mattered, by telling Olivia that these 'new poems interrupted' his rewriting of *A Vision*. 'Perhaps were that finished,' he concludes jocoseriously, 'I might find some third interest' (L, 730).

It would take a decade to rewrite his major occult text, first published in January 1926 (though dated 1925), a volume reflecting his own esoteric preoccupations but also based on years of collaboration with his wife in transcribing the 'automatic writing' at which she became adept. *A Vision* is dominated by Yeats's driving dynamic, in both his thought and his poetry: the perpetual tension between apparent opposites, or Blakean Contraries, the polarity between what he calls (always employing italics), the *primary* (or 'objective') and the *antithetical* (or 'subjective'). Many of his central concepts—this *primary-antithetical* dualism, Mask, Will, the Daimon, Unity of Being, the two-thousand-year cycles of history, the posthumous process labeled the Dreaming Back—receive their fullest exposition in *A Vision*. But they only come to life for most readers in the poetry and plays, where (in Wallace Stevens's phrase from 'Notes Toward a Supreme Fiction') these concepts become 'abstractions blooded.'

For that reason, even in Part One of the present volume, I will have little to say of *A Vision*, and even of 'The Phases of the Moon' (1918), the engaging poem in which Yeats foreshadows, synopsizes, and dramatizes the 'system' of lunar phases later elaborated in prose. Since I neglect it later (unfairly, since it is much more fun than *A Vision*), I will say here that 'The Phases of the Moon' takes the form of one of Yeats's many dialogue-poems—in this case, between Owen Aherne and Michael Robartes, Yeatsian personae who first appeared in the 'nineties.' They now reappear at night outside Yeats's Tower, an austere 'place set out for wisdom,' where, according to Robartes, the poet-mage, burning the midnight oil, 'seeks in book or manuscript/ What he shall never find.' At the end of the poem, mischievous Aherne, having been rehearsed in the details of the system by his companion, thinks to cross the Tower threshold and 'mutter' just enough of Robartes' 'mysterious wisdom' to torment Yeats, who would

> crack his wits
> Day after day; yet never find the meaning.
> *And then he laughed to think that what seemed hard*
> *Should be so simple—a bat rose from the hazels*
> *And circled round him with its squeaky cry,*
> *The light in the tower window was put out.*

But the last laugh may not be Aherne's. As I read that final line, the light in the tower window has been put out, not because Yeats the 'Apprentice Mage,' as R. S. Foster described him, has given up in frustration, but because Yeats the Poet has finished writing his poem, the creator having triumphed over the personae he himself created.

In keeping with that priority, the present volume engages in close reading of selected poems. Part One, examining Yeats as spiritual Seeker and Romantic Poet, focuses on the attractions of the Otherworld (whether Fairyland, Byzantium, or the Christian Heaven) and the gravitational pull of *this* world, with the focus always on the poetry itself, including Yeats's remarkable mastery of a wide range of lyric forms. Throughout, I attempt to unfold the latent processes of Yeats's thought. In engaging the creative tension between spiritual Seeker and Romantic Poet, which plays out in the polarity between soul and body (the latter 'embodied' in the most crucial debate-poems as Self or Heart), I follow Yeats, both in maintaining the polarity and in emphasizing the claims of the body, even in texts which, like the 'Byzantium' poems, seem soul directed.

Though Aherne is *primary* and Robartes *antithetical*, they agree, in conversing in 'The Phases of the Moon,' that 'All dreams of the soul/ End in a beautiful man's or woman's body' (62–64). By 1918, when he wrote these Robartes poems, Yeats's old 1890s character had become something close to a stand-in for the poet himself. The mask is dropped toward the end of the occult poem 'The Double Vision of Michael Robartes'— centered on a sphinx, a Buddha, and a girl dancing between them—that closes *The Wild Swans at Coole*. In the third and final movement, Robartes knows that he has 'seen at last/ That girl' he dreams of, and even if his dreams fly, they 'yet in flying fling into my meat/ A crazy juice that makes the pulses beat,' as though he had 'been undone/ By Homer's paragon/ Who never gave the burning town a thought.' That is to say, Yeats's Helen of Troy, Maud Gonne.

The very next poem, the opening and title poem of the volume following *The Wild Swans at Coole*, presents Robartes in dialogue with a dancer, though a girl based not on Maud Gonne—paramount among those 'beautiful women' who, like Helen of Troy, 'eat/ A crazy salad with their meat'—but, according to Yeats's wife, on Maud's daughter, Iseult. 'Michael Robartes and the Dancer,' a sophisticated variation on the *carpe diem* theme, emphasizes the body in so intriguing a way, at once seductive and chauvinistically off-putting, that it compels one to engage in the debate.

§

Robartes is 'He,' lecturing 'She,' that Iseult-like Dancer. He begins by asserting that 'Opinion is not worth a rush.' Two years earlier, in the 1916 poem 'The Dawn,' Yeats himself had wished to 'be—for no knowledge is worth a straw—/ Ignorant and wanton as the dawn': a parallel that helps, along with this dialogue-poem's urbane playfulness, to save 'Michael Robartes and the Dancer' from being a misogynistic tract against female education. 'Opinion,' this poem's first word; 'knowledge' in 'The Dawn'; accursed 'opinion' in 'A Prayer for my Daughter,' where Maud Gonne, 'because of her opinionated mind,' bartered away the Horn of Plenty 'For an old bellows full of angry wind': all are forms of what Yeats most dreaded: abstract, opinionated, disembodied thought.

That is the enemy targeted throughout by Robartes, who is, of course, patronizingly opinionated himself and something of an intellectual show-off. Drawing the Dancer's attention to a Renaissance painting featuring a dragon-slayer, a dragon, and a lady, he offers an allegorical interpretation of the altar-piece:

> the knight,
> Who grips his long spear so to push
> That dragon through the fading light,
> Loved the lady; and it's plain
> The half-dead dragon was her thought.

Though half-dead, draconic 'thought' is, like most dragons, difficult to permanently subdue; 'every morning [it] rose again/ And dug its claws and shrieked and fought.' This dragon of thought comes between not only the lady and the knight who desires her, but between the lady and her own physical beauty. Robartes informs the Dancer that the lady's 'lover thought' that if his beloved would but look in her mirror, she 'on the instant would grow wise': a carnal knowledge Yeats repeatedly terms 'the thinking of the body' (E&I, 292). This integrated, instinctive, intuitive form of thought is closely aligned with what Wordsworth called (in 'The Tables Turned') 'spontaneous wisdom,' in contrast to mere intellection and book-learning. Lovers, Robartes continues, 'turn green with rage/ At all that is not pictured' in the looking glass, which reflects of course only a woman's body, not 'her thought'—that abstract intellect the knight opposes with his own 'thought,' not to mention 'his long spear.'

The young Dancer, artistically aware of her own body, has a mind as well. Mingling seriousness and wit, she asks, 'May I not put myself to college?' Robartes responds with an imperative: 'Go pluck Athena by the hair.' The point of this reversal of those two dramatic moments in the *Iliad* (Books I and XXII), when the goddess of reason and wisdom, Athena, yanks impetuous Achilles by his hair, is that the young Dancer, perhaps all women, should seize wisdom boldly, physically, rather than submit passively to the sort of book-centered education Robartes claims destroys Unity of Being, cleaving body and mind:

> Go pluck Athena by the hair;
> For what mere book can grant a knowledge
> With an impassioned gravity
> Appropriate to that beating breast,
> That vigorous thigh, that dreaming eye?
> And may the Devil take the rest.

In his daughter-maddened misogynistic rant King Lear consigned to the Devil all that is below a woman's waist; here, what is dismissed as the damnable 'rest' is what is above the neck. The Dancer, perhaps teasing, perhaps annoyed, persists: 'And must no beautiful woman be/ Learned like a man?' In 'real' as opposed to fictive life, Yeats encouraged Iseult's study of Dante, even of Sanskrit. But since, in the poem, He and She are discussing art, Robartes—who believes as Yeats did that 'all art is sensuous,' and that 'no painting could move us at all, if our thought did not rush out to the edges of our flesh' (E&I, 293, 292)—turns to the last of the great sixteenth-century Venetian painters who succeeded in unifying mind and body, intellect and the senses: 'Paul Veronese/ And all his sacred company/ Imagined bodies all their days [...] /For proud, soft, ceremonious proof/ That all must come to sight and touch.'

Yeats is putting in his alter ego's mouth that 'doctrine of Nietzsche' he himself had quoted in his 1912 Introduction to Tagore's *Gitanjali* 'that we must not believe in the moral or intellectual beauty which does not sooner or later impress itself upon physical things' (E&I, 389). Robartes continues his obviously Yeatsian art lesson on the physical embodiment of the spiritual by turning to Michelangelo's Sistine Chapel paintings, and his 'Morning' and 'Night' Medici Chapel sculptures, which 'disclose/ How sinew that has been pulled tight,/ Or it may be loosened in repose,/ Can rule by supernatural right/ Yet be but sinew.' Repeating hearsay, the Dancer responds, playfully but also reflecting conventional pieties learned by rote at home, in church, and in school: 'I have heard said/ There is great danger in the body.'

Faced with religious admonitions about the sinful flesh, Robartes cunningly gets God on his side, posing a rhetorical question: 'Did God in portioning wine and bread/ Give man his thought or his mere body?' Yeats had recently, in a 1916 essay, answered that question: 'The Deity gives us not His thought or His convictions but His flesh and blood' (E&I, 235). Jesus portioned out in the Eucharist what was, in himself, integrated (what Yeats elsewhere praises as 'blood, imagination, intellect running together'). This Donne-like mixture of sacramental seriousness, sex, and wit is too much for the Dancer. She cries out, 'My wretched dragon is perplexed.' As is 'plain,' that dragon is 'her thought.' Dryden famously said of Donne that, even in his 'amorous verses,' he 'affects the metaphysics' and '*perplexes* the minds of the fair sex with nice speculations of philosophy'; and, as Keats reminds us, imagination can be hindered when 'the dull brain *perplexes* and retards.'[1] Such echoes remind us that, like Pope's, Yeats's is a poetry of allusion.

In the poem's final turn, Robartes, having dismissed book-learning as nonchalantly as had early Wordsworth, cites an abstruse text—as

---

1   Dryden, *A Discourse Concerning the Original and Progress of Satire* (1693). Keats, 'Ode to a Nightingale.'

Yeats will have his woman do in 'Chosen' and as he himself does in 'For Anne Gregory.' In having him turn to a book to prove his argument, Yeats reminds us that Robartes is, after all, an occultist, and a pedantic one at that. And yet, Robartes' position, though mildly parodied, is, of course, Yeats's as well: an argument for a Unity of Being in which (as in the conclusion of 'Among School Children') 'the body is not bruised to pleasure soul,' but incorporates soul, achieving a secular blessedness which is 'uncomposite,' rather than composed of divided parts. Half tongue-in-cheek, but only half, Robartes asserts that he has 'principles to prove me right':

> It follows from this Latin text
> That blest souls are not composite,
> And that all beautiful women may
> Live in uncomposite blessedness,
> And lead us to the like; if they
> Will banish every thought, unless
> The lineaments that please their view
> When the long looking-glass is full,
> Even from the foot-sole think it too.

'And lead *us to the like.*' That is the final saving grace in Robartes' playful but apt if overbearing lecture on 'the thinking of the body': the one form of thought he endorses, but the only one that unites rather than divides the normally denigrated body and privileged soul. Robartes' pivotal conjunction, 'unless,' anticipates its more famous appearance in 'Sailing to Byzantium,' where, reversing Robartes' emphasis on the body, 'an aged man is but a paltry thing,' an old scarecrow, 'unless/ Soul clap its hands and sing' as the tattered body decays. Though the Latin text Robartes cites may be Marsilio Ficino's Latin translation of Plotinus, Yeats seems to be thinking more of John Donne, whose work he had been studying for a half-dozen years before he drafted this poem. Writing to H. J. C. Grierson to thank him for the gift of his 1912 edition of Donne (which 'has given me and shall give me I think more pleasure than any other book I can imagine'), Yeats emphasized the mixture, in Donne's poetry, of pedantry and sexuality, 'the rock and the loam of his Eden.' The 'more precise and learned the thought the greater the beauty, the passion; the intricacies and subtleties of his imagination are the lengths and depths of the furrow made by his passion' (L, 570).

In 'Michael Robartes and the Dancer,' Yeats may be thinking, as Seamus Heaney was in a moving late poem, of Donne's lines, in 'The Ecstasy' (71–72), on the soul's need to express itself through the body: 'Love's mysteries in souls do grow,/ But yet the body is his book.'[2] Like Yeats's poem, 'The Ecstasy' is addressed to a woman and written in alternately rhymed tetrameters, but the conclusion of 'Michael Robartes and the Dancer' recalls in particular the elegiac lines on Elizabeth Drury, the daughter of Donne's patron, dead at fifteen: 'She of whose soule,' if we may describe it as gold, 'Her body was th'Electrum.' Her 'pure and eloquent blood/ Spoke in her cheeks and so distinctly wrought/ That one might almost say, her body thought.'[3]

That thinking of the body is a pre-eminent Yeatsian ideal, quarried from Blake, Nietzsche, and, most recently, Donne. Responding to Robartes, the Dancer concludes: 'They say such different things at school,' a line recalling the less playful observation made a decade and a half earlier by Maud Gonne's sister in 'Adam's Curse': 'To be born a woman is to know—/ Although they do not talk of it at school—/ That we must labour to be beautiful.'

§

If 'All dreams of the soul/ End in a beautiful man's or woman's body,' many of Yeats's dreams, spiritual and erotic, began and ended with that woman whose 'face and body had the beauty' and nobility of a classical 'goddess' (Mem, 40). The second part of this book, subtitled 'Love's Labyrinth,' explores the 'great labyrinth' that *was* Maud Gonne, Yeats's Homeric paragon. Though I discuss the actual woman who inspired Yeats, I will, again, be occupied primarily with the poems produced by that obsessive and unrequited love: bittersweet fruit which were also,

---

2   Used as epigraph to 'Chanson D'Aventure,' Heaney's love poem to his wife in the immediate aftermath of his 2006 stroke. The opening section, set in the ambulance, ends: 'we might, O my love, have quoted Donne/ On love on hold, body and soul apart.'

3   Lines embedded in *The Second Anniversary*, 'Of the Progress of the Soul,' 241–46. Coleridge, the one Romantic who appreciated Donne's metaphysical poetry (wreathing 'iron' into 'true love-knots' in 'Wit's forge'), may echo those final lines in the conclusion of 'Phantom,' his dream-vision of the woman he loved, Sara Hutchinson: 'She, she herself and only she/ Shone through her body visibly.' Yeats quoted the Coleridge poem in full in *Per Amica Silentia Lunae* (Myth, 347).

in Maud Gonne's own striking and gender-bending description in 1911, 'children' *she* had 'fathered' and *he* 'mothered'—and of whom she said, 'our children had wings' (G-YL, 302).

This second section of the book offers a guide to readers navigating the poetry Yeats wrote to and about her. Not since Keats and Fanny Brawne and the Brownings has there been a poetic love affair this engaging. The difference is that the poetry inspired by Maud Gonne is, as Joseph Hassett, author of *W. B. Yeats and His Muses*, has said, 'the most sustained and fully developed tribute to a Muse in the history of literature in English.' Conceding Yeats's greatness as an 'arch-poet,' Harold Bloom, resistant to aspects of Yeats's thought, acquiesces when it comes to Yeats as a love poet, doubting that 'any poet of our century enters into competition here with him.'

As many have lamented (Bloom prominent among them), the number of common or general readers of demanding literature, and of poetry in particular, has steadily diminished, becoming, to a degree unimagined by Milton, 'fit audience though few.' But readers are also human beings, and as such retain interest in experiences in any way spiritual, and in human love, with all its mingling of ecstasy and anguish. No one has exceeded Yeats in bringing these perennial subjects to vivid, aesthetic life through the power and beauty of poetry. In lieu of that vanishing common reader, I hope to interest readers intrigued, as I am, by two phenomena: first, Yeats's vacillation in engaging the spiritual, the pull between Body (or Heart) and Soul, between flesh and spirit and second, the related tensions in the Gonne-Yeats relationship—a relationship at once erotic and spiritual, for Yeats was writing in the Petrarchan tradition and his Muse was both aloof and herself an occultist.

Serious Yeatsians will find here much that is new, and even the familiar presented in unexpected ways. One surprise involves a modest proposal I make about Yeats's intended final poem. His 'last word,' the little lyric titled 'Politics' but about love, is, I suggest, yet another poem about Maud Gonne—a 'last kiss given to the void' (LTSM, 154). Part Two now seems to me a companion piece to a short book written half a lifetime ago: *A Wild Civility: Interactions in the Poetry and Thought of Robert Graves*. There, I addressed the conflict, at least on Graves's part, with Yeats, his obvious and more successful rival among twentieth-century poets devoted to a lunar Muse. The conflict this time is between what

Yeats hoped for and what his Muse felt she could offer, resulting in the sublimation of thwarted desire into poetry: 'all I had rhymed of that monstrous thing/ Returned and yet unrequited love.' That was in 1915, in 'Presences,' a poem in which Maud appears as a 'queen,' a woman who relished her role as Muse to a great poet, who cared for 'Willie' but did not love him as he did her, and who never fully understood his plans for them, or for Ireland.

In the same year he wrote 'Presences,' the poet anticipated books like this one, and indeed the labors of the whole Yeats industry. In 'The Scholars,' in the course of mocking passionless pedants laboring over the codices of 'their Catullus,' including those poems of 'hate and love' inspired by 'Lesbia,' Yeats slips in a reference to his own plight as a poet of passionate but tormented and often unhappy love. The 'scholars' are respectable old baldpates who, forgetful of their own youthful sins, 'cough in ink' as they

> Edit and annotate the lines
> That young men, tossing on their beds,
> Rhymed out in love's despair
> To flatter beauty's ignorant ear.

Maud Gonne was hardly 'ignorant,' but, contemplating the mysteriously 'vague look' in her eyes, Yeats, writing privately between 1915 and 1917, acknowledges that he 'often wondered at its meaning—the wisdom that must surely accompany its symbol, her beauty, or lack of any thought' (Mem, 60). It would seem that the lack of 'thought' and 'knowledge' advocated two or three years later as an ideal for 'beautiful women' in 'Michael Robartes and the Dancer' is not always to be desired. And yet Yeats was also, like Robartes, aware of a potentially negative consequence of knowledge. If it were actually true, as he momentarily imagined in the poem 'Words,' that 'My darling understands it all'—that Maud Gonne fully comprehended his love for her, his poetry, and his vision for Ireland—who 'can say/ What would have shaken from the sieve?/ I might have thrown poor words away/ And been content to live.'

1. Introduction: Bodily Decrepitude and the Imagination

Contemplating the Irish poet's occultism, W. H. Auden puzzled publicly, 'How on earth, we wonder, could a man of Yeats's gifts take such nonsense seriously?' However sympathetic I may be personally to that famous, or infamous, rhetorical question, or to William York Tindall's less well-known but equally memorable dismissal of the poet's collaboration with his wife in the automatic writing that culminated in *A Vision*—'a little seems too much, his business none of ours'—the time is long since past when serious readers of Yeats could cavalierly dismiss the intensity of his imaginative, intellectual, and spiritual engagement in the supernatural.[1] Far removed from the late nineteenth-century context of recoil from increasing materialism and scientific skepticism, a recoil that flowered in a notably widespread Victorian interest in spiritualism, sophisticated readers have tended to be condescendingly tolerant of, even as they were enchanted by, the evocations of Fairyland by the poet of the Celtic Twilight (whose Irishness only intensified the contrast between Celtic imagination and British empiricism), and either puzzled or put off by his early and sustained interest in magic and the occult.

At the same time, Yeats's literally enchanting early fairy-poem 'The Stolen Child' remains for many readers the gateway to his later, more complex quests for an Otherworld, shadowed by an awareness of the potential human cost. There is abundant evidence that the interest in magic, the occult, and even fairies is back in fashion. Not to mention the Harry Potter books, there is the almost equally astonishing success of Susanna Clarke's thousand-page novel of magicians in Regency

---

1   Auden, 'Yeats as an Example' (1948), in Hall and Steinmann, 345. W. Y. Tindall, *W. B. Yeats*, 27.

   https://doi.org/10.11647/OBP.0275.01

England, *Jonathan Strange and Mr. Norell*, the 2004 *Time Magazine* Book of the Year, with over four million copies sold. The novel's copiously footnoted backstory features a race of malicious fairies who kidnap mortals, transporting their unhappy victims to 'Other Lands' of 'Losthope': Yeats's 'The Stolen Child' writ large.

That resonance and the magic of Yeats's language explain why one can still admire and love his poetry while acknowledging what Auden, referring not only to Yeats's occultism and interest in fairies but to his sexual dalliances in old age, called his 'silliness.' We will get to the late sexuality. But it is no longer possible, if it ever was, to deny the centrality to his life and work as a poet and playwright of Yeats's engagement, early and late, in the supernatural—especially in the wake of George Mills Harper's work on the now multi-volume *Vision* papers, on the Golden Dawn, and on Yeats's engagement in the occult in general, pioneering studies continued by his daughter, Meg. Their work, and that of others, including Kathleen Raine and F. A. C. Wilson, Warwick Gould and Deirdre Toomey, was buttressed by the publication of the multi-volume Oxford edition of Yeats's letters, and by two massive and deeply researched biographies: Ann Saddlemyer's life of Mrs. Yeats, *Becoming George* (2002), and 'The Apprentice Mage,' the first volume (1997) of R. S. Foster's magisterial *W. B. Yeats: A Life*.[2]

Yeats's early interest in Theosophy and Hermeticism, which led to decades of membership in the Order of the Golden Dawn, was always mixed, under the auspices of Helena Blavatsky and her emissary to Dublin, Mohini Chatterjee, with Eastern mysticism—an interest to which Yeats returned in his final years. And Yeats retained a lifelong fascination with the revelations that emerged from his wife's automatic writing— for which, to her own surprise, George Yeats, who had initially turned to it to stimulate the flagging interest of her new and troubled husband,

---

2   The collaboration between George and Yeats is also discussed by Margaret Mills Harper in *Wisdom of Two* (2006). That same year, Harper laid out four 'quadrants' of Yeats's esoteric interest: Theosophy; Magic; Spiritualism; and Hindu mysticism. In her endnotes, she supplies a concise guide to scholarly work on the subject, not least that of her father, a mentor and friend to me as well. Harper, 'Yeats and the Occult,' in Howes and Kelly, 144–66. See also Wayne Chapman's '"Something Intended, Complete": Major Work on Yeats, Past, Present, and to Come,' the splendid introductory chapter to *Yeats, Philosophy and the Occult*, ed. Matthew Gibson and Neil Mann (2016). This volume also contains Mann's lengthy (64-page) and important essay, 'W. B. Yeats, Dream, Vision, and the Dead.'

found she had a genuine gift. Whether or not that marriage—which was to prove so crucial to his later, and greatest, creativity—would take place at all hung on the shifting indications of their astrological charts. In short, to revert to Auden's glib dismissal, Yeats 'took such nonsense' very 'seriously' indeed. It all becomes considerably less nonsensical when we understand that his inextricable, and primary, interest, amid all the esoterica, remained his poetry. For Yeats, Seamus Heaney rightly insisted, 'True poetry had to be the speech of the whole man. It was not sufficient that it be the artful expression of daylight opinion and conviction; it had to emerge from a deeper consciousness of things and, in the words of his friend Arthur Symons, be the voice of "the mystery which lies all about us, out of which we have come and into which we shall return".'[3]

It is not my purpose, in this first of a two-part exploration, to engage in a sustained contemplation of Yeats and the occult. His wife's 'Communicators' told Yeats, or so he claimed, 'we have come to bring you metaphors for poetry' (Vis, 8); my principal interest is in that poetry, and in the various ways in which the tension plays out between this world and the other, the Here and the There, the *antithetical* and the *primary*. Second only to the poetry, I emphasize, following Yeats, the importance he assigns, even in pursuit of the spiritual, to the physical senses, to the body, and to sexual desire.

Two formulations illuminate my dual emphasis, and in fact link the two parts of the present book. The first is from Graham Hough, from his *The Mystery Religion of W. B. Yeats*. Combining three of his 1983 lectures with a fourth chapter on *A Vision*, Hough, in this concise book offers an illuminating introduction to the subject. But while he provides a humane counterweight to crabbed studies threatening to bury Yeats in esoteric commentary, Hough, though a fine reader, discusses very few of the poems, and none at length. Among many insights, Hough perceptively observes of Yeats: 'His aim was to redeem passion, not to transcend it, and a beatitude that passed beyond the bounds of earthly love could not be his ideal goal.'[4]

---

3   Heaney, 'William Butler Yeats,' *Field Day*, II. 783–90. Heaney cites (784) Symons's *Symbolist Movement in Literature* (1899), a book that meant as much to T. S. Eliot as it did to Yeats.

4   *The Mystery Religion of W. B. Yeats*, 119.

The second formulation is from Harold Bloom, contrasting Yeats's mentor William Blake with 'the Anglo-Irish Archpoet' posing as an old codger singing to 'maid or hag:/ *I carry the sun in a golden cup,/ The moon in a silver bag.*' Aware that he was on the threshold of death, Bloom was haunted, as Yeats was, by Blake's questions (in the motto to the *Book of Thel*), 'Can Wisdom be put in a silver rod?/ Or Love in a golden bowl?'[5] Both Blake and Yeats were echoing Ecclesiastes 12, where we are told that even before the body breaks down (before the 'silver cord be loosed, or the golden bowl be broken'), 'desire shall fail,' and soon, 'the dust return to the earth as it was.'

Those lines are recalled by T. S. Eliot in his Dantean encounter with the 'familiar compound ghost' (essentially that of the recently deceased Yeats) in 'Little Gidding,' the last and greatest of *Four Quartets*. In the most dramatic section of the poem, Eliot puts in the breathless mouth of the ghost inexorable and comfortless wisdom fusing language of Ecclesiastes and Yeats with, surprisingly, that of Shelley, a poet loved by Yeats but usually despised by Eliot:

> Let me disclose the gifts reserved for age
>   To set a crown upon your lifetime's effort.
>   First, the cold friction of expiring sense
> Without enchantment, offering no promise
>   But bitter tastelessness of shadow fruit
>   As body and soul begin to fall asunder. (II, 129–34)[6]

The ghost's grim disclosure is cast in an unrhymed replica of the *terza rima* pioneered by Dante, employed once and magnificently by Yeats (in 'Cuchulain Comforted'), and in the ironically titled *The Triumph of Life* (the one Shelley poem Eliot admired). The dark wisdom and nobility of these lines justify Eliot's audacious act of ventriloquism in using Yeats's own ghost to refute the living poet's emphasis, especially as he aged, on the body. Since that emphasis informs much of Yeats's poetry,

---

5   Bloom, *Possessed by Memory*, 192. The book was published posthumously.
6   The Shelley parallel is discussed below. Eliot's echoes of 'Vacillation,' 'Man and the Echo,' and 'Cuchulain Comforted,' in the ghost-encounter confirm that the spirit is primarily that of Yeats, as Eliot acknowledged in letters. See Gardner, 64–67, and Diggory, 115–17. That Swift is also part of the compound ghost reaffirms Yeats's presence; Eliot's reference to 'lacerating laughter at what ceases to amuse' echoes Yeats's poem 'Swift's Epitaph,' and nods toward the presence of Swift's own ghost in Yeats's *The Words upon the Window-pane*. For Eliot's responses to Yeats over the years, evolving from patronizingly dismissive to reserved but respectful to largely admiring, see Donoghue, 'Three Presences: Yeats, Pound, Eliot,' 563–82.

even beyond the love poems to and about Maud Gonne; and since the emphasis becomes more pronounced as he ages and the body fails, I've chosen, violating chronology, to address the issue early on, as Yeats does in one of his best-known poems, 'Sailing to Byzantium':

> An aged man is but a paltry thing,
> A tattered coat upon a stick, unless
> Soul clap its hands and sing, and louder sing
> For every tatter in its mortal dress,
> Nor is there singing school but studying
> Monuments of its own magnificence;
> And therefore I have sailed the seas and come
> To the holy city of Byzantium.

Though the aged man is ostensibly sailing in quest of a spiritual life to replace that of the deteriorating body, Yeats's Byzantium was not only a 'holy city,' but a city of imagination and art, aesthetic monuments of soul's magnificence. In this stanza, Yeats combines two passages from Blake, both emphasized in Yeats's Preface to his and Edwin Ellis's 1893 edition of Blake's *Works*. The tactile image of the soul clapping its hands and singing, and singing louder for every tatter in the body's mortal dress, recalls Blake's vision of his beloved brother Robert's liberated soul at the moment of his death in 1787. As Yeats noted, Blake, refusing to leave Robert's bedside, 'had seen his brother's spirit ascending and clapping its hands for joy.' Four months before his own death forty years later at the biblical age of seventy, Blake, who had been ill, began a letter to a friend: 'I have been very near the Gates of Death & have returned very weak & an old man feeble & tottering, but not in Spirit & Life [,] not in the Real Man [,] The Imagination which Liveth for Ever. In that I am stronger & stronger as this Foolish Body decays.'[7]

That inverse ratio, imagination waxing as body wanes, exemplified in 'Sailing to Byzantium,' was stressed three years earlier in his 1923 Nobel Prize acceptance speech. Examining the Nobel medal, depicting a young man listening to a Muse, Yeats thought, 'I was good-looking once like that young man, but my unpractised verse was full of infirmity, my Muse old as it were; and now I am old and rheumatic, and nothing to look at, but my Muse is young. I am even persuaded that she is like those Angels in Swedenborg's vision and moves perpetually "towards the day-spring

---

7   Yeats, Preface to Blake's *Works*. The letter, dated 12 August 1827, was written to George Cumberland.

of her youth"' (Au, 541). That persuasion seems demonstrated in the trajectory of his career as a whole, Yeats being prominent among lyric poets whose imaginative power survived into advanced age. 'The poetry of later years is a small, select genre. Yeats is no doubt its master.'[8] One of his masterpieces, 'Cuchulain Comforted,' was written virtually on his deathbed. But it might not have been so had it not been for something even more unseemly than Yeats's occult preoccupations: the famous or infamous Steinach sexual rejuvenation operation.

§

After the pinnacles of *The Tower* (1928) and the two editions of *The Winding Stair* (1929, 1933), there had been a falling off in imaginative power, which Yeats associated with a parallel decline in sexual energy. As his life and poetry demonstrate, Yeats was always at least as painfully aware as Harold Bloom and T. S. Eliot of fleshly limitations and mutability, of 'bodily decrepitude.' Now, with imagination failing, he knew precisely what Blake meant by a 'Foolish Body.' In the opening lines of 'The Tower,' the lines immediately following 'Sailing to Byzantium,' Yeats cried out, 'What shall I do with this absurdity—/ O heart, O troubled heart—this caricature,/ Decrepit age that has been tied to me/ As to a dog's tail?' But that was in 1925/26, when he was at the height of his imaginative powers. Thus, he can boldly claim (recalling Blake's assertion that 'I am stronger & stronger as this Foolish Body decays'), that 'Never had I more/ Excited, passionate, fantastical/ Imagination, nor an eye and ear/ That more expected the impossible.' He has the strength to be playful even about the prospect of succumbing utterly to his pre-eminent spiritual guides and to the dreaded 'abstract':

> It seems that I must bid the Muse go pack,
> Choose Plato and Plotinus for a friend
> Until imagination, ear and eye,
> Can be content with argument and deal
> In abstract things; or be derided by
> A sort of battered kettle at the heel.

---

8   Peter Filkins, 'A Reckoning,' 225. A remark made in the course of a review of the 2020 volume, *So Forth*, by Rosanna Warren, a poet working, at the age of sixty-seven, at the height of her powers.

In the late 1920s, bodily decrepitude was largely though not completely compensated for by the imaginative power so exuberantly on display in this title poem and elsewhere in *The Tower*. By the mid-1930s, however, Yeats, his Muse gone packing, felt the full weight of Shelley's lines on sexual decay and impotence, in the long *terza rima* poem sardonically titled *The Triumph of Life*—a masterpiece interrupted by Shelley's death by water, drowned at the age of twenty-nine. Eliot felt the desolate power of those lines as well, registered, as I've already suggested, in what he called in 'Little Gidding,' the 'bitter tastelessness of shadow fruit/ As body and soul begin to fall asunder.'

Eliot's glib dismissal of Shelley (his emotions adolescent, 'his ideas repellent') had a notable exception. In one of his 1932/33 Norton lectures, Eliot conceded that 'in his last, and to my mind greatest though unfinished poem, *The Triumph of Life*, there is evidence not only of better writing than in any previous long poem, but of greater wisdom.' As revealed, I believe, by those lines earlier quoted from 'Little Gidding,' Eliot remained impressed by the terrifying passage in which Shelley dramatizes the 'destruction' and 'desolation' attending sexual love, in particular, the dance of death of still sex-tormented 'Old men, and women,' who 'shake their grey hairs,' straining 'with limbs decayed/ Limping to reach the light which leaves them still/ Farther behind and deeper in the shade,' surrounded by 'impotence' and 'ghastly shadows' as they sink 'in the dust whence they arose.'[9]

Having experienced symptoms of premature impotence at sixty, a condition all but acknowledged in 'Sailing to Byzantium,' Yeats, convinced that sexual potency and imaginative creativity were connected, underwent in 1934 the famous Steinach operation, as had Freud before him. Yeats's surgery was performed by the celebrated sexologist Norman Haire, who, eager to test its efficacy, immediately introduced Yeats to the exotically beautiful and accomplished Ethel Mannin, having suggested that she dress provocatively for the occasion. Though his erectile dysfunction persisted, the psychological result was what Yeats called his 'second puberty,' a phrase lifted a half-century

---

9   *The Triumph of Life*, 143–74. Though Eliot's shallow comments on Shelley were demolished by C. S. Lewis, in his brilliant 'Dryden, Shelley, and Mr. Eliot,' Eliot's dismissal of Shelley, reinforced by F. R. Leavis, had lasting influence, explaining much, though not all, of Bloom's antipathy to Eliot.

later by Richard Ellmann in his 1984 Library of Congress lecture, 'W. B. Yeats's Second Puberty' (published in 1986).

The poet himself insisted that the vasoligature 'revived my creative power,' which may be demonstrated in the outburst of poetry in his final five years. Minor surgery, even if it became in some Dublin circles the occasion of jokes, seems a small price to pay if it helped in any way to produce poems like the perhaps appropriately titled sequence, 'Supernatural Songs,' 'Lapis Lazuli,' the matched poems 'An Acre of Grass' and 'What Then?,' 'The Municipal Gallery Revisited,' 'Cuchulain Comforted,' 'News for the Delphic Oracle,' 'Long-legged Fly,' 'A Bronze Head,' 'Man and the Echo,' 'The Circus Animals' Desertion,' 'Politics,'' and at least the opening and final movements of the flawed 'Under Ben Bulben.' The operation, Yeats continued, 'revived also sexual desire; and that in all likelihood will last me until I die.'[10]

Whatever Yeats's actual capacity, his sexual 'desire' did not fade in his final years. 'Those Dancing Days Are Gone' (1930), the pre-Steinach poem Bloom cites, insists that even a man who 'leans upon a stick' may 'sing, and sing until he drop,/ Whether to maid or hag:/ *I carry the sun in a golden cup,/ The moon in a silver bag.*' It takes a great deal to bring Harold Bloom and T. S. Eliot into agreement; but on this aspect of Yeats, the old man's preoccupation with sex, they concur. Though he does not turn to his bête noir Eliot for support, nor to Shelley, Bloom writes that Yeats, in 'swerving' from his other Romantic precursor, Blake, 'renders as triumph what Blake regards as a rhetorical question ['Can Wisdom be put in a silver rod?/ Or Love in a golden bowl?'] with an implied answer in the negative mode.' For Yeats, Bloom continues, 'the wisdom of the body had to be sufficient, despite all his occult yearnings. Blake finds a great unwisdom in all those who seek to reason with the loins. D. H. Lawrence shares Yeats's heroic vitalism, but for Blake, more is required than sexual exaltation if we are to become fully human.'[11]

That is true, and yet Yeats, trying to 'put all into a phrase' in his final letter, written in the month he died, insisted, 'Man can embody truth but

---

10   Diana Wyndham offers a psychological analysis in 'Versemaking and Lovemaking,' 25–50. On Haire's near-solicitation, see Ethel Mannin, *Privileged Spectator*, 80–81.

11   *Possessed by Memory*, 193. Despite his hostility to Eliot, Bloom excepted 'Little Gidding,' which he admired, just as Eliot, despite his general hostility to Shelley, admired *The Triumph of Life*.

he cannot know it.' He continued, allying himself with *both* the *primary* and the *antithetical* in the struggle against a shared enemy: 'The abstract is not life and everywhere draws out its contradictions. You can refute Hegel but not the Saint or the Song of Sixpence' (L, 922). Yeats rejects all those 'thoughts men think in the mind alone,' since he that 'sings a lasting song/ Thinks in a marrow-bone.' That is from a poem, 'A Prayer for Old Age,' written in 1934, in the wake of the Steinach operation: a prayer that he 'may seem, though I die old,/ A foolish, passionate man.' 'Seem' is a crucial qualifier, though some, even his friend and former fellow-Senator Oliver St. John Gogarty (Joyce's Buck Mulligan), thought he'd become a sex-obsessed fool confusing himself with his own 'Wild Old Wicked Man' (1937), 'mad about women' and 'a young man in the dark.'

But Yeats, unwilling to divorce imagination from the senses, often cited Blake as an ally in repudiating the abstract in favor of embodied wisdom. In 'The Thinking of the Body,' he insists that 'art bids us touch and taste and hear and see the world, and shrinks from what Blake calls mathematic form, from every abstract thing, from all that is of the brain only, from all that is not a fountain jetting from the entire hopes, memories and emotions of the body' (E&I, 292–93). Blake, for whom the body lacking 'The Imagination' is 'Foolish,' surrounded his Laocoön engraving with visionary axioms: 'The Eternal Body of Man is The IMAGINATION,' and 'Art can never exist without Naked Beauty displayed.'[12]

In the magnificent third and final movement of 'The Tower,' writing his 'will' in vital, pulsing trimeters, Yeats declares his 'faith' by mocking 'Plotinus' thought' and crying 'in Plato's teeth.' Instead, he tells us, even amid 'the wreck of body,/ Slow decay of blood,' 'dull decrepitude,' or worse:

> I have prepared my peace
> With learned Italian things
> And the proud stones of Greece,
> Poet's imaginings
> And memories of love,
> Memories of the words of women.

---

12   *The Poetry and Prose of William Blake,* 271–72.

And at the end, there is still a vestige of the natural world, faint but audible: 'a bird's sleepy cry/ Among the deepening shades.'

At the opposite pole, the mystical ideal has never been more austerely expressed than by St. John of the Cross: 'the soul cannot be possessed of the divine union until it has divested itself of the love of created things.' T. S. Eliot employed the statement as an epigraph to *Sweeney Agonistes* (a performance of which Yeats attended on 16 December 1934). When challenged by a friend who regarded the sentiment expressed in the epigraph 'with horror,' Eliot replied that 'for people seriously engaged in pursuing the Way of Contemplation,' and 'read in relation to that way, the doctrine is fundamentally true.'[13] For Yeats, in stark, or, rather, 'fruitful' contrast, the 'Way' of St. John and of Eliot, 'a sanctity of the cell and of the scourge,' was the most perverse form of the *primary*, 'objective' tendency. 'What is this God,' he asked in a cancelled note to his play *Calvary*, 'for whom He [Christ] taught the saints to lacerate their bodies, to starve and exterminate themselves, but the spiritual objective?' Since 'the Renaissance the writings of the European saints [...] has ceased to hold our attention.' We know that we must eventually forsake the world of created things, 'and we are accustomed in moments of weariness or exaltation to consider a voluntary forsaking. But how can we, who have read so much poetry, seen so many paintings, listened to so much music, where the cry of the flesh and the cry of the soul seem one, forsake it harshly and rudely? What have we in common with St. Bernard covering his eyes that they may not dwell upon the beauty of the lakes of Switzerland?'[14]

The cry of the flesh and the cry of the soul seem one in much of Yeats's later poetry: a poetry celebrating embodied wisdom. As we have seen, Yeats's surrogate, Michael Robartes, tells the Dancer that women can achieve 'uncomposite blessedness' and lead men to a similar state, if they 'banish every thought, unless/ The lineaments that please their view/ When the long looking-glass is full,/ Even from the foot-sole think it too.' In 'Among School Children,' the 'body swayed to music' is swept up into such Unity of Being that we cannot 'know

---

13   Bonamy Dobrée, 'T. S. Eliot: A Personal Reminiscence,' 81.
14   This cancelled but thematically crucial note is cited by F. A. C. Wilson, *Yeats's Iconography*, 323n41.

the dancer from the dance.' In *Words for Music Perhaps*, featuring the 'Crazy Jane' and 'Woman Young and Old' sequences, we have frequent distinctions between, and final fusions of, spirit and flesh. In Poem IV of the sequence 'Vacillation,' in a climactic moment foreshadowed at the conclusion of *Per Amica Silentia Lunae* (Myth, 364), the sixty-six-year-old poet recalls sitting, a decade and a half earlier, 'solitary' in a crowded London shop, a receptively 'open book and empty cup' on the tabletop. Echoing the equally climactic moment in 'A Dialogue of Self and Soul,' when 'sweetness flows into the breast,' and 'We are blest by everything,/ Everything we look upon is blest,' epiphany and reciprocal blessing occur. But, more explicitly than in the prose passage in *Per Amica*, or even in the secular beatitude attained in 'Dialogue,' it is the *body* that is set ablaze:

> While on the shop and street I gazed
> My body of a sudden blazed;
> And twenty minutes more or less
> It seemed, so great my happiness,
> That I was blessèd and could bless.

In what follows, after a preamble establishing context, I intend to focus on specific poems, often quest- or dialogue-poems, which tend to reassert the wisdom of the body, putting in contention the provisionally opposing claims of the temporal and spiritual worlds, body and soul. More often than not, these opposites turn out to be Blakean Contraries, polarities without whose dialectical friction, Blake tells us in *The Marriage of Heaven and Hell* (Plate 3) 'no progression' would be possible. The second part of the book focuses on Yeats's poems to and about Maud Gonne, arguably the most remarkable, though somewhat scattered, sequence of love poems in Western literature since the *Canzoniere* of Petrarch, in whose spiritual-erotic tradition of obsessive and unrequited love Yeats was consciously writing.

Here, too, the spiritual and the erotic are in fruitful if often bittersweet polarity and confluence. For all his 'occult yearning,' as Bloom notes, the body and sexual exaltation mattered enormously to Yeats, and had to be 'sufficient.' Part of Yeats realized that it wasn't sufficient and, in fact, could never suffice; that it took more than sex, even more than sexual love, to resolve what he called, borrowing from Kant, 'the antinomies.'

He endorsed that dark truth by synopsizing, in a resonant phrase, a passage to which I will return: Lucretius as translated by Dryden: 'The tragedy of sexual intercourse is the perpetual virginity of the soul.'

And yet, it also remains true, as Hough observes, and the poems demonstrate, that for Yeats, passion was to be redeemed rather than transcended, and that 'beatitude' required, more than Eliot's 'shadow fruit,' earthly consummation. That 'ideal goal' doomed the actual relationship of W. B. Yeats and Maud Gonne, while giving birth to what Maud called, in a 1911 letter to Yeats, their 'children,' who 'had wings' (G-YL, 302). She was referring, not to human offspring, but to the poems that had emerged from unfulfilled love, fecundity replacing barrenness and frustration. In the pursuit of both occult wisdom and of Maud Gonne, the void is somehow made fruitful.

2. Hermeticism, Theosophy, Gnosticism

'Her favorite reading as a child was Huxley and Tyndall,' Virginia Woolf tells us of Clarissa Dalloway. As Yeats was fond of saying, 'We Irish think otherwise.' He was quoting the most famous Irish-born philosopher, George Berkeley, reinforcing that Idealist's resistance to Locke's materialist version of empiricism with his own defense of visionary powers in an era unsettled by philosophic and scientific skepticism. In the section of *The Trembling of the Veil* covering the period 1887–91, Yeats says he was '

> unlike others of my generation in one thing only. I am very religious, and
> deprived by Huxley and Tyndall, whom I detested, of the simple-minded
> religion of my childhood, I had made a new religion, almost an infallible
> Church of poetic tradition, of a fardel of stories, and of personages, and
> of emotions [...] passed on from generation to generation by poets and
> painters with some help from philosophers and theologians.[1]

Though Yeats was not religious in the normative sense, he *did* seek a world, as he says later in this passage, that reflected the 'deepest instinct of man,' and would be 'steeped in the supernatural.' That was his own instinct. It was his conscious intention, as well, to offset the scientific naturalism of John Tyndall and T. H. Huxley, 'Darwin's bulldog,' and to buttress his rebellion against his father's forcefully expressed agnostic skepticism. In making up his own religion, Yeats relied essentially on 'emotions' (with the *heart* as their repository) and on *art* ('poetic tradition,' 'poets and painters'). But he included in his 'fardel' strands from interrelated traditions Western and Eastern. Seeing them all as a single perennial philosophy, 'one history and that the soul's,' he gathered

---

1   Yeats, Au, 114–15. For Clarissa's reading, see Virginia Woolf, *Mrs. Dalloway*, 106–07.

    https://doi.org/10.11647/OBP.0275.02

together elements from Celtic mythology and Irish folklore, British Romanticism (especially Shelley and Blake, whose Los 'must create a system or be enslaved by another man's'); Platonism and Neoplatonism; Rosicrucianism and Theosophy, Cabbalism, Hinduism, and Buddhism, along with other varieties of spiritualist and esoteric thought, including Gnosticism. Though Yeats was not a scholar of Gnosticism, there are persistent themes and emphases in his thought and poetry that Gnostics would find both familiar and congenial. Others, not so much. Most obviously, whereas Gnosticism (with the exception of two sects I will later discuss) stressed the conflict between body and spirit, with the ultimate goal freedom from the body, Yeats's instinct was to heal this breach in favor of what he called Unity of Being.

After this preamble, I will, in discussing the spiritual dimension in Yeats's work, sometimes focus on Gnostic elements. But this is an essay on Yeats rather than Gnosticism. I bring in historical Gnosticism and the tenets of certain Gnostic sects only where they illuminate particular poems; for example, 'The Secret Rose,' 'A Dialogue of Self and Soul,' 'Crazy Jane and Jack the Journeyman,' and 'What Then?' Otherwise, I will have little to say of the religious movement drawing on, but competing with, Judaism and Christianity in the Eastern Mediterranean in the first and second centuries, CE.[2] Instead, I will emphasize *gnosis* as differentiated from historical Gnosticism, precisely the distinction made at the 1966 international conference, the Colloquium of Messina, convened to examine the origins of Gnosticism. In the colloquium's final 'Proposal,' the emphasis was on the attainment of *gnosis*, defined as 'knowledge of the divine mysteries reserved for an elite.'

Such knowledge was individual and intuitive. For most Gnostics, this intuitive esoteric knowledge had little to do with either Western philosophic reasoning or with the theological knowledge of God to be found in Orthodox Judaism or normative Christianity. For spiritual

---

2   Even that Gnosticism is syncretist and complex, steeped not only in Hebrew and early Christian writing, but with roots in India, Iran, and of course in Greece (Orphism and Pythagoreanism, Platonism and Neoplatonism). That kind of cross-fertilization simultaneously enriches the tradition and complicates analysis. In addition, the various sects were secret. Because of its value as the way to break out of our imprisonment by the flesh and the material world, and thus the path to salvation, the knowledge was kept hidden, reserved for the spiritual elite capable of achieving and exercising *gnosis*.

adepts, such intuition derived from knowledge of the divine One. For poets like Yeats, it was identified with that '*intuitive* Reason' which, for the Romantics—notably, Wordsworth, Coleridge, and their American disciple, Emerson—was virtually indistinguishable from the creative imagination. Yeats was also steeped in the dialectical thinking of Blake, and much of his strongest poetry derived its power from the tension between the spiritual 'perennial philosophy' of Plato and Plotinus and the formidable and welcome challenge presented, after 1902, by 'that strong enchanter, Nietzsche,' who, Yeats believed, 'completes Blake and has the same roots' (L, 379). It was, above all, Nietzsche, enemy of all forms of the otherworldly, who provided Yeats with the *antithetical* counterweight required to resist the *primary* pull of body-denigrating spiritualism, whether Christian, Neoplatonic, or (in most forms) Gnostic.

At the same time, there is no denying the centrality of spiritual quest, of esoteric knowledge, mysticism and 'magic,' in Yeats's life and work. In July 1892, preparing to be initiated into the Second Order of the Golden Dawn, he wrote to one of his heroes, the Irish nationalist John O'Leary, in response to a 'somewhat testy postcard' the kindly old Fenian had sent him. The 'probable explanation,' Yeats surmised, was that O'Leary had been listening to the poet's skeptical father, holding forth on his son's 'magical pursuits out of the immense depths of his ignorance as to everything that I am doing and thinking.' Yeats realizes that the word 'magic,' however familiar to *him*, 'has a very outlandish sound to other ears.' But it was 'surely absurd' to hold him 'weak' because

> I chose to persist in a study which I decided deliberately four or five years ago to make, next to my poetry, the most important pursuit of my life [...] If I had not made magic my constant study I could not have written a single word of my Blake book, nor would *The Countess Kathleen* have ever come to exist. The mystical life is the centre of all that I do and all that I think and all that I write [...] I have always considered myself a voice of what I believe to be a greater renaissance—the revolt of the soul against the intellect—now beginning in the world. (L, 210–11)

Just as he had emphasized art and a 'Church of poetic tradition' in the creation of his own 'new religion,' even here, in his most strenuous defense of his mystical and magical pursuits, Yeats inserts the caveat that they were paramount, 'next to my poetry.' But this is hardly to dismiss the passionate intensity of Yeats's esoteric and mystical pursuits. What seemed to W. H. Auden, even in his great elegy, 'In Memory of W. B. Yeats,' to be 'silly' or, worse, to Ezra Pound, to be 'very very very bughouse' (it takes one to know one), or by T. S. Eliot to be dreadfully misguided, was taken, not with complete credulity, but very very very seriously, by Yeats himself. His esoteric pursuits, in many heterodox guises, remained an energizing stimulus, if not an obsession, throughout his life. In his elegy, written just days after the poet's death in January 1939, Auden says, 'You were silly like us; your gift survived it all.' But the interest in mysterious wisdom, dismissed by Auden and Eliot and Pound, actually enhanced Yeats's artistic gift—as Virginia Woolf perceived the very first time he engaged her in conversation.

When she met Yeats in November 1930, at Lady Ottoline Morrell's, Woolf knew little of his thought and not all that much of his poetry, but she was overwhelmed by his personality and by an immediate sense of a body of thought underlying his observations on 'dreaming states, & soul states,' on life and art: 'I perceived that he had worked out a complete psychology that I could only catch on to momentarily, in my alarming ignorance.' When he spoke of modern poetry, she recorded in her diary, Yeats described deficiencies inevitable because we are at the end of an era. 'Here was another system of thought, of which I could only catch fragments.' She concludes on a note seldom found in Bloomsbury self-assurance: 'how crude and jaunty my own theories were besides his: indeed I got a tremendous sense of the intricacy of his art; also of its meaning, its seriousness, its importance, which wholly engrosses this large active minded immensely vitalized man. Wherever one cut him with a little question, he poured, spurted fountains of ideas.'[3]

§

The Golden Dawn was a major source of that 'system of thought,' that abounding glittering jet of ideas, that so impressed Virginia Woolf. Yeats was, along with his friend George Russell (AE), a founding member, in 1885, of the Dublin Hermetic Society, which, the following April, evolved into the Dublin Theosophical Society. Though he 'was much among the Theosophists, having drifted there from the Dublin Hermetic Society,'

---

3   *The Diary of Virginia Woolf*, 3:329.

Yeats declined to join, believing that 'Hermetic' better described his own wider interests as a devotee of what he called the study of 'magic.' He did join the Theosophical Society of London, in which, eager to push mystical boundaries, he enlisted in the 'Esoteric Section.' He resigned in 1891, amid tension, though not, despite rumor, expelled, let alone 'excommunicated.' Yeats was for more than thirty years a member of the Hermetic Order of the Golden Dawn, which he joined in London in March 1890; he stayed with the Golden Dawn until it splintered, then joined one of its offshoot Orders, the Stella Matutina. During its heyday in the 1890s, the G.D. and its Inner Order of the Rose of Ruby and the Cross of Gold (R.R. & A.C.) was 'the crowning glory of the occult revival in the nineteenth century,' having succeeded in synthesizing a vast body of disparate material and welding it into an effective 'system.'[4]

Yeats took as his Golden Dawn motto and pseudonym *Demon Est Deus Inversus* (D.E.D.I.). That sobriquet's recognition of the interdependence of opposites is a nod to both William Blake and Helena Petrovna Blavatsky, the eleventh chapter of whose seminal text, *The Secret Doctrine* (1888), bears this title. The most extraordinary of the many exotic figures that gathered in societies and cults, making Victorian London ground zero in the revolt against reductive materialism, Madame Blavatsky (HPB to her acolytes) was, of course, the co-founder and presiding genius of the Theosophical Society. In a letter to a New England newspaper, Yeats referred to her with wary fascination as 'the Pythoness of the Movement,' and as a half-masculine 'female Dr. Johnson.'[5] Unless we accept her own tracing of Theosophy to ancient Tibetan roots, the movement was born in 1875, in part in Blavatsky's New York City apartment, where she kept a stuffed baboon, sporting under its arm a copy of Darwin's *On the Origin of Species* to represent the creeping tide of scientific materialism she was determined to push back—though it should be mentioned that

---

4   Ellic Howe, ix. The admission ceremony to the R.R. & A.C. required an initiate to commit to the 'Great Work': to 'purify and exalt my Spiritual nature,' and thus, with divine help, to 'gradually raise and unite myself to my Higher and Divine Genius.' The main point of Yeats's 1901 pamphlet *Is the Order of R.R. & A.C. to Remain a Magical Order?* was that frivolous 'freedom' was inferior to 'bonds gladly accepted.' That emphasis illuminates his later philosophy in *A Vision*, as well as the tension in his poetry between freedom and traditional forms.

5   Yeats, *Letters to the New Island*, ed. Bornstein and Witemeyer, 84. The volume collects pieces Yeats sent between 1888 and 1892 to *The Boston Pilot* and the *Providence Sunday Journal*.

The Secret Doctrine was promoted as an audacious attempt to synthesize science, religion, and philosophy.

While he never shared the requisite belief in Blavatsky's Tibetan Masters, Yeats, without being anti-Darwinian, did share her determination to resist and turn back that materialist tide. And he was personally fascinated by the Pythoness herself, whom he first met in the formidable flesh in 1887 when he visited her at a little house in Norwood, a suburb of London. She was just fifty-six at the time but looked older (she would live only four more years). Young Yeats was kept waiting while she attended to earlier visitors. Finally admitted, he 'found an old woman in a plain loose dark dress: a sort of old Irish peasant, with an air of humor and audacious power.' Their first conversation was a whimsical exchange on the vagaries of her cuckoo clock, which Yeats thought had 'hooted' at him. On subsequent visits he found her 'almost always full of gaiety [...] kindly and tolerant,' and accessible—except on those occasions, once a week, when she 'answered questions upon her system, and as I look back after thirty years I often ask myself, "Was her speech automatic? Was she a trance medium, or in some similar state, one night in every week?"'[6]

Her alternating states were adumbrated in the phases, active and passive, HPB called, in *Isis Unveiled* (1877), 'the days and nights of Brahma.' Yeats had read that book and Blavatsky's alternating phases may have influenced his lifelong emphasis on polarity, the antinomies: the tension between quotidian reality and the spiritual or Romantic allure of the Otherworld, in forms ranging from the Celtic Fairyland to that city of art and spirit, Byzantium; and, early and late, between things that merely 'seem' (Platonic 'appearance,' Hindu *maya*) and the spiritual reality perceived by Western visionaries and Hindu hermits contemplating on Asian mountains. After reading *Isis Unveiled*, Yeats had delved into a book given him by AE. This was *Esoteric Buddhism*

---

6   Yeats, *The Trembling of the Veil* (1922), in Au, 173–74, 179. The report issued on Blavatsky by Richard Hodgson, a skilled investigator employed by the Society for Psychical Research, assessed her claimed activities in India to be fraudulent, but concluded that she was no 'mere vulgar adventuress. We think she has achieved a title to a permanent remembrance as one of the most accomplished, ingenious, and interesting imposters of history' (cited in Peter Washington, 83.) Yeats, writing in 1889, and registering Blavatsky's magnetism and skills as an eclectic magpie, found that conclusion simplistic, noting, with his usual mixture of skepticism and credulity, that 'the fraud theory,' at least at 'its most pronounced,' was 'wholly unable to cover the facts' (Mem, 281).

(1883) by Madame Blavatsky's fellow Theosophist and sometime disciple, A. P. Sinnett, whose earlier book, *The Occult World* (1881), had already had an impact on Yeats. 'Spirituality, in the occult sense,' Sinnett declared, 'has nothing to do with feeling devout: it has to do with the capacity of the mind for assimilating knowledge at the fountainhead of knowledge itself.' And he asserted another antithesis crucial to Yeats: that to become an 'adept,' a rare status 'beyond the reach of the general public,' one must 'obey the inward impulse of [one's] soul, irrespective of the prudential considerations of worldly science or sagacity' (101).

That Eastern impulse is evident in Yeats's three hermit poems in *Responsibilities* (1914). It was even more evident a quarter-century earlier, in three poems in his first collection of lyrics. 'The Indian upon God,' 'The Indian to his Love,' and the lengthy (91-line) 'Anashuya and Vijaya,' were written under a more direct and visceral influence.[7] For the lure of the East had another source, also related to Madame Blavatsky. Yeats had been deeply impressed with the roving ambassador of Theosophy she had sent to Dublin in April 1886, to instruct the members of the Dublin Hermetic Society in the nuances of Theosophy. The envoy was the charismatic young Bengali swami, Mohini Chatterjee, described by Madame Blavatsky, with perhaps more gaiety than tolerance, as 'a nutmeg Hindoo with buck eyes,' for whom several of his English disciples 'burned with a scandalous, ferocious passion,' that 'craving of old *gourmands* for *unnatural* food.'[8] Despite his inability to resist the sexual temptations presented to him (he was eventually dispatched back to India), Chatterjee preached the need to realize one's individual soul by contemplation, penetrating the illusory nature of the material world, and abjuring worldly ambition. His 1887 book, *Man: Fragments of a Forgotten History*, described reincarnational stages, and ascending states of consciousness. The fourth and final state, which 'may be called transcendental consciousness,' is ineffable, though 'glimpses' of it 'may be obtained in the abnormal condition of *extasis*' (64).

---

7   The latter anticipates Yeats's later and greater debate-poems as well as two late mountain-poems: the sonnet 'Meru' (1933), centered on caverned Hindu hermits, and 'Lapis Lazuli' (1936), which ends with a mountain vision. In 'Anashuya and Vijaya,' the young priestess Anashuya compels Vijaya to swear an oath by the gods 'who dwell on sacred Himalay,/ On the far Golden Peak' (66–70). Like Meru, Golden Peak is a sacred mountain.

8   Quoted in Washington, 88–89. Italics in original.

'Ecstasy,' an *antithetical* state, whether spiritual or sexual or both, became a crucial term in Yeats's lexicon, at war with abstract wisdom or knowledge, though not with a deeper *gnosis*. Perhaps Yeats was not completely hyperbolic in later saying that he learned more from Chatterjee than 'from any book.' There is no doubt that he was permanently affected by the swami's concept of ecstasy and by the idea of ancient and secret wisdom being passed on orally from generation to generation, fragmentary glimpses of an ineffable truth. There are distinctions between East and West, but, as in Gnosticism and Neoplatonism, the Theosophy of Madame Blavatsky and Mohini Chatterjee presents an unknown Absolute, from which souls emanate as fragments, or 'sparks,' separated from the divine substance, and longing to return to the One from which they came. The principal Eastern variation is that, to achieve that ultimate goal requires a long pilgrimage through many incarnations, living through many lives, both in this world and the next.

Many years later, in 1929, Yeats wrote an eponymous poem, 'Mohini Chatterjee.' Its final words, 'Men dance on deathless feet,' were added by Yeats 'in commentary' on Chatterjee's own words on reincarnation. There is no reference to a God, and we are to 'pray for nothing,' but just repeat every night in bed, that one has been a king, a slave, a fool, a rascal, knave. 'Nor is there anything/ [...] I have not been./ And yet upon my breast/ A myriad heads have lain.' Such words were spoken by Mohini Chatterjee to 'set at rest/ A boy's turbulent days.' When that boy, almost forty years later, published 'Mohini Chatterjee' in *The Winding Stair and Other Poems* (1933), he placed it immediately preceding what is certainly his most 'turbulent' poem of spiritual purgation and reincarnation: 'Byzantium,' in which impure spirits, 'complexities of mire and blood,' are presented 'dying into a dance,/ An agony of trance,/ An agony of flame that cannot singe a sleeve.' Yet, like most of the other poems we will examine, 'Byzantium' participates, though in this case with unique fury and surging energy, in the dominant Yeatsian *agon* between Time and Eternity, flesh and spirit.

§

As we've seen, Yeats wondered if, on heightened occasions, HPB's speech might not be 'automatic,' and she herself a 'trance medium.' But, since he never gave full credence to the astral dictations of Blavatsky's

Tibetan Masters, it is ironic that his own major esoteric text had a related genesis. His book *A Vision*, first published in 1925 and revised in 1937, is based on the 'automatic writing' for which Mrs. Yeats discovered a gift when, in the early days of their marriage in 1917, she sensed that her husband's thoughts were drifting back to the love of his life and his Muse, the unattainable Maud, and to her lush daughter, Iseult, to whom Yeats had also proposed before marrying his wife. Whatever its origin, psychological or occult, the wisdom conveyed to George by her 'Communicators,' and then passed on to her husband, preoccupied the poet for years. Alternately insightful and idiosyncratic, beautiful and a bit bananas, *A Vision* may not be required reading for lovers of the poetry, except for advanced students. Informed scholarship has illuminated the collaboration that led to *A Vision*, but Tindall's old witticism still resonates: 'a little seems too much, his business none of ours.'

But Yeats's purpose was serious, and, as always, a balancing attempt to exercise individual creative freedom within a rich tradition. In dedicating the first edition of *A Vision* to 'Vestigia' (Moina Mathers, sister of MacGregor Mathers, head of the Golden Dawn), Yeats noted that while some in the Order were 'looking for spiritual happiness or for some form of unknown power,' clearly Hermetic or Gnostic goals, he had a more poetry-centered object, though that, too, reflects the intuitive Gnosticism of creative artists seeking their *own* visions. As early as the 1890s, he claimed in 1925, he anticipated what would emerge as *A Vision*, with its circuits of sun and moon, its double-gyre, its tension between Fate and Freedom: 'I wished for a system of thought that would leave my imagination free to create as it chose and yet make all that it created, or could create, part of one history and that the soul's.'[9] Contemptuous of Yeats's specific supernatural beliefs ('obstacles' he had to overcome to achieve his 'greatness'), T. S. Eliot had himself memorably described creative freedom operating within a larger and necessary historical discipline as the interaction between 'Tradition and the Individual Talent.'[10]

---

9   *A Vision* (1925), xi.
10   Rejecting Yeats's occultism, along with other forms of 'modern heresy,' Eliot opined that Yeats had 'arrived at greatness against the greatest odds.' *After Strange Gods*, 50–51.

If it is not mandatory that those drawn to the poetry read *A Vision*, it was absolutely necessary that Yeats write it. It illuminates the later poetry, and even provides the skeletal structure for some of his greatest poems, the best known of which, 'The Second Coming,' was originally accompanied by a long note, reproducing the double-gyre, that central symbol of *A Vision*. Yeats tells us, in the Introduction to the second edition of *A Vision*, that, back in 1917, he struggled for several days to decipher the 'almost illegible script,' which he nevertheless found 'so exciting, sometimes so profound,' that he not only persuaded his wife to persevere, but offered to give up poetry to devote what remained of his own life to 'explaining and piecing together those scattered sentences' which he believed contained mysterious wisdom. The response from one of the unknown writers was conveniently welcome news for him and for *us*: '"No," was the answer, "we have come to give you metaphors for poetry"' (Vis, 8).

Yeats was a man at once credulous and rational, a believer among skeptics, a skeptic among believers. In a letter to Ethel Mannin, written a month before his death, Yeats asked and answered his own jocoserious question: 'Am I a mystic?—no, I am a practical man. I have seen the raising of Lazarus and the loaves and the fishes and have made the usual measurements, plummet line, spirit-level and have taken the temperature by pure mathematic' (L, 921). Though always open to the possibility of miracle, when confronted by it, he tended to test, as he did in surreptitiously sending samples of blood said to be dripping from a religious icon off to the lab for scientific analysis. The response of Maud Gonne, who had crossed the Channel with Yeats in wartime to view the bleeding icon in the village of Mirebeau, was quite different: having long since converted to Catholicism, she dropped devoutly to her knees.[11]

Yeats's lifelong quest for spiritual knowledge was countered by the circumspection of a self-divided man and notably dialectical poet, who also wanted to '*remain faithful to the earth*,' to cite the opening imperative of the Zarathustra[12] of 'that strong enchanter, Nietzsche,' whose astringent and electrifying impact on Yeats, beginning in 1902, changed the poet, if

---

11   George Mills Harper, '"A Subject for Study": Miracle at Mirebeau,' in *Yeats and the Occult*, ed. Harper, 172–89. For Maud's reaction to the bleeding holograph, see Cardozo, 292.

12   Prologue to 'Thus Spoke Zarathustra,' in *The Portable Nietzsche*, 125. Italics in original

not utterly, substantially. But unlike Nietzsche, Yeats had no doubt that there was a spiritual realm. He strove to acquire knowledge of that world through any and all means at hand: studying the 'perennial philosophy,' but not excluding the occasional resort to hashish and mescal to induce occult visions, and belief in astrology and séances, of which he attended many. A séance is at the center of one of his most dramatic plays, *Words upon the Window-pane* (1932), which helps explain the emphasis on 'a medium's mouth' in his cryptic poem 'Fragments,' written at the same time, and which—since it condenses a world of history, philosophy, and mythology in its ten lines and forty-five words—I will later explicate at some length.

Though it is difficult to track and disentangle intertwined strands of thought and influence, let alone make conclusive pronouncements, two significant Yeats scholars, Allan Grossman (in his 1969 study of *The Wind Among the Reeds*, titled *Poetic Knowledge in Early Yeats*) and Harold Bloom, in his sweeping 1970 study, grandly titled *Yeats*, both concluded that their man was essentially a Gnostic. The same assertion governs an unpublished 1992 PhD thesis, written by Steven J. Skelley and titled *Yeats, Bloom, and the Dialectics of Theory, Criticism and Poetry*. My own conclusion is less certain. What *is* certain is that Yeats envisioned his life as a quest: first as a search for the secret and sacred, whether a book, a system, or an Otherworldly paradise; but also, early and finally, as a quest for the power to *create*, which meant elevating the role of the Poet over that of the Saint. It therefore meant refusing to submit to the authoritative and prescriptive demands of any 'religion,' orthodox or occult, Christian or Neoplatonic or Gnostic, that he deemed, whatever its attractions, ultimately hostile to imaginative creativity and to human life itself.

3. The Seeker

Yeats was a lifelong Seeker. He was influenced, early on and powerfully, by Shelley's visionary quester in *Alastor*, and Tennyson's in 'Ulysses,' heroic solitaries who engage in idealist quests, unconstrained by conventional ties, and whose version of the archetypal *peregrinatio vitae* ends in death. The crucial lines Yeats puts in the mouth of his nameless death-foreseeing Irish airman—'A lonely impulse of delight/ Drove to this tumult in the clouds'—echo the lines (304–5), in which the narrator of *Alastor* epitomizes what impels Shelley's nameless Seeker, in quest of an ideal represented by an irresistible but inaccessible woman: 'A restless impulse urged him to embark/ And meet lone death on the drear ocean's waste.'[1]

'An Irish Airman Foresees his Death,' a concise fusion of solitary ecstasy, fate, and *gnosis* (the poem begins 'I know'), is deservedly one of Yeats's best-known short lyrics. In referring in my subtitle and throughout to Yeats as a Seeker, I am alluding to a very early, little-known 'dramatic poem in two scenes' with that title. Though Yeats later struck *The Seeker* from his canon, its theme—the perennial quest for secret knowledge, usually celebrated but always with an acute awareness of the attendant dangers of estrangement from 'mere' human life—initiates what might be fairly described as the basic and archetypal pattern of his life and work.

The Seeker of the title is an aged knight who has been made 'a coward in the field,' and been 'untouched by human joy or human love,' sacrificing 'all' in order to follow a beckoning voice. In his dying moments, he discovers that the alluring voice he has been pursuing all

---

1   The Irish airman was, of course, Robert Gregory, with Yeats himself supplying the dead pilot's supposed final words. The profound influence of *Alastor* on Yeats's thought and poetry is well known. George Mills Harper once told me that 'one of the controls in an unfinished notebook of *Vision* materials is named "Alastor".'

    https://doi.org/10.11647/OBP.0275.03

his 'dream-led' life is that of a 'bearded witch,' who knows not what she is, though men call her 'Infamy.' That final turn looks back to Spenser's *Faery Queen* (I, ii), where the evil witch Duessa, outwardly 'faire,' is actually 'fowle,' and to Banquo describing the witches he and Macbeth encounter as 'bearded.' There are also hints of Keats's wasted and doomed knight-at-arms in 'La Belle Dame sans Merci.' In the final exchange, the bearded figure, bending triumphantly over the dying knight, sardonically whispers, 'What, lover, die before our lips have met?' With his last breath, the knight responds: 'Again, the voice! The Voice!' (VP, 681–85).[2]

Celtic mythology has thematic variations, often exacting a price. In the most famous modern version, Yeats's 1902 play *Cathleen ni Houlihan*, written for and starring Maud Gonne, the old hag is climactically transformed into a beautiful woman: 'a young girl with the walk of a queen,' Ireland herself, her regal beauty rejuvenated by blood-sacrifice. In that sense she is a devouring female, Ireland as Stephen Dedalus's 'old sow that eats her farrow,' a queen anticipating Wallace Stevens's devouring earth mother, whose male victim's 'grief' is that she 'should feed on him.' Resembling as well the 'bearded witch' of Yeats's *The Seeker*, 'Madame La Fleurie' is revealed in Stevens's final line as 'a bearded queen, wicked in her dead light.'[3]

The first of two points to be made concerns Yeats's ambivalence in such quests. What was sought, once achieved, turns out to be more, or less, than the Seeker bargained for. A variation on the theme occurs in a famous poem written a year after *The Seeker*. In 'The Stolen Child,' the naïve mortal is an abducted child rather than an active Seeker. He is seduced by the fairies into an Otherworld at once remote and localized in Sligo, a hauntingly beautiful natural world as ominous as it is enchanting. The fairies' italicized choral refrain, until the final iteration, is certainly enticing:

---

2   The grotesque ending in *The Seeker* also anticipates Rebecca du Maurier's 'Don't Look Now,' in which the father of a drowned daughter pursues and is slain by a serial-murdering dwarf he mistakes for that dead daughter: a short story turned by director Nicholas Roeg into a haunting film starring Donald Sutherland and Julie Christie.

3   On this lethal archetype, see my *Terrible Beauty: Yeats, Joyce, Ireland, and the Myth of the Devouring Female*.

Come away, O human child!
To the waters and the wild
With a faery, hand in hand,
For the world's more full of weeping than you can understand.

The fairies themselves are childlike, immortal yet mischievous and not to be trusted. Despite the poem's beauty, signs of impending trouble abound. On 'a leafy island/ Where flapping herons wake/ The drowsy water-rats,' the fairies have 'hid our faery vats/ Full of berries/ And of reddest stolen cherries.' On the moonlit sands 'Far off by furthest Rosses,' where the souls of sleepers are said to have been stolen by fairies, they 'foot it all the night,/ Weaving olden dances,/ Mingling hands and mingling glances': conspiratorial, knowing looks to which the child is not privy. The fairies leap to and fro, chasing 'frothy bubbles,/ While the world is full of troubles/ And is anxious in its sleep.' In the penultimate and most beautiful stanza, set 'Where the wandering water gushes/ From the hills above Glen-Car' (the waterfall on the side of Ben Bulben, a little cataract particularly loved by Yeats), there are tiny 'pools among the rushes/ That scarce could bathe a star,' but large enough to contain fish. There the fairies

Seek for slumbering trout
And whispering in their ears,
Give them unquiet dreams;
Leaning softly out
From ferns that drop their tears
Over the young streams.

In the final stanza, the focus shifts (as it does, though more subtly, in the 'Byzantium' poems) to the world left behind, to be heard and seen 'no more.' We have a backward glance, not to a world of felt but incomprehensible adult weeping, but to the warm, pre-Disneyesque images of a home now irretrievably lost to the deceived child taken away by the sinister fairies:

Away with us he's going,
The solemn-eyed;
He'll hear no more the lowing
Of the calves on the warm hillside
Or the kettle on the hob
Sing peace into his breast,

> Or see the brown mice bob
> Round and round the oatmeal chest.
> *For he comes, the human child,*
> *To the waters and the wild*
> *With a faery hand in hand,*
> *From a world more full of weeping than he can understand.*

As Yeats acknowledged two years later in a letter to his friend Katharine Tynan, his early poetry 'is almost all a flight into fairy land from the real world,' a theme 'summed up,' he says, by the 'chorus' to 'The Stolen Child.' That is 'not,' he continued, 'the poetry of insight but of longing and complaint—the cry of the heart against necessity. I hope some day to alter that and write a poetry of insight and knowledge' (L, 63). But of course, as in 'What Then?'—a poem written half a century later, and again pitting the song of the supernatural against the pleasures of this world—'The Stolen Child' consists of more than its refrain. As the title suggests and the poem gradually reveals, culminating in the perspective-altering final 'chorus,' the child is now in the power of the fairies. As Emerson tells us, 'nothing is got for nothing'; longing and susceptibility to the siren song of the fairies has led to 'solemn-eyed' buyer's remorse, a palpable sense of terror at having lost forever a world full not only of weeping but of familiar things to be cherished on this warm earth. Even as early as 'The Stolen Child' (1886), Yeats was already writing a poetry of ambivalence, and thus of 'insight and knowledge.'[4]

The second point to be emphasized is that it was precisely such 'insight and knowledge' Yeats was seeking. Whether poetic or Hermetic, it was knowledge aligned with the quest for an intuitive knowledge of spiritual truth. On the other hand, Yeats wanted, as he told 'Vestigia,' to participate in a spiritual tradition that 'would leave my imagination free to create as it chose.' The imaginative power and passionate intensity of much of his best poetry derive from Yeats's

---

4   Yeats's *The Land of Heart's Desire* (1894) equates this seduction by the fairies with death, as in Goethe's famous ballad, often set to music, *Der Erlkönig*. The elf-king tries to seduce a child, being carried on horseback by his father, with promises of a blissful world where the demonic king's daughters will 'dance thee and rock thee and sing thee to sleep.' The child is aware of the danger, but the father remains oblivious, until it is too late. When he arrives home, the child is dead in his arms: '*In seinem Armen das Kind in war tot.*'

commitment to the paradox that the 'sacred,' unquestionably valid, was to be found through the 'profane' and in the here and now, in the tangible things of this earth.

A profound point was made precisely eight decades ago by a perceptive student of Yeats's life and work, Peter Allt, later the editor of the indispensable *Variorum Edition* of the poems. Allt argued persuasively that Yeats's 'mature religious *Anschauung*' consists of 'religious belief without any religious faith, notional assent to the reality of the supernatural' combined with 'an emotional dissent from its actuality.'[5] As a student of secret wisdom, Yeats responded, not to the orthodox Christian emphasis on *pistis* (God's gift of faith), but to *gnosis*, derived from individual intuition of divine revelation. What Allt refers to as emotional dissent illuminates Yeats's resistance to Christianity, and his occasional need to 'mock Plotinus' thought/ And cry in Plato's teeth,' as he does in the final section of 'The Tower' in the very act of preparing his 'peace' and making his 'soul'. But emotional dissent and the making of one's own soul in an act of self-redemption are hardly alien to the concept of individual *gnosis*.

Paramount to understanding Yeats as man and poet is a recognition of the tension between the two worlds, between the *primary* and the *antithetical*, the never fully resolved debate between the Soul and the Self (or Heart). That tension plays out from his earliest poems to the masterpieces of his maturity. Though foreshadowed by the uncanonical *The Seeker*, the theme is publicly established with 'The Stolen Child,' in which the human child, torn between realms, is 'taken,' irretrievably absorbed into the Celtic Otherworld. Three years later, the tension is developed at length in *The Wanderings of Oisin* (1889), Yeats's quest-poem anchored by another debate between paganism and Christianity, here embodied by the Celtic warrior Oisin and St. Patrick. The theme continues with his pivotal Rosicrucian poem, 'To the Rose upon the Rood of Time' (1892), and culminates in the great debate-poems of his maturity: 'A Dialogue of Self and Soul' (1927) and the career-synopsizing debate between 'Soul' and 'Heart' in section VII of the sequence revealingly titled 'Vacillation,' which appeared in 1933, forty years after 'To the Rose upon the Rood of Time.'

---

5   Peter Allt, "W. B. Yeats," *Theology* 42 (1941), 81–99.

The eighth and final section of 'Vacillation' ends with the poet blessing—gently and gaily, if somewhat patronizingly—yet rejecting the Saint, here represented by the Catholic theologian Baron von Hügel, who had, in his 1908 book *The Mystical Element of Religion*, stressed 'the costingness of regeneration.' In the last of his *Four Quartets*, T. S. Eliot aligns himself with von Hügel by endorsing, in the conclusion of 'Little Gidding' (lines 293–94), 'A condition of complete simplicity/ (Costing not less than everything).' In section II, in the Dantesque ghost-encounter (seventy of the finest lines he ever wrote and, by his own admission, the ones that had cost him the most effort, Eliot respectfully but definitively differentiated himself from the recently deceased Yeats. In that nocturnal encounter with a largely Yeatsian 'familiar compound ghost,' Eliot echoes in order to alter Yeats's poem 'Vacillation,' and the refusal of 'The Heart' to be 'struck dumb in the simplicity of fire!' In the present context, the contrast between Eliot and Yeats is illuminating; and Eliot is right to perceive as his mighty opposite in spiritual terms the man he pronounced in his 1940 memorial address, 'the greatest poet of our time—certainly the greatest in this language, and so far as I am able to judge, in any language,' but who was also, from Eliot's Christian perspective, an occultist and a pagan.[6]

The charges were hardly far-fetched. In the final section of 'Vacillation' the poet wonders if he really must 'part' with von Hügel, since both 'honor sanctity' and 'Accept the miracles of the saints'—the report, for example, that the dead 'body of St. Teresa' of Avila was discovered 'undecayed in tomb,/ Bathed in miraculous oil' and exuding 'sweet odours.' Yeats was not being casual about Teresa's supposedly uncorrupted corpse. He had alluded to the same phenomenon five years earlier, in 'Oil and Blood,' and once asked a skeptic how he accounted for 'the fact that when the tomb of St. Teresa was opened her body exuded miraculous oil?' (LTSM, 122)

---

6   Though Eliot later removed that phrase, perhaps judging it too fulsome, his final tribute to Yeats is registered more powerfully at the end of this ghost-encounter in 'Little Gidding.' Fusing the pivotal 'unless' of 'Sailing to Byzantium' with the 'agony of flame' in which blood-begotten spirits are depicted 'Dying into a dance' in 'Byzantium,' Eliot has the ghost conclude on what amounts to a rapprochement: 'From wrong to wrong the exasperated spirit/ Proceeds, unless restored by that refining fire/ Where you must move in measure, like a dancer.'

Yet he *must* part with von Hügel. His heart 'might find relief/ Did
I become a Christian man and choose for my belief/ What seems most
welcome in the tomb,' but he is fated to

> play a predestined part.
> Homer is my example and his unchristened heart.
> The lion and the honeycomb, what has Scripture said?
> So get you gone, von Hugel, though with blessings on your head.

In sending the poem to Olivia Shakespear, his first lover and most
intimate lifetime correspondent, Yeats, having just re-read all his lyric
poetry, cited that line, and observed: 'The swordsman throughout
repudiates the saint, but not without vacillation. Is that perhaps the
sole theme—Usheen and Patrick—"so get you gone Von Hugel though
with blessings on your head?"' (L, 798). Having, in the preceding line,
cited scripture (Samson's riddle in Judges 14) to insist that sweetness
comes out of strength, Yeats ends by blessing the Catholic mystic even
as he asserts as his own exemplar pagan Homer and 'his unchristened
heart.' As we will see in the next chapter, Yeats adopted Nietzsche's
agon of Homer and paganism versus Plato and Christ. The choice of a
Nietzschean 'Homer and his unchristened heart' is doubly exemplary,
since this is the central line of the stanza Yeats himself chose to represent
his life's work in his *Oxford Book of Modern Verse*, published three years
after 'Vacillation.'

§

Marked by tension between the material and spiritual worlds, the
Seeker theme, at once Gnostic and high Romantic, illuminates, along
with several of Yeats's most beautiful early quest-lyrics, two explicitly
Rosicrucian poems: 'To the Rose upon the Rood of Time' and, a poem I
will get to in due course, 'The Secret Rose.'

   'To the Rose upon the Rood of Time,' the italicized poem opening the
group known after 1895 as *The Rose*, establishes, far more powerfully
than *The Seeker*, this poet's lifelong pattern of dialectical vacillation, of
being pulled between the temporal and spiritual worlds. In his 1907
essay 'Poetry and Tradition,' Yeats would fuse Romanticism (Blake's
dialectical Contraries without which there can be 'no progression')
with Rosicrucianism. 'The nobleness of the Arts,' Yeats writes, 'is in

the mingling of contraries, the extremity of sorrow, the extremity of joy, perfection of personality, the perfection of its surrender; and the red rose opens at the meeting of the two beams of the cross, and at the trysting place of mortal and immortal, time and eternity' (Myth, 255). In 'To the Rose upon the Rood of Time,' the symbolist poet seeks to *'find'* the immortal within the mortal; yet there is an inevitable tension between *'all poor foolish things that live a day'* and *'Eternal Beauty wandering on her way.'* That mingling, or contrast, concludes the first of the poem's two 12-line movements. The second part begins by invoking the Rose to *'Come near, come near, come near—,'* only to have the poet suddenly recoil from total absorption in the eternal symbol. He may be recalling Keats, who, at the turning point of the 'Ode to a Nightingale,' suddenly realizes that if he were to emulate the nightingale's 'pouring forth thy soul abroad/ In such an ecstasy,' by dying, he would, far from entering into unity with the 'immortal Bird,' be divorced from it, and everything else, forever: 'Still wouldst thou sing, and I have ears in vain—/ To thy high requiem become a sod.'

Yeats's recoil is no less abrupt, and thematically identical: *'Come near, come near, come near—Ah, leave me still/ A little space for the rose-breath to fill!'* Marked by a rare exclamation point, this seems a frightened defense against the very beauty he remains in quest of. A hesitant Yeats is afraid that he will be totally absorbed, engulfed, in the spiritual realm symbolized by the rose. Along with Keats at the turning point of the 'Ode to a Nightingale,' another parallel, with St. Augustine, may be illuminating. The Latin Epigraph to *The Rose*—*'Sero te amavi, Pulchritudo tam antiqua et tam nova! Sero te amavi'* [Too late I have loved you, Beauty so old and so new! Too late I have loved you]—is from *The Confessions*, a passage (X, 27) in which Augustine longs to be kindled with a desire that God approach him. Yeats would later, in 1901, quote these same Latin lines to illustrate that the religious life and the life of the artist share a common goal (E&I, 207). But the plea in the poem for 'a little space' may remind us of a more famous remark by Augustine, also addressed to God, but having to do with profane rather than sacred love. A sinful man, still smitten with his mistress, he would, Augustine tells us, pray: '"*O Lord, give me chastity and continency, but not yet!*" For I was afraid, lest you should hear me soon, and soon deliver me from the disease of concupiscence, which I desired to have satisfied rather than extinguished' (*Confessions* XIII, 7:7; italics in original).

In pleading with his Rose-Muse to *'leave me still/ A little space for the rose-breath to fill,'* Yeats also fears a too precipitous deliverance from the temporal world. Augustine is 'afraid, lest you [God] should hear me too soon.' Yeats is afraid *'Lest I no more hear common things that crave.'* Becoming deaf to the transient world with its *'heavy mortal hopes that toil and pass,'* he worries that he will *'seek alone to hear the strange things said/ By God to [...] those long dead,'* and thus *'learn to chaunt a tongue men do not know.'* The hidden wisdom and eternal beauty symbolized by the rose is much to be desired. But this quester is also a poet; and a poet, as Wordsworth rightly said in the Preface to *Lyrical Ballads*, is above all, 'a man speaking to other men.' Early and late, Yeats, thinking of the warning example of the eccentric MacGregor Mathers, head of the Golden Dawn, was aware that 'meditations upon unknown thought/ Make human intercourse grow less and less' ('All Soul's Night,' 74–75). The *'rose-breath'* is the crucial breathing / speaking *'space'* between the two worlds. Here, as always, self-divided Yeats is pulled in two antithetical directions. Hence the debates, implicit and often explicit, embodied in so many of his poems, over thirty in all.

A memorable paragraph in his most beautiful prose work, *Per Amica Silentia Lunae*, begins, 'We make out of the quarrel with others, rhetoric, but of the quarrel with ourselves, poetry' (Myth, 331). Almost forty years after he wrote 'To the Rose upon the Rood of Time,' Yeats presented, in section VII of 'Vacillation,' a stichomythic debate between 'The Soul' and 'The Heart,' already cited as the second of my epigraphs to Part One. Once again, and more dramatically, the more Yeatsian of the interlocutors resists the option of chanting in *'a tongue men do not know.'* The Soul offers 'Isaiah's coal,' adding, in an imperious rhetorical question, 'what more can man desire?' But the Heart, 'a singer born,' refuses to be 'struck dumb in the simplicity of fire,' his tongue purified but cauterized by the spiritual fire of that live coal the angel took from God's altar and brought to the prophet's lips in Isaiah 6:6–7. Having refused to 'seek out' spiritual 'reality,' the Heart goes on, after indignantly rejecting Isaiah's coal and 'the simplicity of fire,' to adamantly spurn Soul's final promise and threat: 'Look on that fire, salvation walks within.'

The Heart anachronistically but dramatically responds, 'What theme had Homer but original sin?' Though it firmly stands its *antithetical* ground, the Heart does not deny the lot-darkening concept of original sin, and accepts the notional distinction (Platonic and Neoplatonic, Hindu and Christian) between spiritual 'reality' and material 'things that [merely] seem.' But since it is these things of the world that fuel an artist's fire and provide a resinous theme, the Heart emotionally dissents. I am here alluding to the final Dionysian lines of the curtain-closing song (written the year before 'Vacillation,' VII) for Yeats's play, *The Resurrection*: 'Whatever flames upon the night/ Man's own resinous heart has fed.' In this second of 'Two Songs from a Play,' Yeats echoes and alters Virgil's Fourth, so-called Messianic, Eclogue. In the song as in the play, ambivalent Yeats remains torn between the world of spirit and more human images. As a reader of Nietzsche, who celebrated Dionysus rather than 'the Crucified,' Yeats is recalling that torches of resinous pine were carried by the Bacchantes: the devotees of Dionysus, whose heart was torn out of his side in the opening song. With that marvelous adjective 'resinous,' Yeats ends by emphasizing Dionysus as much as Jesus, even in a play focused on Christ's Resurrection. The tension between interdependent contraries, the divine and the human, and the titular vacillation, persists—as does the desire to merge the antinomies at some 'trysting place,' Yeats's heart-language characteristically 'mingling' the spiritual and the erotic.

But we have jumped ahead four decades. Before turning to 'The Secret Rose,' which appeared in Yeats's next volume, three other poems from *The Rose* merit comment. The first of these, 'The Rose of the World,' is also the first to suggest a connection linking Celtic and Greek mythology with Maud Gonne, her beauty resembling that of Deirdre and of Helen, for whose red lips, 'Troy passed away in one high funeral gleam.' The other two—'Who Goes with Fergus?' (later added to *The Rose*) and, immediately following, 'The Man who Dreamed of Faeryland'—are both beautiful, and both embody the tension between the two worlds. The first suggests that the peace promised by an alluring Otherworld is more tumultuous than it appears; the second, like *The Seeker* and 'The Stolen Child,' stresses the human cost of seduction by Otherworldly dreams. I will return to 'The Man who Dreamed of Faeryland' later in this volume, juxtaposing it with 'What Then?,' a poem written almost a half-century later, and which, I believe, amounts to a point-by-point refutation of the earlier poem—except, crucially, for the refrain.

The 'Faeryland' poem is a catalog of might-have-beens. The 'tenderness' of love; the 'prudent years' that might have freed him from 'money cares and fears'; the 'fine angry mood' leading to 'vengeance' upon mockers; and, finally, 'unhaunted sleep in the grave': all have been lost, spoiled by the repeated 'singing' of 'an unnecessary cruel voice' that 'shook the man out of his new ease,' paralyzing him so that he dies without ever having lived.[7] The voice—a variation on the siren call of the fairies in 'The Stolen Child' (*Come away, O human child!*) and on the 'voice' that beckons and deceives the victim of *The Seeker*—emanates, ultimately, from the Otherworld, in this case from a Celtic 'woven world-forgotten isle,' where

> There dwelt a gay, exulting, gentle race
> Under the golden or the silver skies;
> That if a dancer stayed his hungry foot
> It seemed the sun and moon were in the fruit;
> And at that singing he was no more wise.

The poem ends, 'The man has found no comfort in the grave.' But that closing line is immediately preceded by a rather cryptic couplet: 'Why should those lovers that no lovers miss/ Dream, until God burn Nature with a kiss?' In Fairyland, where the boughs are 'changeless' and the waves 'dreamless,' all dreams are presumably fulfilled, as are the desires of those perfect lovers. There is no need for further dreaming, 'until God burn Nature with a kiss.' The poems of early Yeats have their apocalypses, the most dramatic the windblown Blakean conflagration in 'The Secret Rose.' But the apocalypse in the 'Fairyland' poem is unexpected—unless one knows Yeats's Celtic Twilight tale, 'The Untiring Ones,' where fairies dance on and on, 'until God shall burn up the world with a kiss' (Myth, 78).

We also have a supposedly perfect world, with the 'deep wood's woven shade' and lovers who 'dance upon the level shore,' in 'Who Goes with Fergus?' Originally a song in the earliest version (1892) of Yeats's

---

7   In his jauntily bleak 'Miniver Cheevy' (1910), American poet Edward Arlington Robinson gave us another frustrated Romantic dreamer (as chivalry-intoxicated as Don Quixote) who, wasting his life, 'sighed for what was not,/ And dreamed, and rested from his labors.'

play *The Countess Kathleen*, it was a favorite among the early Yeats poems memorized by James Joyce—the song he sang in lieu of the requested prayer at his mother's deathbed and whose words haunt his alter ego, Stephen Dedalus, throughout Bloomsday. The King of Ulster who put aside his crown to be 'no more a king,/ But learn the dreaming wisdom' of the Druids, now lives in the deep woods. He invites, or tempts, others, specifically a pair of troubled lovers, to join him (is he lonely?) in his ostensibly perfect and peaceful paradise:

> Who will go drive with Fergus now,
> And pierce the deep wood's woven shade,
> And dance upon the level shore?
> Young man, lift up your russet brow,
> And lift your tender eyelids, maid,
> And brood on hopes and fear no more.
>
> And no more turn aside and brood
> Upon love's bitter mystery;
> For Fergus rules the brazen cars,
> And rules the shadows of the wood,
> And the white breast of the dim sea
> And all disheveled wandering stars.

As indicated by the chiasmus linking the last line of the first stanza with the first line of the second, these two 6-line stanzas partially mirror each other. But while the wood and the sea of the second sestet parallel 'the deep wood's woven shade' and the 'level shore' of the first, the final and most striking line of the poem, elevating and expanding our gaze to those 'disheveled wandering stars,' has no precursor. As such, it requires particular attention. Fergus's otherworld seems peaceful and untroubled, but there are echoes of the false paradise offered by Milton's Satan; and the final three lines (anticipating the turbulent final lines of 'Byzantium') amount to a disturbance of the peace. For despite the emotional respite promised by Fergus, the poem's culminating imagery—'shadows' of the wood, the 'white breast' of the dim sea, above all those 'disheveled' wandering stars—extends to the forest, the sea, and the heavens themselves, all the erotic tumult of 'love's bitter mystery,' albeit naturalized and sublimated.

This sublimated erotic tumult is not unprepared for; it is foreshadowed in retrospect by the displaced sexuality of Fergus's poem-opening verbs, 'drive' and 'pierce.' But the enchanting and disturbing final line suggests, by allusion, other erotic connections. 'All disheveled wandering stars' fuse the 'golden tresses' Eve 'wore/ Disheveled' and in 'wanton ringlets' in *Paradise Lost* (IV. 305–6) with Pope's echo in *The Rape of the Lock*, which ends with Belinda's shorn tresses consecrated 'midst the Stars': 'Not Berenice's Locks first rose so bright,/ The Heavens bespangling with disheveled Light.' Those sexual undercurrents are also present in 'Who Goes with Fergus?'

In the next chapter, we will move from quest to reincarnation, from Fairyland to Byzantium, and, via the final 'Rose' poem, the violent but benignly apocalyptic 'The Secret Rose,' to the far better-known and bestial apocalypse of 'The Second Coming.'

4. The Byzantium Poems and Apocalypse in 'The Secret Rose' and 'The Second Coming'

The quest-theme, first established crudely in *The Seeker*, beautifully if ambivalently in 'The Stolen Child,' 'The Man who Dreamed of Faeryland,' and 'Who Goes with Fergus?,' and, perhaps most seminally in 'To the Rose upon the Rood of Time,' also provides the structure for the two 'Byzantium' poems. Before discussing the last of the Rose poems, 'The Secret Rose,' I would therefore like to jump ahead three decades, leaving behind for a few moments Fairyland and the Celtic Twilight in order to engage the more vigorous poetry attending the imaginary voyages to a very different Otherworld. Taken together, the two 'Byzantium' poems feature, first, a sailing after knowledge and, second, a process of purgation, both of which turn out to be simultaneously spiritual and erotic. The *subject* of both 'Byzantium' poems is the opposition of flesh and spirit, natural flux and spiritual form; but their shared *theme* is that these antitheses are polarities—Blakean Contraries inextricably interdependent. The 'Byzantium' poems seem proof of the artistic truth of Yeats's Golden Dawn name, *Demon Est Deus Inversus*, and of Blake's proverb, 'Eternity is in love with the productions of time.' That proverb, the tenth, is from *The Marriage of Heaven and Hell*, Blake's affirmation of the polar nature of being, privileging, in the dialectic of necessary Contraries, 'Energy' and the active 'Prolific' over the 'Devouring,' the passive and religious (Plates 3, 7, 16). Yeats is pulled between these Contraries.

In 'Sailing to Byzantium' (1926), a sixty-year-old and temporarily impotent poet, painfully aware that the world of youth and sexual vitality is 'no country for old men,' sets sail for and has finally 'come/

    https://doi.org/10.11647/OBP.0275.04

To the holy city of Byzantium.' But is all changed? The opening stanza's 'young/ In one another's arms, birds in the trees,/ —Those dying generations—at their song' are reversed yet mirrored in the final stanza. 'Once out of nature,' the aging speaker, his heart 'sick with desire/ And fastened to a dying animal,' imagines that heart, purged in 'God's holy fire,' consumed away and himself (with what Denis Donoghue once wittily characterized as 'the desperate certainty of a recent convert') transformed into a bird of 'hammered gold and gold enameling,' set 'upon a golden bough to sing/ To lords and ladies of Byzantium/ Of what is past, or passing, or to come.'

In a 1937 BBC broadcast, Yeats glossed the golden bird and Virgilian golden bough as symbolic 'of the intellectual joy of eternity, as contrasted to the instinctual joy of human life.' That Platonic/Plotinian contrast with nature is most certainly there. But these golden artifacts are still, however changed, recognizable 'birds in the trees,' so that, whatever the ostensible thrust of the poem, the undertow of the imagery recreates— as in the 'white breast' and 'disheveled' stars of the supposedly tumult-free final stanza of 'Who Goes with Fergus?'—the world being 'rejected.' Further, the now-avian poet is singing to 'lords and ladies' of Byzantium, the sexual principle surviving even in that 'holy city'; and his theme, 'What is past, or passing, or to come,' repeats—in a Keatsian 'finer tone,' to be sure—the three-stage cycle of generation presented in the opening stanza: 'Whatever is begotten, born, and dies.' 'Caught in that sensual music,' those 'dying generations [...] neglect/ Monuments of unageing intellect.' But the golden bird set on the golden bough, however symbolic of ageless intellect, still seems partially caught in that sensual music, singing of the cycle of time to lords and ladies. Despite the poem's haughty dismissal of 'any natural thing,' nature is the source of art, which, in turn, expresses nature; and the audience will always necessarily be men and women.

I've referred to 'Byzantium'—borrowing the adjective from 'Mohini Chatterjee,' the poem that immediately precedes it—as Yeats's most 'turbulent' engagement in the tension, marked by conflict and continuity, between flesh and spirit, natural and supernatural, Time and Eternity. Though he admired the first 'Byzantium' poem, Yeats's friend Sturge Moore expressed a serious reservation: 'Your "Sailing to Byzantium," magnificent as the first three stanzas are, lets me down in the fourth, as such a goldsmith's bird is as much nature as a man's body, especially if it only sings like Homer and Shakespeare of what is past or passing or to come to Lords and Ladies' (LTSM, 164). It's difficult to believe that this was news to Yeats; but, agreeing with Moore to the extent that his friend had shown him that 'the idea needed exposition,' he set out to address the issue in a second poem.

The result, written in September 1930, was 'Byzantium,' a poem that complicates rather than resolves Sturge Moore's intelligent quibble. Holy and purgatorial though the city may be, as the 'unpurged images of day recede,' the 'Emperor's' soldiery are described as 'drunken' and 'abed,' perhaps exhausted from visiting temple prostitutes, since we hear, as night's resonance recedes, 'night-walkers' song/ After great cathedral gong.' Amid considerable occult spookiness, including a walking mummy (more image than shade or man), two images of the eternal emerge: the works of architect and goldsmith, both transcending and scorning the human cycle, sublunary and changeable: 'A starlit or a moonlit dome disdains/ All that man is,/ All mere complexities,/ The fury and the mire of human veins.'

The second emblem of eternity reprises the first poem's icon of 'hammered gold and gold enameling,' the form the speaker of 'Sailing to Byzantium' imagined himself taking once he was 'out of nature.' This avian artifact,

> Miracle, bird, or golden handiwork,
> More miracle than bird or handiwork,
> Planted on the starlit golden bough,
> Can, like the cocks of Hades crow,
> Or, by the moon embittered, scorn aloud
> In glory of changeless metal
> Common bird or petal
> And all complexities of mire and blood.

However golden and immutable it may be, that the miraculous bird can be moon-embittered and scornful suggests that it may be 'almost as much nature' as the golden bird Moore found insufficiently transcendent in the first Byzantium poem. Even in the overtly *primary* or soul-directed 'Byzantium' poems, the *antithetical* or life-directed impulse is too passionate to be programmatically subdued. We remember (as with the 'Byzantium' poems' precursors, Keats's 'Nightingale' and 'Grecian Urn' odes) the rich vitality of the sexual world being 'rejected' in the first poem, and the possible ambiguity of the famous phrase, 'the artifice

of eternity.' And the final tumultuous stanza of 'Byzantium,' especially
its astonishing last line, evokes a power almost, but not quite, beyond
critical analysis.

The multitude of souls ('Spirit after spirit!') riding into the holy city,
each 'Astraddle on the dolphin's mire and blood,' cannot be controlled,
even though that surging power is said to be broken by the Byzantine
artificers and artifacts. The poem ends with a single extraordinary burst,
asserting one thing thematically, but, in its sheer momentum and syntax,
suggesting quite another:

> The smithies break the flood,
> The golden smithies of the Emperor!
> Marbles of the dancing floor
> Break bitter furies of complexity,
> Those images that yet
> Fresh images beget,
> That dolphin-torn, that gong-tormented sea.

The marbled floor is not only the site for the preceding stanza's ritual
of purgation, where the spirits are envisioned 'dying into a dance'; the
floor itself seems to be 'dancing,' the city almost lifted off its dykes under
the inundation of the prolific sea of generation. There is a protective
barrier against the full impact of the waves. The Emperor's smithies and
marbles, we are twice told, 'break' (defend against, order, tame) these
'furies,' these 'images,' and the sea itself. All three are the direct objects of
that one verb; but, as Helen Vendler has observed, 'Practically speaking,
the governing force of the verb "break" is spent long before the end
of the sentence is reached.'[1] The artistic defenses erected to order and
transform the flood end up emphasizing instead the turbulent plenitude
of nature, and those spawning 'images that yet/ Fresh images beget.'

We end with what is, phonetically and in tension-riddled power,
one of the most remarkable single lines in all of English literature: 'That
dolphin-torn, that gong-tormented sea.' Along with the images that yet
fresh images 'beget,' that final line overpowers even the teeming fish
and flesh—all that is 'begotten, born, and dies,' the 'salmon-falls, the
mackerel-crowded seas'—of 'Sailing to Byzantium.' The dolphin is at

---

1   Vendler, *Yeats's* Vision *and the Later Plays*, 118. The floor is ambiguously 'marbled.'
     One draft, referring to the 'emperor's bronze & marble,' suggests statuary, as in the
     statues of 'Among School Children,' that 'keep a marble or a bronze repose.'

once the mythological savior and transporter of souls to paradise and kin to us, who share its complexities of 'mire and blood.' Inversely, the 'gong,' though emblematic of Time, also, since it recalls the semantron of the opening stanza, the 'great cathedral gong,' has to be seen and heard as tormenting the surface of life, yet pulling the sea of generation up, to the spiritual source of life's transcendence. Once again—though more powerfully than usual—we are caught up in the dialectical conflict between time and eternity, sexuality and spirituality, self and soul.

§

We may now return to 'The Secret Rose' (1896) which appeared in Yeats's third collection, the autumnal *The Wind Among the Reeds* (1899). This *fin-de-siècle* and *symboliste* volume (his friend Arthur Symons's influential *The Symbolist Movement in Poetry* appeared the same year), evokes a fallen world, soon to be visited by a longed for apocalyptic wind. This volume includes what may be Yeats's most beautiful early poem. The exquisite 'Song of Wandering Aengus' projects ultimate union between the temporal and eternal as a sublime yet sexual mingling (as in that dreamt of 'Faeryland,' where 'the sun and moon were in the fruit') of lunar apples of silver and solar apples of gold: a marriage of alchemy and Deuteronomy. I discuss this poem in Part Two in connection with Maud Gonne.

Less entrancing poems in *The Wind Among the Reeds* feature a world-weary speaker who, to quote the longest-titled poem in a volume of many long titles, 'mourns for the Change that has come upon him and his Beloved, and longs for the End of the World.' That consummation devoutly to be wished is far more dramatic in 'The Secret Rose,' which I have deliberately delayed discussing until now. The last of Yeats's explicit 'Rose' poems, it begins and ends, 'Far off, most secret, and inviolate Rose': a rondure suggesting that all will be enfolded (the verb 'enfold' appears twice in the poem) within the petals of the symbolic flower. The Seeker is among those questers who have 'sought thee in the Holy Sepulchre, / Or in the wine vat,' a questing alternately Christian or Dionysian. Wandering Aengus sought his elusive beauty (the 'apple-blossom in her hair' allying her with Maud Gonne, associated from the day Yeats met her with apple blossom) through hollow lands and hilly lands suggestive of a woman's body. The Seeker in 'The Secret Rose'

also, over many years, 'sought through lands and islands numberless
[...]/ Until he found'—unsurprisingly since this poem, too, was written
for Maud Gonne—'a woman, of so shining loveliness' that *one* desired
consummation suggests another. No sooner is the beautifully tressed
woman of shining loveliness 'found' (a state projected in 'The Song of
Wandering Aengus,' where 'I *will* find out where she has gone') than
we are told:

> I, too, await
> The hour of thy great wind of love and hate.
> When shall the stars be blown about the sky,
> Like the sparks blown out of a smithy, and die?
> Surely thine hour has come, thy great wind blows,
> Far off, most secret, and inviolate Rose?

This early apocalypse, with its approaching 'hour' and final questions,
looks before and after. That 'surely' anticipates ('Surely some revelation
is at hand;/ Surely the Second Coming is at hand') Yeats's most powerful,
terrifying, yet longed-for apocalypse: his reversal of the *Parousia* of
Christ in the century's most-quoted poem. '*Surely thine hour has come*':
foreshadowing the advent of the rough beast, 'its hour come round at
last,' this line echoes and reverses Jesus' initial retort to his mother, who
suggests that he miraculously resupply the wine that has run out during
the wedding at Cana: 'Woman, what has this to do with me? My hour
is not yet come' (John 2:4). As Helen Vendler has recently suggested,
that allusion is compounded by its Shakespearean reverberation in the
remark of the French nobleman on the eve of the battle of Agincourt,
who looks forward to English corpses and the carrion crows that will 'Fly
o'er them, all impatient for their hour.' That line from *Henry V*, Vendler
observes, 'adds the malice and impatience that will be incorporated by
Yeats in his image of the rough beast.'[2]

Just as the apocalyptic 'hour' of 'The Secret Rose' looks before as
well as after; and just as 'The Second Coming' had a genesis both occult
and literary, so too with the apocalypse of 'The Secret Rose.' In both
cases, the primary literary source is Blake. The slouching rough beast
of the later poem fuses (among other creatures) Blake's sublime Tyger

---

2   'Loosed Quotes,' 133–34. Vendler argues that critical focus on the opening octave
     of 'The Second Coming' has caused this 'intricate' poem *as a whole*—in which Yeats
     ultimately repudiates and disavows the 'vain human temptation to prophesy'—to
     be 'regularly misread' (139).

with his striking illustration (in *The Marriage of Heaven and Hell* and elsewhere) of bestial Nebuchadnezzar slouching on all fours. In 'The Secret Rose,' whatever its Rosicrucian sources, the precursor passage is Blake's description, in the apocalyptic final 'Night' of *The Four Zoas*, of 'The stars consumed like a lamp blown out,' which reappear as Yeats's 'stars,' extinguished after being 'blown about the sky/ Like the sparks blown out of a smithy.' Even Yeats's substitution of a smithy for a lamp pays tribute to Blake's blacksmith-god, Los (in Eternity, Urthona).

The Blakean echo is hardly accidental. Of Yeats's three 1890s Rosicrucian short stories, the first, *Rosa Alchemica*, is most closely related to 'The Secret Rose.' The hero of *Rosa Alchemica*, the magician Michael Robartes, is a student of comparative literature, especially drawn, as was Yeats, to the prophetic poems of William Blake. Blake's epic *The Four Zoas* (first titled *Vala*, and abandoned in manuscript in 1807) was rediscovered and published in 1893 by none other than Yeats (and Edwin Ellis). In the finale, from which Yeats lifted his image of stars dying after being 'blown' about the sky like 'sparks,' redeemed 'Man' (meaning the redeemed human being), having finally purged all the evil in himself, looks at infinity unharmed. Los 'rose in all his regenerative power'; the hour of transformation has arrived:

> The sun has left his blackness & found a fresher morning,
> And the mild moon rejoices in the clear & cloudless night,
> And Man walks forth from midst of the fires, the evil is all consumed:
> His eyes behold the angelic spheres arising night & day;
> The stars consumed like a lamp blown out, & in their stead, behold:
> The expanding eyes of Man behold the depths of wondrous worlds.
> (IX.822–27)

Here we have the potentially divine 'Man' envisioned by so many Gnostics, Hermeticists, Cabbalists, Rosicrucians, and Alchemists. The great Gnostic Valentinus was unknown to Yeats, who was, however, familiar with the half-mythological medieval alchemist, Basilius Valentinus, whose 'Twelve Keys' are cited by Yeats in *Rosa Alchemica*. This Valentinus compares 'the fire of the Last Day to the fire of the alchemists, and the world to the alchemist's furnace,' in which 'all must be dissolved before the divine substance, material gold or immaterial ecstasy, awake' (Myth, 270). Basilius Valentinus' 'new man, more noble in his glorified state' than he was before 'the conflagration,' is a 'Man' fully human, liberated from all imprisoning limitations, whether of materialism, the

Lockean / empiricist senses, or political tyranny.[3] In the final lines of
The Four Zoas, Urthona, the eternal form of Los, 'rises from the ruinous
walls/ In all his ancient strength.' (One of Yeats's, and Joyce's, favorite
phrases of Blake comes from an 1800 letter to William Hayley: 'The ruins
of Time build mansions in Eternity.') In Blake's anything-but-static
Eternity, Urthona, though still ready for the creative strife of Contraries
in the Blakean Eden, is now armed to wage 'intellectual war,' the 'war
of swords' having 'departed' (IX.849–51). In his most famous appeal
(in what is now known as the hymn 'Jerusalem') for an imaginative
art prophetically inspired and intended to achieve individual and
societal redemption, building a new 'Jerusalem' in England, Blake says
his 'sword' will not 'sleep' in his hand. But his weaponry (sword, 'Bow
of burning gold,' 'Arrows of desire,' spear, and 'Chariot of fire') is to
be employed in ceaseless '*Mental* Fight.' He has, Gnostics would say,
achieved *gnosis*, a state anticipated in Yeats's longed for apocalypse in
'The Secret Rose.'

These two apocalypses are benign. That of 'The Second Coming,'
though also anticipated and partially longed for, is different. The 'vast
image' of the sphinx-beast that rises up from 'sands of the desert' had
its occult (as opposed to literary / Blakean) origin in an 1890 symbolic-
card experiment conducted with Yeats by MacGregor Mathers, head of
the Golden Dawn, an experiment also participated in by Florence Farr,
not only a great beauty, accomplished actress and musician to whom
Yeats was attracted, but a gifted adept. Yeats suddenly saw 'a gigantic
Negro raising up his head and shoulders among great stones' (Mem,
71), changed in its published version to 'a desert and a Black Titan' (Au,
180). In his description of the occult experiment with Mathers, Yeats
acknowledges that (unlike the 'crowning moment' achieved by Florence
Farr) 'sight came slowly, there was not that sudden miracle as if the
darkness had been cut with a knife' (Au, 185). That simile reappears in
the drafts of 'The Second Coming.' Introducing the moment preceding
the vision of the vast image rising up out of *Spiritus Mundi*, Yeats first
wrote: 'Before the dark was cut as by a knife.' That he cancelled the

---

3   In *Rosa Alchemica*, Yeats cites the 'ninth key,' to which should be added the 'Fourth
    Key': 'At the end [...] the world shall be judged by fire,' and, the alchemist adds,
    alluding to Isaiah, 'After the conflagration, there shall be formed a new heaven and
    a new earth, and the new man will be more noble in his glorified state than he was
    before.' Waite, I, 331.

line is one of several indications of the shift from the poem's opening certitude to the *un*certainty of the second movement, beginning with that twice repeated but nevertheless equivocal 'Surely.'[4]

Like 'The Secret Rose,' 'The Second Coming' ends in a mysterious question mingling breathless anticipation with ambiguity, in an uncertain certitude. The final movement begins 'But now I *know*,' yet ends with a question, the mark of the excited yet terrified reverie that defines the Sublime. Whatever visionary certitude is claimed, knowledge was reserved, in the drafts, to the apocalyptic 'rough beast' itself: 'And now at last *knowing its hour* come round/ *It* has set out for Bethlehem to be born.' In the published text, Yeats ends, grammatically, with an assertion. But his subjective perplexity, at variance with the objective omniscience of the opening eight lines, compels him to conclude with a question mark—a terrified and humbling response reflecting that of the Hebrew apocalyptic visionary, Daniel.

In his long note to the poem, occultist Yeats anticipated and welcomed a post-Christian civilization. But then there is the actual poem. Unlike the opening octave of oracular declarations (a parody of naively *optimistic* Christian certitude), the second part, its fourteen lines taking the unexpected form of an unrhymed sonnet, is less aloofly visionary than human and uncertain. In the Ninth Night of *The Four Zoas* and 'The Secret Rose,' destruction is the prerequisite to re-creation, the consummation of time and the onset of eternity, or at least the re-emergence of a better historical era. That archetypal pattern dominates Yeats's occult note to the poem, in which, having reproduced the double cone of *A Vision*, he informs us that 'the end of an age' is represented by 'the coming of one gyre to its place of greatest expansion and of the other to that of its greatest contraction.' What will be swept away is not only *primary* Christianity but 'all our scientific, democratic, fact-finding [...] civilization,' to be replaced by an *antithetical* aristocratic civilization, based on the esoteric materials allegedly given to Michael Robartes by a fictive Arab sect (the 'Judwalis'), but sounding decidedly Nietzschean. 'When the revelation comes it will not come to the poor but to the great and learned and establish again for two thousand years prince & vizier. Why should we resist?' (VP, 823–25)

---

4   I quote the drafts as transcribed in my *Yeats's Interactions*, 65, and, for the beast 'knowing *its* hour', 100.

This is the welcome change, the confident occultist assures us, to be ushered in by the birth of the rough beast. But the poem itself has a decidedly different tale to tell. For, 'surely,' the newborn age is likely to take the *un*-civilized, chaotic shape prefigured by its brutal engendering. With that plot shift or *peripeteia*, the theoretician and cold-eyed clairvoyant in Yeats yields to the poet and man whose vision of the beast, however titillating, *truly* 'troubles my sight.' Yeats is here in accord with the response of Daniel (two centuries before an echoing John of Patmos in Rev. 13) to the final and most 'terrifying and dreadful' of the 'four great beasts' he sees in a dream: 'my spirit was troubled within me, and the visions of my head terrified me [...] I was dismayed by the vision and did not understand it' (Dan 7:19–20, 8:15–27).

This deeper insight, knowing that we do not know, in a Daniel or a Yeats, is also a form of *gnosis*, but a higher form, more human and accurate than recklessly prophetic and oracular.[5] In her 1996 Nobel Prize acceptance speech, Polish poet Wislawa Szymborska celebrated the three words, 'I don't know,' a small phrase that 'flies on mighty wings.' She noted that 'Poets, if they're genuine, must also keep repeating "I don't know."' Her predecessor as a Nobel laureate, the man who wrote that long note about history-determining gyres and cycles, was an occultist and something of a right-wing crank. The man who envisioned and wrote 'The Second Coming' was a poet, and the poem that emerged burst the limits of Yeats's own accompanying prose note. As D. H. Lawrence reminds us, 'Never trust the teller, trust the tale. The proper function of the critic is to save the tale from the artist who created it.'[6]

---

5   The dangers of pseudo-historical cyclicism are exemplified by *The Fourth Turning: What the Cycles of History Tell Us About America's Next Rendezvous with Destiny* (1997), by William Strauss and Neil Howe, a book that asserts that violence must necessarily precede full 'Awakening.' The projected crisis may not 'require total war, but it does require a major discontinuity or *ekpyrosis*—the death of an old order and the rebirth of something new' (51). Barely tolerable in Yeats, this apocalyptic gibberish has been enthusiastically endorsed by Steve Bannon and other architects of the seditious attempt on 6 January 2021 by Donald Trump and his more conspiracy-addled followers (QAnon, Proud Boys, Oath Keepers, et al.) to carry out a violent insurrection in an attempt, with the passive complicity of a craven Republican Party, to overturn the 2020 US presidential election. See Adele M. Stans.

6   Lawrence, *Studies in Classic American Literature*, 14. Szymborska, 'The Poet and the World.'

5. Gnosis and Self-Redemption

Gnosis takes many forms. I just noted what the visionary poet of 'The Second Coming' claims to 'know,' and the very different acknowledgment in the punctuation and in the drafts, where the role of seer is usurped by the rough beast itself, 'knowing its hour come round.' The annunciation to the Virgin Mary two thousand years earlier, though it resulted in the Incarnation, left Yeats's Magi, the star-led Seekers who had come to Bethlehem, 'unsatisfied' by the subsequent crucifixion on Calvary. Thus, they long—to quote the memorable final line of 'The Magi' (1913)—for another 'uncontrollable mystery on the bestial floor.' As with so many questers in Yeats, they would be disappointed by the coming, two thousand years later, of something bestial indeed but hardly what they hoped for. 'Leda and the Swan,' the fused sonnet (a Shakespearean octave and Petrarchan sestet) initiating the three-part cycle that ends with the rough beast slouching 'towards Bethlehem to be born,' also prefigures that mystery on the stable floor. Itself bestial, 'Leda and the Swan' signals and embodies the annunciation of the Classical era, and it, too, involves a sexual engendering accompanied by a hint of *gnosis*. Did Leda, raped by the swan-god Zeus, 'put on his knowledge with his power/ Before the indifferent beak could let her drop?' Here is another poem, like 'The Secret Rose' and 'The Second Coming,' ending in a question, the mystery-marker of the Sublime.

There is, of course, *no* question about the brutality of the sudden rape, and the indifference of the God following the 'shudder in the loins,' which, impregnating Leda, completes Zeus's mission. For in fathering Helen of Troy, he also 'engenders there' the Trojan War (depicted in imagery at once military and sexual: 'The broken wall, the burning roof and tower') and its sequelae ('And Agamemnon dead'), initiating an historical cycle destined to last until, two thousand years later, another

 https://doi.org/10.11647/OBP.0275.05

lady, the Virgin Mary, would be visited by the Holy Spirit in the form of a dove: another divine bird, his 'great wings beating about the room' in Yeats's 'The Mother of God.' (Before appearing in *The Tower*, 'Leda and the Swan' introduced the 'Dove or Swan' chapter of *A Vision*.) 'The Mother of God' (1931) is a dramatic monologue spoken by the terrified village girl singled out to bear 'the Heavens in my womb.' Mary's questions ('What is this flesh I purchased with my pains,/ This fallen star my milk sustains [...] ?') concern the central human / divine mystery. And the question raised at the end of 'Leda and the Swan' is not merely rhetorical. Did Leda, whose 'loosening thighs' (an echo of Sappho's famous 'limb-loosening Love'?) are rather tenderly '*caressed/ By the dark webs*,' so intrigue the swan-god that he inadvertently held her just long enough ('Before the indifferent beak *could* let her drop') for her to participate momentarily in 'his knowledge,' the divine *gnosis* of Zeus?

§

Gnosis also figures in the cryptic poem, 'Fragments,' which features, like 'The Mother of God' and its more celebrated cousins, 'Leda and the Swan' and 'The Second Coming,' a strange birth, and a revelation derived from counter-Enlightenment intuition. Written between 1931 and 1933, but placed in later editions of *The Tower* (1928),[1] this epigrammatic poem is in two short sections, both of which require considerable unpacking. Here is the first part, a quatrain:

> Locke sank into a swoon;
> The Garden died;
> God took the spinning-jenny
> Out of his side.

In this parody of Genesis, the role of sleeping Adam, from whose rib God created Eve, is usurped by John Locke, whose empiricist

---

1   Yeats emphasized the connection among various miraculous births and rebirths. First appearing in the canon in the 1933 *Collected Poems*, 'Fragments' was, in the final collection, inserted in the 1928 *The Tower*, with Yeats carefully placing this poem about the birth of the spinning jenny immediately after the equally epigrammatic 'Two Songs from a Play' (*The Resurrection*) and just before 'Wisdom' (with its strange account of the begetting of Jesus) and that history-telescoping dramatization of another mythological begetting, the sonnet 'Leda and the Swan.'

epistemology and distinction between primary and secondary qualities seemed to Yeats, as to George Berkeley and Blake before him, to have fractured the organic unity of the living world, and thus destroyed not only nature but its archetype, the Edenic 'Garden.' That the resultant birth, of the 'spinning-jenny,' bears a woman's name accentuates the irony, and the horror. It was not altogether to the benefit of humanity and a sign of progress, Yeats once mordantly observed, for the home spinning-wheel and the distaff to have been replaced by the robotic looms and masculinized factories of the Industrial Revolution. Blake's god of the fallen world, Urizen, presides over an Enlightenment world-machine perceived as 'the Loom of Locke' washed by the 'Water-wheels of Newton,' all 'cruel Works' with 'cogs tyrannic' moving each other 'by compulsion' (*Jerusalem* Plate 15:15–19).

Yeats is never closer to Blake than in this first part of 'Fragments,' where he emulates not only his mentor's attack on Locke (and Newton), but also his genius for epigram and crystallization, Blake being 'perhaps the finest gnomic artist in English literature.' In Yeats's gnomic vision in 'Fragments' (I), which has been called 'certainly the shortest and perhaps not the least comprehensive history of modern civilization,' the Enlightenment is revealed as a nightmare for the creative imagination; and the monster that rides upon this spirit-sealing sleep of reason is the mechanistic conception of matter, indeed the whole mechanistic rather than organic way of thinking (a crucial contrast Yeats knew from Coleridge, who had borrowed it from A. W. Schlegel), here symbolized by the invention that epitomizes the Industrial Revolution.[2] Yeats replaces the divinely anesthetized flesh of Adam with Locke's imaginatively inert body (sunk into that fall into division Blake called 'Single Vision & Newton's sleep'), and substitutes for Eve, the beautiful embodiment of Adam's dream, a mechanical contraption, a patriarchal cog in the dark satanic mills of which it is proleptic.

But how does Yeats know all this, and know it to be the 'truth'? It wasn't only from absorbing Blake. Or only from reading Alfred North Whitehead's *Science and the Modern World* (1925), a chapter of which, 'The Romantic Reaction,' Yeats synopsized with a related variation on

---

2   For Blake's 'gnomic' genius, see Northrop Frye, *Fearful Symmetry*, 5. On Yeats's synopsis of modern civilization in 'Fragments,' see Douglas Bush, *Science and English Poetry*, 158.

the creation metaphor in the second chapter of Genesis, jotting in the margin: 'The dry rib (Pope) becomes Eve (Nature) with Wordsworth.'[3] Yeats answers his own question in 'Fragments' (II), not, however, by turning to Wordsworth, whose French Revolution-centered books of *The Prelude* figure prominently in the evolution of 'The Second Coming,' but to the occult:

> Where got I that truth?
> Out of a medium's mouth.
> Out of nothing it came,
> Out of the forest loam,
> Out of dark night where lay
> The crowns of Ninevah.

Is this mere occult mumbo-jumbo, intended to twist the tail of positivists and empiricists? Well, yes and no. But before coming to conclusions, let's pause to appreciate the wit of the three couplets, alive with reversals and allusions. Yeats's ironic reversal of the birth 'out of' the side of Locke takes the form of a counter-'truth,' born 'out of' (repeated four times in succession) a variety of sources. The anaphora is Whitmanian—'Out of the cradle endlessly rocking,/ Out of the mocking-bird's throat, the musical shuttle,/ Out of the Ninth-month midnight.' And Whitman's poem-opening birth images may have suggested Yeats's equally fertile sources: the female 'medium's mouth,' the 'forest loam,' and 'dark night,' all in organic and fecund contrast to the mechanical, sterile 'birth' of the spinning jenny.

Yeats deliberately begins with what rationalists would dismiss as among the least reputable sources of truth: 'Out of a medium's mouth.' Even Madame Blavatsky, whose own experiments had been discredited, told Yeats, who reported it to John O'Leary in a May 1889 letter, that she 'hates spiritualism vehemently—says mediumship and insanity are the same thing' (L, 125). In 'Fragments'(II) Yeats is having some fun, but it is worth mentioning that the poem was written shortly after the first production of Yeats's dramatic ghost-play, *The Words upon the Window-pane*, which centers on a séance, climaxing with our shocked

---

3   Edward O'Shea, *A Descriptive Catalog*, item 2258. And see 'Revolutions French and Russian: Burke, Wordsworth, and the Genesis of Yeats's "The Second Coming",' in my *Yeats's Interactions with Tradition*, 72–105.

recognition that the female medium is authentic. The one scholarly skeptical character attending the séance, a specialist in the life and work of Jonathan Swift, is refuted once the post-séance stage is bare except for the female medium, who is suddenly revealed, not to be faking it as he had been sure all along, but to be channeling the tormented ghost of Swift, and thus speaking the sort of spiritual truth Yeats, half-skeptic himself, sought all his life. 'All about us,' he concludes his Introduction to the play, 'there seems to start up a precise inexplicable teeming life, and the earth becomes once more, not in rhetorical metaphor, but in reality, sacred' (Ex, 369).

The second source is philosophically and theologically scandalous. Subverting the venerable axiom, *ex nihilo nihil fit*, employed by metaphysicians from Parmenides on and by theologians arguing for the necessary existence of God, Yeats boldly declares that the 'truth' revealed to him came 'Out of *nothing*,' only to instantly add details that deepen the mystery and sharpen his thrust against the Enlightenment. Coming 'Out of the forest loam,/ Out of dark night,' Yeats's 'truth' is generated from fecund earth, once more become 'sacred,' and teeming with inexplicable 'life,' replacing or restoring the 'Garden' earlier said to have 'died.' It also comes out of a mysterious, or occult, 'dark night.'

If the spinning jenny epitomizes the Industrial Revolution, Alexander Pope's intended epitaph for Isaac Newton epitomizes the Scientific Revolution and the Enlightenment: 'Nature and Nature's laws lay hid in night,/ God said, *Let Newton be!* And all was light.' Pope's couplet, like Yeats's opening quatrain, plays off scripture, with Newton now assuming God's role as creator by verbal fiat: 'And God said, "Let there be light," and there was light' (Genesis 1:3). Pope avoids blasphemy; after all, it was *God* who said, 'Let Newton be!' Until the advent of the principal scientific genius of the European Enlightenment, the universe existed, but 'Nature and Nature's laws lay hid in night.' Adopting that darkness, and reversing the laws that prior to Newton 'lay hid in night,' Yeats tells us that his counter-Enlightenment truth came 'Out of dark *night* where *lay*,' not Nature's scientific laws, but 'The crowns of Ninevah.'

Why Ninevah in particular? For one thing, Yeats loved Arthur O'Shaughnessy's 'Ode' celebrating poets as music makers and prophets. The famous final stanza (and these are the lines Yeats always cited) begins: 'We, in the ages lying/ In the buried past of the earth,/ Built

Ninevah with our sighing,/ And Babel itself with our mirth.' When, in 'Fragments,' the golden crowns of Ninevah flame up 'Out of dark night,' what is evoked is more O'Shaughnessy's city of the poetic imagination than Ashurbanipal's capital, majestic as that may have been. Yeats was looking, not merely back to old Ninevah, but cyclically ahead, to the resuscitation of the ancient—a past buried, dark, chthonic, and, here, female. For, as Yeats seems to have known, the Assyrians named their capital city Nin-evah—after 'Holy Mother Eve': the Mother-womb, or Goddess of the Tree of Life in their mythology. Displaced by a machine in the withered garden of the first part of 'Fragments,' Eve, in a return of the repressed, is restored, re-surfacing in the final word of Part II, in the disguised but detectable form of the city named for her. Like 'the holy city of Byzantium,' Ninevah emerges as another Yeatsian variation on, or occult alteration of, the biblical *topos* of the lost Edenic garden become a city, which, in Romans, in Revelations, and in Blake is also a woman: the 'holy city, new Jerusalem,' adorned as the 'bride' of the Lamb of God. Recalling the role of *Sophia*, often opposed to the male *Logos* in esoteric tradition, including Gnosticism, one is reminded as well that *gnosis* is a Greek female noun.

At his most winning, Yeats reminds us of Hamlet's rejoinder to his skeptical and scholastic friend: 'There are more things in heaven and earth, Horatio, than are dreamt of in your philosophy.' But we are right to be wary when Yeats crosses the threshold into the occult. Though concurring in, in fact shaping, Yeats's cavalier dismissal of Locke and Newton as Enlightenment icons, Blake would be appalled by his disciple's delving into the occult darkness. Though Yeats tended to mystify him and turn him into an occultist, Blake in fact condemned the heathen 'God of this World & the Goddess Nature/ Mystery, Babylon the Great' (*Jerusalem* Plate *93*: 22–25). But what Blake rejects here are the very things his prodigal son celebrates as the matrix of vision: the forest loam and the mysterious dark night where lay the crowns of ancient Ninevah, repository of Assyro-Babylonian mythology.

Of course, Yeats's recourse to the occult is one measure of the intensity of his need to expedite what he called in that earlier-cited 1892 letter to John O'Leary 'the revolt of the soul against the intellect' (L, 211). That is, somewhat reductively, a description of the Romantic revolution, the noble attempt to beat back, through restored wonder at a re-enchanted nature and the transformative power of the creative imagination, the passivity of mind and mechanistic materialism that had reigned (Yeats insists in introducing his 1936 anthology of modern poetry) since 'the end of the seventeenth century' down to the present. With, he emphasizes—as had Alfred North Whitehead, though his Romantic hero was Wordsworth rather than Blake or Shelley—'the exception of the period beginning at the end of the eighteenth century and ending with the death of Byron': that is to say, the 'brief period' of the Romantic revolt, a span 'wherein imprisoned man beat upon the door.'[4]

That compelling metaphor was repeated that November in 'An Acre of Grass,' a companion of 'What Then?,' in which Yeats prays to be granted the creative 'frenzy' and 'old man's eagle mind' he had been reading of at just this time in Nietzsche's *Daybreak* (§347, §575). He also specifically invokes 'That William Blake/ Who beat upon the wall/ Till truth obeyed his call'—a 'truth' related to, but not identical to, the 'truth' Yeats claimed in 'Fragments' (II) came to him 'Out of' counter-Enlightenment sources both Romantic and, most dubiously, out of a mysterious 'dark night' whose counter-Enlightenment *frisson* will be offset for many readers by resistance to the dangerously irrational aspect of the occult. And yet, to again quote Heaney on Yeats's power and appeal, 'true poetry' had to be more than the 'artful expression of daylight opinion and conviction; it had to emerge from a deeper consciousness of things,' evoking 'the mystery which lies all about us, out of which we have come and into which we shall return.' Reading Yeats, Heaney remarked in a private letter to Joseph Hassett, 'every time you part the drapes and enter into that inner chamber of his, you realize you've only been surfacing an external, daylight world, while the real thing has been going on in the poetry sanctum.'

§

Though, as we shall see in Part Two, Yeats was alternately fascinated and fearful of the creative yet potentially maddening power of a lunar Muse, night was not normally privileged over day in Yeats's thinking. Blake and Nietzsche, his great mentors, were both celebrants of 'daybreak,'

---

4   Yeats, 'Introduction' in *The Oxford Book of Modern Verse*, xxvi-vii. In Whitehead's account of the 'Romantic Reaction,' the principal figure was Wordsworth, influenced by Coleridge on imagination and organicism.

of Blake's 'glad day.' In 1902, enthralled by his 'excited' reading of Nietzsche, Yeats drew in the margin of page 122 of an anthology of 'choice' selections (*Nietzsche as Critic, Philosopher, Poet and Prophet*) given to him as a gift by John Quinn, a diagram crucial to understanding much if not all of his subsequent thought and work. Annotating primarily *On the Genealogy of Morals*, Yeats grouped under the heading 'NIGHT': 'Socrates' (as presented by Plato), 'Christ,' and 'one god'—symbolizing what he would later call the *primary*: the 'denial of self, the soul turned toward spirit seeking knowledge.' And, under 'DAY': 'Homer' and 'many gods'—symbolizing the *antithetical* 'affirmation of self, the soul turned from spirit to be its mask & instrument when it seeks life.' 'Plato versus Homer': *that*, proclaimed Nietzsche in the *Genealogy* (III.25), 'is the complete, the genuine antagonism—there the sincerest advocate of the "Beyond," the greatest slanderer of life, here the distinctive deifier, the *golden* nature' (italics in original). Reminiscent of Madame Blavatsky's alternating 'days and nights of Brahma,' that diagrammatical skeleton is fleshed out in the pull between eternity and the temporal from such early poems as 'To the Rose upon the Rood of Time' to the late 'What Then?,' where the achievements of earthly life are countered by the Otherworldly singing of 'Plato's ghost.' The tension is embodied in Yeats's own chosen exemplar in 'Vacillation'—'Homer is my example and his unchristened heart'—and made tangible in Self's choice, in 'A Dialogue of Self and Soul,' of Sato's sword wound in silken 'embroidery' of 'Heart's purple': 'all these I set/ For emblems of the day against the tower/ Emblematical of the night.' And yet that sword is also described as a 'consecrated blade,' and 'Unspotted by the centuries.' Ultimately, it is the emblem of a life-seeking poet who, without 'denial of self,' attempts to transcend the antithesis set up a quarter-century earlier in that Nietzsche anthology, usurping Soul's role by also being oriented 'toward spirit seeking knowledge,' or *gnosis*.

'A Dialogue of Self and Soul' is in many ways Yeats's central poem since its ramifications reach before and after, and it features perhaps the greatest of Yeats's fused symbols: the 'ancient blade' (a 1920 gift from Japanese admirer, Junzo Sato) scabbarded and bound in complementary 'female' embroidery. That sword and winding silk are not only 'emblems of the day against the tower/ Emblematical of the night.' Fusing East and West, the sacred and profane, war and love, the phallic and the vaginal, the sheathed and silk-wound sword becomes Yeats's symbol of gyring life, set against the vertical ascent urged by the Neoplatonic Soul. What Neoplatonists and Gnostics put asunder, body and spirit, Yeats unites. And yet, as we will see, Self's final act of self-redemption, magnificent but heretical, is as Gnostic as it is Nietzschean.

In the opening movement of the poem, the half in which there is still a semblance of actual dialogue, hectoring Soul repeatedly demands that Self 'fix' every thought 'upon' the One, 'upon' the steep ascent, 'upon' the occult Pole Star, 'upon' the spiritual quarter where all thought is done. But the recalcitrant Self remains diverted by the Many, by earthly multiplicity, by the sword wound in embroidery replicating the windings of mortal nature. In unpublished notes, Yeats describes 'Dialogue' as 'a variation on Macrobius' (the 'learned astrologer' of 'Chosen,' the central poem of 'A Woman Young and Old'). Yeats had been directed by a friend (Frank P. Sturm) to Macrobius's Neoplatonic *Commentary* on Cicero's *Somnium Scipionis*. In Cicero's text (*De re publica*, Book 6:17–20), despite the admonition of Scipio's ghostly ancestor, 'Why not *fix* your attention *upon* the heavens and contemn what is mortal?' young Scipio admits he 'kept turning' his 'eyes back to earth.' According to Macrobius, Scipio 'looked about him everywhere with wonder. Hereupon his grandfather's admonitions recalled him to the upper realms.' Though the *agon* between the Yeatsian Self and Soul is identical to that between young Scipio and his grandfather's spirit, the Soul in Yeats's poem proves a much less successful spiritual guide than that ghost.[5]

Turning a largely deaf ear to Soul's advocacy of the upward path, Self (revealingly called 'Me' in the poem's drafts) has preferred to focus downward on life, brooding on the blade upon his knees with its tattered but still protective wrapping of 'Heart's purple,' Tower and Winding Stair writ small. Its 'flowering, silken, old embroidery, torn/ From some court-lady's dress and round/ The wooden scabbard bound and wound' makes the double icon 'emblematical' not only of 'love and war,' but of the ever-circling gyre: the eternal, and archetypally female, spiral. When Soul's paradoxically physical tongue is turned to stone

---

5   For these unpublished notes, connecting Cicero's *Dream of Scipio* and *Macrobius's Commentary* with Balzac's Swedenborgian novel *Séraphita*, see my *Yeats's Interactions with Tradition*, 142–47.

with the realization that, according to his own austere doctrine, 'only the dead can be forgiven,' Self takes over the poem. He goes on to win his way, despite difficulty, to a *self-redemptive* affirmation of life.

Self begins his peroration defiantly: 'A living man is blind and drinks his drop./ What matter if the ditches are impure?' This 'variation' on Neoplatonism, privileging life's filthy downflow, or 'defluction,' over the Plotinian pure fountain of emanation, is followed by an even more defiant rhetorical question: 'What matter if I live it all once more?' 'Was *that* life?' asks Nietzsche's Zarathustra. 'Well then! Once more!'[6] But Self's grandiose and premature gesture is instantly undercut by the litany of grief that Nietzschean Recurrence, the exact repetition of the events of one's life, would entail—from the 'toil of growing up,' through the 'ignominy of boyhood' and the 'distress' of 'changing into a man,' to the 'pain' of the 'unfinished man' having to confront 'his own clumsiness,' then the 'finished man,' old and 'among his enemies.' Despite the Self's bravado, it is in danger of being shaped, deformed, by what Hegel and, later, feminist critics have emphasized as the judgmental Gaze of Others. Soul's tongue may have turned to stone, but malignant *ocular* forces have palpable designs upon the assaulted Self:

> How in the name of Heaven can he escape
> That defiling and disfigured shape
> The mirror of malicious eyes
> Casts upon his eyes until at last
> He thinks that shape must be his shape?

The triple repetition of 'shape' is significant. For this malicious imposition would involve, as Yeats says in 'Ancestral Houses' (the 1921 opening poem of his sequence 'Meditations in Time of Civil War'), the loss of the ability to 'choose whatever shape [one] wills,' and (echoing Browning's arrogant Duke, who 'choose[s] never to stoop') to 'never stoop to a mechanical/ Or servile shape, at others' beck and call.' As the aristocratic language of 'Ancestral Houses' makes clear, this is Yeats's rejection of 'slave morality' in favor of Nietzschean 'master morality.' In the 'Dialogue,' master morality takes the apolitical and far more appealing form of self-redemptive autonomy, but not without a struggle.

---

6   'Thus Spoke Zarathustra,' III.2:1; in *The Portable Nietzsche*, 269. Italics in original.

The centrality of 'A Dialogue of Self and Soul' is enhanced by its repercussions elsewhere in Yeats's own work and by its absorption of so many influences outside the Yeatsian canon. Aside from the Body / Soul debate-tradition, from Cicero to Milton and Marvell, and the combat between Nietzsche on the one hand and Neoplatonism on the other, this Yeatsian *psychomachia* incorporates other poems in the Romantic tradition. Among them is another Robert Browning poem, 'Childe Roland to the Dark Tower Came,' which supplies those 'malicious eyes' that cast upon Self a distorting lie so powerful that he temporarily falls victim to it, and Blake's remarkably feminist text, *Visions of the Daughters of Albion.*[7] Self's eventual victory, like Oothoon's in *Visions*, is over severe moralism, the reduction of the body to a defiled object. In Yeats's case, Self's victory is a triumph over his own Neoplatonism. Gnosticism, too, seeks liberation from the body, but the heterodox Gnostic emphasis on self-redemption makes it compatible with Blake, Nietzsche, and Yeats. 'Dialogue' represents Nietzschean *Selbstüberwindung*, creative 'self-overcoming,' for, as Yeats said in *Per Amica Silentia Lunae*, 'we make out of the quarrel with others, rhetoric, but of the quarrel with ourselves, poetry' (Myth, 331).

Since this 'Dialogue' is a quarrel with himself, the spiritual tradition is not simply dismissed, here any more than in the 'Crazy Jane' or 'A Woman Young and Old' sequences. For Yeats, the world of experience, however dark the declivities into which the generated soul may drop, is never utterly divorced from the world of light and grace. The water imagery branching through Self's peroration subsumes pure fountain and impure ditches. There is a continuum. The Plotinian fountain cascades down from the divine One through mind or intellect (*nous*) to the lower depths. As long, says Plotinus, as *nous* maintains its contemplative

---

7   In the opening stanza of Browning's quest-poem, Childe Roland first thought was that he was being 'lied' to by that sadistic cripple, 'with *malicious eye*/ Askance to watch the working of *his lie/ On mine.*' (The earlier allusion, to Browning's Duke, refers of course to 'My Last Duchess.') Even closer to Self's temporarily mistaken belief that that 'defiling' shape 'cast upon' him by mirroring eyes 'must be *his* shape' is the initially deluded, masochistic cry of Blake's Oothoon (2:36–39) for her '*defiled bosom*' to be rent away so that she 'may *reflect/* The image' of the very man (the moralistic sadist, Theotormon, who, having raped her, now brands her 'harlot') whose 'loved' but unloving 'eyes' have cast upon her this 'defiled' shape—one of Blake's, now Yeats's, grimmest ironies. But both—Oothoon and the Yeatsian Self—recover.

gaze on the divine 'Father,' it retains God's likeness (*Enneads* 5.2.4). But, writes Macrobius (*Commentary* 1.14.4), by increasingly 'diverting its attention,' the soul, though itself incorporeal, 'degenerates into the fabric of bodies.'

Viewed from Soul's perspective, Self is a falling off from higher Soul. When the attention, supposed to be fixed on things above, is diverted below—down to the blade on his knees wound in tattered silk and, further downward, to life's 'impure' ditches— Self has indeed degenerated into the 'fabric,' the tattered embroidery, of bodies. And yet, as usual in later Yeats, that degradation is also a triumph, couched in terms modulating from stoic contentment through fierce embrace to a casting out of remorse, leading to self-forgiveness and redemption:

> I am content to live it all again
> And yet again, if it be life to pitch
> Into the frog-spawn of a blind man's ditch,
> A blind man battering blind men;
> Or into that most fecund ditch of all,
> The folly that man does
> Or must suffer, if he woos
> A proud woman not kindred of his soul.
>
> I am content to follow to its source
> Every event in action or in thought;
> Measure the lot, forgive myself the lot!
> When such as I cast out remorse
> So great a sweetness flows into the breast
> We must laugh and we must sing,
> We are blest by everything,
> Everything we look upon is blest.

Following everything to the 'source' *within*, Self spurns Soul's tongue-numbing Neoplatonic doctrine that 'only the dead can be forgiven.' Instead, having pitched with vitalistic relish into life's filthy frogspawn, Self audaciously (or blasphemously) claims the power to forgive *himself*. In a similar act of self-determination, Self 'cast[s] out' remorse, reversing the defiling image earlier 'cast *upon*' him by the 'mirror of malicious eyes.' The sweetness that 'flows into' the self-forgiving breast redeems the frogspawn of the blind man's ditch and even that 'most fecund ditch of all,' the painful but productive folly that is the bitter-sweet fruit of unrequited love. (There is no need to name that 'proud woman not kindred of his soul.')

That sweet in-flow also displaces the infusion (*infundere*: 'to pour in') of Christian grace through divine forgiveness. Despite the repeated 'must' ('We must laugh and we must sing'), it is a claim to autonomy at once redemptive and heretical, and a fusion of Yeats's two principal precursors. 'Nietzsche completes Blake, and has the same roots,' Yeats claimed (L, 379). If, as he also rightly said, Blake's central doctrine is a Christ-like 'forgiveness of sins,' the sweetness that flows into the suffering but *self-forgiving* 'breast' (in which Blake also said 'all deities reside') allies the Romantic poet with Nietzsche. He had been preceded by the German Inner Light theologians, but it took Nietzsche, son and grandson of Protestant ministers, to most radically transvalue the Augustinian doctrine that man can only be redeemed by divine power and grace, a foretaste of predestination made even more uncompromising in the strict Protestant doctrine of the salvation of the Elect as an unmerited gift of God. One must find one's *own* 'grace,' countered Nietzsche in *Daybreak*, a book studied by Yeats. In Nietzsche's words, he who has 'definitively *conquered himself*, henceforth regards it as his own privilege to punish himself, to pardon himself'—or, as rephrased by Yeats, 'forgive myself the lot.' We must cast out remorse and cease to despise ourselves: 'Then you will,' says Nietzsche, 'no longer have any need of your god, and the whole drama of Fall and Redemption will be played out to the end in you yourselves!'[8]

But, as I earlier suggested, this is as Gnostic as it is Nietzschean. The most formidable of the historical Gnostics, Valentinus, claimed that the person who received *gnosis* could purge *himself* of the ignorance associated with matter. He describes the process in the 'Gospel of Truth,' a Valentinian text unearthed at Nag Hammadi in 1945. In stark contrast with the orthodox Christian doctrine of salvation through the grace of God, Valentinus declared that 'It is within Unity that each one will attain himself; within *gnosis* he will purify himself from multiplicity into Unity, consuming matter within himself like a fire, and darkness by light, death by life.' Here, and elsewhere in Gnostic literature, salvation

---

8   Nietzsche, *Daybreak* (§437, §79), 186–87, 48. In *The Marriage of Heaven and Hell*, Plate 11, Blake insists that in setting up a religious 'system' presided over by a ''Priesthood,' men and women "forgot that All deities reside in the human breast.'

is defined, as it is in Romanticism (from which Gnosticism occasionally seems less a deviation than a precursor), as an escape *into* the self, where, through introspective private vision, we find true knowledge, *gnosis*. The spiritual quest tends to be solitary. When Sturge Moore, who was designing the book cover for the volume containing 'Byzantium,' asked if the poet saw 'all humanity riding on the back of a huge dolphin,' Yeats responded, 'One dolphin, one man' (LTSM, 165). There is no real need for any Other; the individual who has attained *gnosis* is the whole and sole agent of redemption. (It should be added that Yeats valued community. In 'What Then?' he cherished 'Friends that have been friends indeed.' He loved the women celebrated in 'Friends,' and meant it when he ended 'The Municipal Gallery Revisited,' after reflecting with emotion on the dead companions whose portraits hung there: 'Think where man's glory most begins and ends,/ And say my glory was I had such friends.')

In the now-celebrated Gospel of Thomas, the most audaciously heterodox of the Nag Hammadi texts, the Gnostic Jesus of Thomas tells us, 'Whoever drinks from my mouth will become as I am.' The central teaching is redemption from within: 'If you bring forth what is within you, what you bring forth will save you. If you do not bring forth what is within you, what you do not bring forth will destroy you.' If Emerson, prophet of self-reliance, hadn't been speaking more than a century before the Gospel of Thomas had been rediscovered, he might have been accused of plagiarizing from it in his Divinity School Address, the bombshell he exploded at Harvard in 1838. Reflecting the spiritual and Romantic concept of divinity within, Emerson celebrated Jesus not as the Lord, but as the religious thinker who first realized that 'God incarnates himself in man.' He informed the shocked ministers and thrilled graduating students in the audience: 'That is always best which gives me to myself. That which shows God in me, fortifies me. That which shows God out of me, makes me a wart and a wen.' As heterodox as Thomas's, Emerson's Jesus is imagined saying, in 'a jubilee of sublime emotion, "I am divine. Through me, God acts; through me, speaks. Would you see God, see me; *or see thee, when thou also thinkest as I now think*".'[9]

---

9   *Emerson: Essays and Lectures*, 81. The Divinity School Address controversy shook
     New England. Condemned as a 'pagan,' an 'infidel,' and a 'cloven-hoofed' pantheist

Despite such assertions of autonomy and of heretical (high Romantic or Gnostic) self-redemption, Yeats never fully appreciated Emerson. But he echoed the American sage's best-known essay, 'Self-Reliance,' in describing, in 'A Prayer for my Daughter,' the radically innocent soul as 'self-delighting,/ Self-appeasing, self-affrighting,' and he embraced Emerson's most ardent European disciple, Nietzsche, with whose thought the Irish poet always associated Blake. It is primarily under the twin auspices of Blake and Nietzsche that the Self of 'Dialogue' finds the bliss traditionally reserved for those who follow the ascending path. Recovering radical innocence, the battered but ultimately childlike Self of 'Dialogue' concludes, 'We must laugh and we must sing,/ We are blessed by everything,/ Everything we look upon is blest.' Though recalling King Lear's projection of happiness with Cordelia ('we'll sing like birds i' the cage'; we'll 'live, and pray, and sing, and laugh'), and the blessing of the water-snakes by Coleridge's Mariner, the more thematic echo is of Oothoon's final affirmation in *Visions*, addressed to everything we bless and are blest by: 'sing your infant joy!/ Arise and drink your bliss, for every thing that lives is holy!' Of that Blakean 'praise of life, "all that lives is holy",' Yeats noted that 'Nietzsche had it doubtless at the moment he imagined the "Superman" as a child,' referring both to Zarathustra's third and final metamorphosis of the spirit (as an 'innocent child,' that 'sacred Yes' to life) and to Nietzsche's evocation, in *The Gay Science*, of 'a second innocence in joy, more childlike and yet a hundred times subtler than one has ever been before.' This childlike second innocence has a Gnostic parallel (the *Logos* dramatically revealed itself to Valentinus in the form of 'a child'); but it would have tallied for Yeats with the final stage of the Blakean dialectical progression from 'Innocence' through 'Experience' to a higher or 'Organiz'd Innocence,' what the American Romantic poet Hart Crane, having read both Blake and Nietzsche, would later call 'an improved infancy.'[10]

---

who had defiled the citadel of Unitarianism, Emerson was ostracized from his alma mater for thirty years. On Thomas's 'bringing-forth' passages, see Pagels, *Beyond Belief*, 49, 32. On the affinity between Gnostic Thomas and the Romantics, see Bloom, *Where Shall Wisdom Be Found?*, 260.

10   *King Lear* V.iii,11–12. Blake, *Visions of the Daughters of Albion*, Plate 8:9–10. 'Thus Spoke Zarathustra' (*The Portable Nietzsche*, 139); *The Gay Science*, Preface. Yeats, 1909 Diary (Au, 474–75). Blake's higher 'innocence' and Nietzsche's 'second innocence' are captured in Crane's 'an improved infancy' (from his poem 'Passage').

Whatever its myriad sources and analogues, Yeats's alteration of the orthodox spiritual tradition in the 'Dialogue' *completes* Blake, for whom cyclicism was the ultimate nightmare, with that Nietzsche whose exuberant Zarathustra jumps 'with both feet' into the 'golden-emerald delight' of self-redemption and Eternal Recurrence, exultantly embraced as the ultimate affirmation of life in the 'Yes and Amen Song' that concludes Part III of *Thus Spoke Zarathustra*:

> In laughter all that is evil comes together, but is pronounced *holy* and *absolved by its own bliss*; and if this is my *alpha* and *omega*, that all that is heavy and grave should become light, all that is body, dancer, all that is spirit, bird—and verily that *is* my alpha and omega: oh, how should I not lust after eternity and the nuptial ring of rings, the ring of recurrence? (III.16:6, *The Portable Nietzsche*, 342)

We might say that Zarathustra here also 'jumps' into a cluster of images and motifs we would call Yeatsian, remembering, along with Self's laughing, singing self-absolution, 'Among School Children,' where 'body is not bruised to pleasure soul,' and we no longer 'know/ The dancer from the dance'; the natural and golden birds of the Byzantium poems; and the final transfiguration of Yeats's central hero, both in *The Death of Cuchulain* and 'Cuchulain Comforted,' into a singing bird. In 'A Dialogue of Self and Soul,' the Yeatsian-Nietzschean Self, commandeering the spiritual vocabulary Soul would monopolize, affirms Eternal Recurrence, the labyrinth of human life with all its tangled antinomies of joy and suffering. (As we will see in Part Two, in 'On Woman,' written a dozen years earlier, Yeats, echoing *The Gay Science* §341, had embraced the joy and despair of Nietzschean Recurrence precisely *because*, brought 'to birth again,' he could 'find what once I had': that 'one/ Perverse creature of chance,' the fatal beloved not kindred of his soul.) In subverting the debate-tradition, Yeats leaves Soul with a petrified tongue, and gives Self a final chant that is among the most rhapsodic in that whole tradition of secularized supernaturalism Yeats inherited from the Romantic poets and from Nietzsche. In a related if somewhat lower register, it is also the vision of Crazy Jane and the Woman Young and Old.

Of course, as even the stanza-form they share in the 'Dialogue' suggests, Self and Soul are aspects of the one man, and, as Yeats jotted in his 1930 diary, 'Man can only love Unity of Being.' The internal 'opponent' with whom we debate 'must be shown for a part of our greater expression' (E&I, 362). This resembles the Valentinian Unity 'each one will attain himself,' overcoming 'multiplicity.' Yeats's friend, AE (George Russell), to whom he sent a copy of the 1929 edition of *The Winding Stair*, said that of the poems in that volume he liked 'best' of all 'A Dialogue of Self and Soul.' Acknowledging his friend's gift, he wrote, 'I am on the side of Soul, but know that its companion has its own eternal claim, and perhaps when you side with the Self it is only a motion to that fusion of opposites which is the end of wisdom.'[11] Having astutely synopsized the central Yeatsian dialectic, Russell was tentatively noting its reflection in the poem's impulse, beneath the manifest debate of opposites, toward fusion. We seem to achieve fusion in the secular beatitude of Self's final chant. But Yeats was not AE, the 'saint,' as Mrs. Yeats described him, to her husband's 'poet,'[12] and the poet in Yeats, the Self, gives us—in the whole of 'A Dialogue of Self and Soul' and particularly in this magnificent final affirmation—an overcoming of Christian and Neoplatonic dualism and defilement of the body by way of a heterodox, 'heretical' self-blessing at once Blakean, Nietzschean, and Gnostic.

---

11   *Letters to W. B. Yeats*, ed. Finneran, et al., 2:560.
12   Yeats quotes George in a letter to Dorothy Wellesley, written after Russell's death in July, 1935: 'My wife said the other night, "AE" was the nearest thing to a saint you and I will ever meet. You are a better poet but no saint. I suppose one has to choose' (L, 838).

6. Sex, Philosophy, and the Occult

Despite Self's triumph in the 'Dialogue,' Yeats remained torn between what he called in 'Vacillation' (echoing Kant) 'the antinomies' of soul and body. As 'On Woman' alone would demonstrate, Yeats's occult speculations were always entangled in his emotional life. 'His aim,' to repeat Graham Hough's conclusion, 'was to redeem passion, not to transcend it, and a beatitude that has passed beyond the bounds of earthly love could not be his ideal goal.'[1] In the alembic of Yeats's paradoxical imagination, the search for hidden spiritual knowledge is often merged with *carnal* knowledge.

Autobiographically and symbolically, the object of desire was Maud Gonne: the never fully attainable Muse that haunts the life and work of the century's greatest love poet. But the beloved proves to be ultimately unattainable, even with physical consummation attained, as it was, in December 1908, with the elusive Maud. Yeats was both impressed and deeply moved by Dryden's translation (Vis, 214) of a famous passage of Lucretius, asserting that sexual union can never provide complete satisfaction.

In a 1931 conversation with John Sparrow, Fellow of All Souls' College, Oxford, Yeats cited and expanded on Lucretius' lines from the end of the long passage (1037–1191) on sexual love concluding Book IV of *De rerum natura.* In glossing Dryden's translation of the Roman poet, Yeats seems to echo the Gnostics' doubly radical dualism, a dualism between man and nature, but also between nature and the transmundane God. Yeats's citation and comment suggest that he is looking back to four of his own poems, three written in 1926/27, the fourth in 1931. Two, 'A Dialogue of Self and Soul' and 'Among School Children,' are indisputably major. The other two, lesser lyrics but closely related to

---

1   Hough, *The Mystery Religion of W. B. Yeats*, 119.

    https://doi.org/10.11647/OBP.0275.06

those major texts, are 'Summer and Spring,' from Yeats's 'A Man Young and Old' sequence, and, the most splendid of the 'Crazy Jane' lyrics, the poignant yet triumphant 'Crazy Jane and Jack the Journeyman,' written in 1931, the same year as his conversation with John Sparrow. But here, finally, is what Yeats told Sparrow:

> The finest description of sexual intercourse ever written was in John Dryden's translation of Lucretius, and it was justified; it was introduced to illustrate the difficulty of two becoming a unity: 'The tragedy of sexual intercourse is the perpetual virginity of the soul.' Sexual intercourse is an attempt to solve the eternal antinomy, doomed to failure because it takes place only on one side of the gulf. The gulf is that which separates the one and the many, or if you like, God and man.[2]

In 'Summer and Spring' (poem VIII of the autobiographical sequence in which the poet is masked as an anonymous 'Man Young and Old'), two lovers grown old reminisce 'under an old thorn tree.' When they talked of growing up, they: 'Knew that we'd halved a soul/ And fell the one in 'tother's arms/ That we might make it whole.' We recall, as we are meant to, 'Among School Children,' written in the same year. In transitioning from the first to the second stanza of this great poem, we shift abruptly from Yeats's external persona as senator and school inspector, 'a sixty-year-old smiling public man,' to the private, inner man, the poet himself reporting an incident Maud Gonne once related from her childhood:

> I dream of a Ledaean body bent
> Above a sinking fire, a tale that she
> Told of a harsh reproof, or trivial event
> That changed some childish day to tragedy—
> Told, and it seemed that our two natures blent
> Into a sphere from youthful sympathy,
> Or else, to alter Plato's parable,
> Into the yolk and white of the one shell.

In 'Summer and Spring' the lovers 'Knew that we'd halved a soul.' Though the blending of our two natures in 'Among School Children'

---

2   Cited by Brian Arkins, *Builders of My Soul*, 148, 52, 135. Yeats improves on Dryden, whose Lucretian lovers, in 'the raging foam of full desire,' twine 'thighs' and lovely limbs, yet couple 'In vain; they only cruze about the coast,/ For bodies cannot pierce, nor be in bodies lost.'

is poignant, the tragedy lies in the qualifying 'seemed' and in the need 'to alter Plato's parable'—a 'Lucretian' alteration, since the merging is empathetic and partial (yolk and white remain separated even within the unity of the 'one shell') rather than the full sexual / emotional union of Aristophanes' haunting fable in Plato's *Symposium*. It is precisely this 'whole' union that the old man claims in 'His Memories' (poem VI of 'A Man Young and Old')[3] and in 'Summer and Spring,' which concludes with a sexual variation on the Unity of Being symbolized by the dancer and 'great-rooted blossomer' of 'Among School Children': 'O what a bursting out there was,/ And what a blossoming,/ When we had all the summer-time/ And she had all the spring!'

But even here, despite that fecund blossoming, it is all memory and heartache. Two decades later, that night in December 1908, no matter how fleeting, remains paramount among the 'memories' of Yeats's 'Man Old.' In 'real life,' however, after their night of lovemaking in Paris, Maud had quickly put the relationship back on its old basis, a 'spiritual marriage,' informing Yeats in a morning-after note that she was praying he could overcome his 'physical desire' for her. In a journal entry the following month (21 January 1909), Yeats referred despairingly but realistically to the 'return' of Maud's 'old dread of physical love' (first confided to him in 1898), which has 'probably spoiled her life [...] I was never more deeply in love, but my desires must go elsewhere if I would escape their poison.' Hence, those 'others,' including Yeats's wife, destined to become 'friends,' or sexual partners, if never a fully satisfactory replacement for *'that* one' (as he refers to her, namelessly and climactically in 'Friends').

Maud was aware that her status as an unattainable Muse-figure was not only a painful but productive source of the poet's creativity, but, ironically, a cause of happiness. 'Poets should never marry,' she repeatedly informed him in what became a Maud-mantra. 'The world should thank me for not marrying you' because 'you make such beautiful poetry out of what you call your unhappiness.' Since Maud was unmarriageable

---

3   Aside from 'To a Young Girl' (1915), addressed to Iseult Gonne, 'His Memories' is the only poem where Yeats claims that his passion for Maud was sexually reciprocated. Readers used to the Maud / Helen association would know who 'The first of all the tribe' was who lay in the speaker's arms, 'And did such pleasure take—/ She who had brought great Hector down/ And put all Troy to wreck—/ That she cried into this ear,/ "Strike me if I shriek".'

and, ultimately, 'not kindred of his soul,' Yeats sought complete union (physical and spiritual) in memory, and in poetry, masked as a 'Man Young and Old'—or, empathetically switching genders in *Words for Music Perhaps*, as embodied in the vision of his 'Woman Young and Old' or of 'Crazy Jane.'

Partly based on an old, crazed Irish woman, Jane is not merely promiscuous. Yeats's occult experiences had led him to a belief in feminized, often sexualized, spirituality, early embodied in the beautiful, highly-sexed actress Florence Farr, one of the most gifted women visionaries of the Golden Dawn (and, briefly, his lover). Such female adepts, whose powers he admired and envied; women of 'second sight' (his own sister, 'Lily,' his uncle George Pollexfen's servant, Mary Battle); and his experiences at séances, where the mediums were almost invariably women: all convinced him of a female and erotic dimension in spirituality. The artistic result was the two powerful poetic sequences, 'A Woman Young and Old' and the 'Crazy Jane' poems. The third poem in the latter sequence, 'Crazy Jane on the Day of Judgment,' begins with Jane insisting that 'Love,' to be satisfied, requires 'all'—by far the most frequent word in the vocabulary of Yeats and of Blake, for whom 'Less than All cannot satisfy Man.'

> 'Love is all
> Unsatisfied
> That cannot take the whole
> Body and soul':
> *And that is what Jane said.*[4]

It ends with Jane still holding forth, now emphasizing her version of *gnosis*, but one that would certainly resonate with most Gnostics. While mystical experience was possible during life, virtually all Gnostics believed that the true ascent, in which (in Jane's phrase) 'all could be known,' took place after death, with the return of the spirit to its divine origins, the spark of life redeemed and reunited with the One from which it had been severed and alienated by its immersion in the material, temporal world. For most of the 'Crazy Jane' sequence,

---

4   Italics in original. 'All' appears 1,019 times in Yeats's poetry, almost twice as frequently as the runner-up, 'old.' 'Less than All cannot satisfy Man' is the fifth axiom in Blake's 'There is NO Natural Religion' (b).

unconventional Jane, making the most of her time on earth, will take a decidedly unorthodox *Itinerarium mentis ad Deum*. But here we find her, yearning for 'Time' to disappear and *gnosis* to be achieved, again with the emphasis on 'all':

> 'What can be shown?
> What true love be?
> All could be known or shown
> If Time were but gone.'

Jane's male interlocutor—responding, 'That's certainly the case'—might be Yeats himself, who thought Lucretius remained justified in insisting on the 'failure,' in this life, to bridge 'the gulf,' the insuperable 'difficulty of two becoming a unity.'

The poem that immediately follows Jane's thoughts on the Day of Judgment, 'Crazy Jane and Jack the Journeyman,' responds more audaciously to the Lucretius- and Epicurus-based assertion that 'The tragedy of sexual intercourse is the perpetual virginity of the soul.' Writing on Lucretius in 1875, the Victorian essayist J. M. Symonds qualified what Dryden before him and Yeats after him designated a 'tragedy,' though Symonds goes on to emphasize, even more than Yeats, the Lucretian, Epicurean—and, I would add, Gnostic—bleakness and frustration of lovers whose immaterial souls are entrammeled in the flesh: 'There is something almost tragic,' writes a sympathetic but austere Symonds, 'in these sighs and pantings and pleasure-throes, and the incomplete fruition of souls pent up within their frames of flesh.'[5] Symonds seems to reflect, along with the frustration described by Lucretius (and Platonism and Neoplatonism in general), the dualism of the Gnostics, concerned above all with freeing the spirit dwelling within the garment of flesh imprisoning the spark of life.

Before birth, we are in what Platonic Shelley called in 'Adonais' the 'white radiance of eternity.' What makes us free, the Gnostics insisted, is the knowledge of who we were then, when we *were* 'in the light' of pre-natal innocence. Crazy Jane, returning to the One, 'Shall leap into the light lost/ In my mother's womb.' That Blakean infant joy marks the

---

5   'Lucretius,' *Fortnightly Review* (1875); reprinted in *The Cambridge Companion to Lucretius*, 12.

exuberant climax of her vision. But she had begun by asserting her own *gnosis*, shaped by earthly experience:

> I know, although when looks meet
> I tremble to the bone,
> The more I leave the door unlatched
> The sooner love is gone,
> For love is but a skein unwound
> Between the dark and dawn.

Her knowledge of the transience of sexual love has not driven Jane to abstinence, despite the hectoring of the Bishop (her antagonist in this sequence) that she should 'Live in a heavenly mansion,/ Not in some foul sty.' In that poem, 'Crazy Jane Talks with the Bishop' (the sixth in the sequence), Jane tells the Bishop, a 'religious' Soul-spokesman nevertheless fixated on 'those breasts,' where *her* God—neither Jehovah nor Jesus, but Eros—has 'pitched' (temporarily set up as one would a tent) his mansion. It is not up among the stars as a 'heavenly mansion' (Yeats has the Bishop borrow that lofty sty-disdaining phrase from Urbino's Platonist, Pietro Bembo, and the Gospel of John, 14:2). Love's mansion is 'pitched' (with a probable pun on darkened), not up but down, *inter urinam et faeces*, 'in/ The place of excrement.' And her final words, definitely punning but serious news for the Bishop, are that 'Nothing can be sole, or whole/ That has not been rent': a sexual / spiritual variation (in keeping with 'Plato's parable') on the archetypal cycle of original unity, division, and reunification and completion.

Despite the graphic nature of her language in Poem VI, Jane is no more a simple materialist than is Augustine, or Swift, or Blake, an unlikely trinity whose shared excremental yet visionary vocabulary Yeats has her echo. What Jane insists on is the beauty of both the physical and the ideal world, with 'Love' the *'tertium quid'* mediating between them. 'Fair and foul are near of kin,/ And fair needs foul,' Jane tells the Bishop. Love is the 'great spirit' or 'daemon' celebrated by that Sophia-figure, Diotima, presented in the *Symposium* by Socrates, whose simplistic dualism between good and evil, 'fair' and 'foul,' she corrects ('Hush,' she quiets him in mid-argument) by presenting Love as 'a mean between them,' a yoker of apparent opposites, a creator of unity out of division. (*Symposium* 202–3).

Whatever its other parallels and sources, Jane's vision is also reflective of *some* aspects of Gnosticism, hostile to 'law,' especially law-orientated scripture, such as in Exodus and Deuteronomy, and the sort of puritanical strictures the Bishop wants to impose on Jane. Historical Gnosticism ran the ethical gamut from extreme asceticism to, at its most unconventional, robust promiscuity. The charges, by early Christian opponents, of Gnostic orgies were exaggerated (or at least unsupported by evidence). However, two Gnostic sects (the Carpocratians and the Cainites) held that, in order to be freed from the Archons, the world-creating angels who would 'enslave' them, men and women had to 'experience everything.' To 'escape from the power' of the Archons, Carpocrates said, one 'must pass from body to body until he has experience of every kind of action which can be practiced in this world, and when nothing is any longer wanting to him, then his liberated soul should soar upwards to that God who is above' the Archons. By 'fulfilling and accomplishing what is requisite,' the liberated soul will be saved, 'no longer imprisoned in the body.'[6] This is certainly in accord with Jane's notably embodied theory of illumination through a sexual liberation that is ultimately spiritual and salvific:

> A lonely ghost the ghost is
> That to God shall come;
> I—love's skein upon the ground,
> My body in the tomb—
> Shall leap into the light lost
> In my mother's womb.
>
> But were I left to lie alone
> In an empty bed,
> The skein so bound us ghost to ghost
> When he turned his head
> Passing on the road that night,
> Mine must walk when dead.

6　The Carpocratian doctrine is synopsized and condemned in *Adversus Haereses* (§2952) by the Bishop of Lyon, Irenaeus, whose work has been invaluable to scholars studying the beliefs of various Gnostic sects. Yeats did not read the Bishop's attack on heresies, but he did (as Warwick Gould recently reminded me in an email) read G. R. S. Mead's *Simon Magus: An Essay* (1892), which draws on Irenaeus for a story in *The Adoration of the Magi.*

Most readers of Yeats, even most Yeatsian scholars familiar with the finale of the *Enneads* of his beloved Plotinus, misread the central and crucial stanza, a misreading based on an understandably negative response, when the word is taken out of context, to the adjective 'lonely.' It is in fact an ultimate affirmation. Jane will come to God as a 'lonely ghost,' the climax of her 'flight of the alone to the Alone.' These, the final words of the *Enneads*, are also memorably recalled by Yeats's friend Lionel Johnson at the climax of 'The Dark Angel,' a poem Yeats rightly admired: 'Lonely unto the lone I go,/ Divine to the Divinity.'[7]

Jane's transcendence is earned not (to echo the final stanza of 'Among School Children') through a body-bruising, soul-pleasuring abstinence, but (since nothing can be sole or whole that has not been rent) by utterly unwinding, through experience, what Blake called (in *The Gates of Paradise* and elsewhere) 'the sexual Garments.' Though 'love is but a skein unwound/ Between the dark and dawn,' if left *un*wound, it would bind her to the earth, condemning her ghost, like that of her true lover, Jack, to 'walk when dead.' That skein fully unwound, we are to go to our graves (to borrow a phrase of Milton, but hardly his meaning), 'all passion spent.' Yeats told an interviewer at this time, 'If you don't express yourself, you walk after you're dead. The great thing is to go empty to your grave.'[8]

In order to liberate the soul, escaping the Archons who would enslave us, we must, Carpocratian Gnostics insisted, exhaust earthly 'experience.' In a letter of January 1932, Yeats confided to Olivia Shakespear, 'I shall be a sinful man to the end, and think upon my death-bed of all the nights I wasted in my youth' (L, 790). He was writing to the one woman on earth best equipped to know what he meant by nights wasted in his youth; he had been a virgin until, at the age of thirty-one, Olivia had relieved him of that burden. Yeats was also fond of a passage from Blake's *Vision of the Last Judgment*: two sentences which, with their emphasis on both the

---

7   My one ally on this point is Elizabeth Butler Cullingford, who accurately notes that Jane claims 'that unsatisfied desire binds us to the earth; the exhaustion of desire through its fulfillment is the precondition for union with the divine.' She follows Yeats in enlisting Aquinas in the political fight against Irish puritanism. In his Senate speech against Catholic censorship, Yeats had cunningly cited the Thomistic formulation, *"anima est in toto corpore'* [the soul inhabits all parts of the body.] See Cullingford, 'Yeats and Gender,' in Howes and Kelly, 182.

8   *W. B. Yeats: Interviews and Recollections*, ed. Mikhail, 2:203.

'realities of intellect' and the need for the passions to 'emanate' in a way alien to Plotinus, would appeal to some Gnostics: 'Men are admitted into Heaven not because they have curbed and governed their passions, but because they have cultivated their understandings. The treasures of heaven are not negations of passion, but realities of intellect, from which the passions emanate uncurbed in their eternal glory' (E&I, 137–38).[9]

The Gnostic Carpocrates would endorse *that* vision of the Last Judgment. Whatever he might have thought of Crazy Jane's promiscuous theology, Blake, though aware of the limitations of sexuality, saw no puritanical line demarcating the human heart and loins from the human head and spirit. Yeats, who habitually couples Blake with Nietzsche, cited with approval the latter's 'doctrine' that 'we must not believe in the moral or intellectual beauty which does not sooner or later impress itself upon physical things' (E&I, 389). As Nietzsche insisted in an epigram (§75) in *Beyond Good and Evil*, 'the kind and degree of a man's sexuality reach up into the ultimate pinnacle of his spirit.' What Yeats described, in the title of a bold 1926 article defending life and art against religious censorship, as 'The Need for Audacity of Thought,' took the form of an increasingly candid celebration of the body. Already present in the 'Solomon and Sheba,' 'A Man Young and Old,' 'A Woman Young and Old,' and 'Crazy Jane' sequences, that candor dominates his final years. Ribh, the unorthodox monk of 'Supernatural Songs,' tells us in the opening poem of that sequence that 'Natural and Supernatural with the selfsame ring are wed,' and reads his 'holy book' in the incandescent Swedenborgian light shed by the sexual 'intercourse of angels.' The graphically sexual 'Three Bushes' sequence was co-written with Dorothy Wellesley, and it was she who best characterized Yeats in old age: 'Sex, philosophy and the occult preoccupy him. He strangely intermingles the three' (LDW, 374).

That intermingling is also prominent in 'A Woman Young and Old,' the eleven-poem sequence written between 1926 and 1929. In the alluring 'Before the World was Made,' which, following the framing 'Father and Child,' is the first poem in her own voice, the young woman applying

---

9   Blake goes on to excoriate those who, lacking passion and intellect, spend their lives 'curbing and governing other peoples.' He is thinking of 'the modern church,' which 'crucifies' the 'true' imaginative Christ 'upside down.' Yeats's Bishop leaps to mind.

her make-up mixes the sensuous with the spiritual, the aesthetically
erotic with Neoplatonic philosophy:

> If I make the lashes dark
> And the eyes more bright
> And the lips more scarlet,
> Or ask if all be right
> From mirror after mirror,
> No vanity's displayed:
> I'm looking for the face I had
> Before the world was made.
>
> What if I look upon a man
> As though on my beloved,
> And my blood be cold the while
> And my heart unmoved?
> Why should he think me cruel
> Or that he is betrayed?
> I'd have him love the thing that was
> Before the world was made.

In Yeats's gender-crossing empathy and in the alembic of his lyricism,
an apparently self-centered coquette and budding *femme fatale* is
transformed into a heroic quester for her archetype in eternity. Any
potential lover courts her at his peril, if, failing to see beyond the surface,
he is not equal to her challenge: a task ironically made more difficult
by her own attempt to align mask and spiritual reality through beauty-
enhancing artifice. Though she lures him on with brightened eyes and
crimsoned lips, her blood will remain cold, her heart unmoved, unless
he is able to love the eerie, non-sensuous 'thing that was/ Before the
world was made'—a Neoplatonizing allusion to God being 'still where
he was before the world was made,' a description by John Donne, whose
work Yeats was reading intensely at this time.[10]

Donne also figures in 'Chosen,' the sixth and central lyric of this
concentrically structured sequence. The flanking poems provide context.
In 'Parting,' the Romeo-and-Juliet-like *aubade* that immediately follows
'Chosen,' the young woman claims that the light they see 'is from the
moon' and the song she and her lover hear that of the nightingale.

---

10   *John Donne: The Sermons.* In Sermon 23, Donne observes that, having planted Adam
     in Paradise, God remained unmoved, 'still where he was before the world was
     made.'

When he points out that it is the dawn-announcing lark and, indeed, that 'Daylight already flies/ From mountain crest to crest,' she ends the debate by making him an offer he cannot refuse: let the bird 'sing on,/ I offer to love's play/ My dark declivities.' In 'Chosen,' the now-mature woman also struggles 'with the horror of daybreak'; but she chooses, along with 'the lot of love,' an esoteric concept to celebrate that serene post-coital moment when she and her lover seemed to exchange hearts. If questioned on

> my utmost pleasure with a man
> By some new-married bride, I take
> That moment for a theme
> Where his heart my heart did seem
> And both adrift on the miraculous stream
> Where—wrote a learned astrologer—
> The Zodiac is changed into a sphere.

Though Yeats, as in 'A Dialogue of Self and Soul,' plays a variation on his esoteric source (the Neoplatonic *Commentary* on Cicero's *Somnium Scipionis* by the Latin encyclopedist Macrobius), readers oblivious to astrology can still perceive the sexual analogue to this transformation of the whirling zodiacal gyre of the poem's opening stanza into the motionless 'sphere'—symbol of perfection not only for Yeats's 'learned astrologer,' Macrobius, but for more prominent thinkers, among them Parmenides and Plato, whose Myth of Er and its 'lottery' in the final sections of *The Republic* (619–620), is the source of the phrase 'the lot of love.'

But why delve into this arcana at all? Because Yeats took it seriously and, at the same time, with the jocoseriousness that allowed him to yoke seeming opposites. After amusing Olivia Shakespear by distilling all that was worthy of attention to two topics: 'sex and the dead' (L, 730), he confided to her in his very next letter that perusing Blake's Dante designs captured 'my own mood between spiritual excitement, and the sexual torture and the knowledge that they are somehow inseparable!' (L, 731). In 'Parting,' the woman is erotically playful; in 'Consolation,' the poem immediately preceding 'Chosen,' she stands orthodox spiritual doctrine on its head with a *felix culpa* variation emphasizing the intensification of erotic pleasure by the awareness of sex as forbidden fruit. She acknowledges 'wisdom' in what is said by the 'sages,' referring to Neoplatonic philosophers like Plotinus and Christian Neoplatonists like Augustine, with his obsessive emphasis on original sin. But, adopting the Yeatsian *agon* between 'wisdom' and 'ecstasy,' she has news for those who would bruise the body to pleasure soul. She tells her lover, 'lay down that head/ Till I have told the sages/ Where man is comforted.'

> How could passion run so deep
> Had I never thought
> That the crime of being born
> Blackens all our lot?
> But where the crime's committed
> The crime can be forgot.

It would not have occurred to Augustine, for all the sexual experience of his youth, that the lot-blackening crime he was convinced we inherited at birth could be so pleasurably forgotten: returning to the scene of the crime by re-entering a woman's 'dark declivities.'

In 'Chosen,' Yeats has his protagonist memorialize her moment of 'utmost pleasure with a man' in arcane language nuanced by what I hear as a note of urbanity. To have her answer the new-married bride with *no* saving urbanity would be to parody the role famously assigned by Dryden to Donne, who (as we saw in discussing 'Michael Robartes and the Dancer'), even in his 'amorous' poems, 'perplexes the minds of the fair sex with nice speculations of philosophy when he should engage their hearts and entertain them with the softness of love.' To capture that post-orgasmic euphoria in which she and her lover were 'both adrift' on a 'miraculous stream,' Yeats's woman cites an abstruse text. In doing so, she mimics the simultaneous detachment and participation of a pedantic scholar. One assumes that the 'new-married bride' questioning the older woman on her utmost sexual pleasure has not come fresh from a perusal of *A Vision*, nor of Macrobius, nor of John Donne—the stanza, meter, and astronomical imagery of whose 'Nocturnall upon S. Lucies Day' Yeats adapted for 'Chosen.' This is the 'just finished' poem Yeats mentions in his 21 February 1926 letter (L, 710) to Donne scholar H. J. C. Grierson, in which he refers to Donne's 'Nocturnall' as a passionate and 'intoxicating' poem, which it is, and 'proof that he was the Countess of Bedford's lover,' which, despite Yeats's revealing insistence, it most certainly is not.

In two late poems, Yeats pushes audacity of thought to the limit. Yeatsian physicality and revulsion from the abstract are at their most blasphemously sensationalistic in the quatrain whose titular 'Stick of Incense' is revealed to be that of St. Joseph, who 'thought the world would melt,' but, probing the 'virgin womb' of Mary, 'liked the way his finger smelt.' Yeats is less sacrilegious than insouciant in 'News for the Delphic Oracle.' Even in this poem's predecessor, 'The Delphic Oracle upon Plotinus' (1931), Yeats had altered the Oracle's report, as given in Porphyry's *Life of Plotinus,* which Yeats had read in both the Thomas Taylor and Stephen MacKenna translations. Porphyry describes clear-eyed Plotinus swimming through the sea of generation to reach the Platonic Choir of Love. Characteristically, *antithetical* Yeats devoted his most sharply memorable line to the temporary obliteration of Plotinus's spiritual vision: 'Salt blood blocks his eyes.' In the poem written seven years later, Plotinus has arrived, 'salt flakes on his breast,/ And having stretched and yawned awhile/ Lay sighing' like the rest of the 'golden codgers.' Yeats mocks his own early pastorals, ending in a salty, sexual tumult that makes even the dolphin-torn finale of 'Byzantium' seem tame by comparison:

> Foul goat-head, brutal arm appear,
> Belly, shoulder, bum
> Flash fishlike,
> Nymphs and satyrs
> Copulate in the foam.

This orgiastic scene would be 'News' indeed, not only for the Delphic Oracle and the 'sages standing in God's holy fire' in 'Sailing to Byzantium,' but for the John Milton of the Nativity Ode. The 'Delphic Oracle' poem's opening lines were scribbled in a copy of Milton's poems, with Yeats's 'sighing' wind and water echoing the suspended calm of wind and water in the Nativity Ode. In revisiting Milton's 'On the Morning of Christ's Nativity,' Yeats had been preceded by Blake, in *Europe: A Prophecy,* and Coleridge, in *Religious Musings* (both 1794), and, a quarter-century later, closer in time and theme, in the 'Ode to Psyche.' Though Keats's warm sexual union of Eros and Psyche is a far cry from the orgiastic doings in the 'Delphic Oracle' poem, those copulating nymphs and satyrs suggest that Yeats may be recalling the excited questions in the 'Grecian Urn' ode: 'What men or gods are these? What maidens loth?/ What mad pursuit? What struggle to escape?/ What pipes and timbrels? What wild ecstasy?'

To return to *Milton's* ode: the great Puritan's fatal news for Apollo, driven from his shrine on 'the steep of Delphos,' is that he, Pan, and the other pagan deities are to be replaced by the newborn infant Jesus. Though Yeats includes in his pagan paradise the 'Innocents' slaughtered by Herod in his attempt to kill infant Jesus, a focus on Christ would not do for *antithetical* Yeats. At the end as at the beginning, in *The Wanderings of Oisin*, a palpably sexual paganism is preferred to Christianity. Yeats's example, 'Homer and his unchristened heart,' is companion to Sophocles' *antithetical* Oedipus, who—Yeats reminds us in the Introduction to *A Vision*, alluding to Oedipus' wondrous end at Colonus—'sank down body and soul into the earth': an earth, Yeats adds to the Greek text, 'riven by love,' in contrast to *primary* Christ who, 'crucified standing up, went into the abstract sky soul and body' (Vis, 27–28).

That preference, the chthonic, earthy *down* over the abstract heavenly *up*, is echoed in the 'Delphic Oracle' poem: 'Down the mountain walls/ From where Pan's cavern is/ Intolerable music falls.' Yeats replaces Milton's 'Pan'—the newborn infant Jesus, his birth accompanied by 'musick sweet'—with the lusty, half-goatish pagan Pan and the fallen but resonant *basso profundo* attending caverned Pan and the copulating nymphs and satyrs: sensual music 'intolerable' to spiritual orthodoxy, Neoplatonic or Christian or both.[11]

In this witty and exuberant poem—part parody of Neoplatonism and of Christian Milton, part mischievous potpourri of mythological personages—Yeats almost debases love to lust. *Almost*, for the Choir, wading in 'some cliff-sheltered bay,' sings of Love, and we are told of Peleus, Thetis' husband, that, gazing on her 'delicate' limbs, 'Love has blinded him with tears.' But it is Thetis' 'belly' that listens to that sexual music. Despite the Neoplatonic sources of his vision of the Isles of the Blest, Yeats emphasizes, not transcendent serenity beyond desire but a generative fecundity that would make Milton's or even Swedenborg's copulating angels blush—to say nothing of the virginal sibyl at the shrine of Apollo, the titular recipient of 'news' actually intended for Plotinus and Porphyry. And, since the infant in Thetis' belly is fetal Achilles, we have another iteration of Yeats's Nietzschean motto: 'Homer is my example and his unchristened heart.'

---

11   In the first edition of *A Vision*, Yeats described the 'sacred and profane' as having 'fallen apart in the hymn "On the Morning of Christ's Nativity",' making Milton's mythology 'an artificial ornament,' whereas 'no great Italian artist' of the Renaissance 'saw any difference between them, and when difference came, as it did with Titian, it was God and the Angels that seemed artificial.' *A Vision* (1925), 205. Yeats's partial parody of Milton's ode was first noted by Daniel Albright, *The Myth against Myth*, 122–23. According to Albright, George gave her husband's annotated copy of Milton to Richard Ellmann as a gift.

7. Mountain Visions and Other Last Things

In Part Two, in dealing with 'last things,' I'll focus on 'The Circus Animals' Desertion,' 'Man and the Echo,' and 'Politics' in the context of Maud Gonne and of Yeats's final affirmation of life. Here, I'll focus on 'Lapis Lazuli,' and on two death-poems, 'Cuchulain Comforted' and the colloquial debate-poem, 'What Then?' If I had to select one final testament of Yeats, the choice might narrow to 'Among School Children,' or Self's chant at the end of 'A Dialogue of Self and Soul,' or to the final movements of 'Lapis Lazuli,' 'Cuchulain Comforted,' and 'Man and the Echo.' Such deeply moving retrospective poems are the fully ripened fruit of an aged but major poet working at the height of his undiminished creative power. Each of these poems constitutes wisdom writing, a quest for *gnosis*, or the acknowledgment that it may not be attainable in this life. That is true as well of the more casual, but no less momentous, 'What Then?'

Written in July 1936, 'Lapis Lazuli,' which Yeats himself recognized as 'almost the best I have made of recent years' (L, 859), was, like 'Politics,' published with war imminent. Yeats is annoyed by those who cannot abide the gaiety of artists creating amid impending catastrophe, unaware of the deep truth—known to Hindu mystics, to the Nietzsche of *gaya scienza*, and to Arthur O'Shaughnessy, whose creative artists 'built Ninevah' and Babel out of their own 'sighs' and 'mirth'—that 'All things fall and are built again/And those that build them again are gay.' To counter the consternation of those who are 'sick of the palette and fiddle-bow,/ Of poets that are always gay,' women dismissed as 'hysterical,' Yeats presents Shakespearean figures who—like Ophelia, Cordelia, and (by implication) Cleopatra—'do not break up their lines to weep.' Above all, 'Hamlet and Lear are gay;/ Gaiety transfiguring all that dread.'

 https://doi.org/10.11647/OBP.0275.07

Fusing Shakespearean heroism with Eastern serenity and Nietzsche's Zarathustrian joy ('Who among you can laugh and be elevated at the same time? Whoever climbs the highest mountains laughs at all tragic plays and tragic seriousness'),[1] the poem turns in its final movement to the mountain-shaped lapis lazuli sculpture given to Yeats as a gift, and which, in turn, giving the poet his title, serves as the Yeatsian equivalent of Keats's Grecian urn. 'Two Chinamen, behind them a third,/ Are carved in lapis lazuli.' Over them flies 'a long-legged bird,' a 'symbol' not of eternity but 'of longevity.' The third carved figure, though 'doubtless a serving man,' is the resident artist; like Keats's piper, he 'Carries a musical instrument.'

Aside from the obvious resemblance of the lapis lazuli sculpture to the Grecian urn, the repeated 'or' in the lines that follow seals the connection, with description yielding to a stunning exercise of the creative imagination, worthy of its precursor, the fourth stanza of Keats's ode. Since the place of origin of the figures in the sacrificial procession is not depicted on the urn, Keats speculates: 'What little town by river or sea-shore,/ Or mountain-built [...]?' Yeats ups the ante to four repetitions of *or*:

> Every discoloration of the stone;
> Every accidental crack or dent
> Seems a water-course or an avalanche,
> Or lofty slope where it still snows
> Though doubtless plum or cherry-branch
> Sweetens the little half-way house
> Those Chinamen climb towards, and I
> Delight to imagine them seated there;
> There, on the mountain and the sky,
> On all the tragic scene they stare.
> One asks for mournful melodies;
> Accomplished fingers begin to play.
> Their eyes mid many wrinkles, their eyes,
> Their ancient glittering eyes are gay.

Yeats turns every discoloration and 'Every accidental crack or dent' (damage I nearly added to in 1995 when, visiting Michael and Gráinne

---

1   'Thus Spoke Zarathustra,' I.7 'On Reading and Writing,' in *The Portable Nietzsche*, 153.

Yeats, I almost dropped the piece of lapis I'd been invited to examine) into a feature of the mountain landscape. But the even greater creative leap in this marvelous final movement is the setting of those sculpted figures, frozen in lapis as Keats's were on the marble urn, into motion, with the poet *delighting* to 'imagine' them having attained the prospect of the gazebo half-way up the mountain. That the perspective is not quite *sub specie aeternitatis*; that the 'little half-way house' is situated at the midpoint rather than on the summit, makes this a human rather than divine vision. To that extent, the Chinese sages' mountain vision may not achieve the *gnosis* attained by the naked hermits caverned on another Asian mountain, in Yeats's 1933 sonnet, 'Meru.' Those hermits, aware of the 'manifold illusion' of one passing civilization after another, 'know/ That day brings round the night, that before dawn/ [Man's] glory and his monuments are gone.' Yet the affirmation of the Chinese sages of 'Lapis Lazuli' is also registered in full awareness of 'all the tragic scene.' The eyes of these Yeatsian visionaries, wreathed in the wrinkles of mutability, glitter with a tragic joy lit by the poet's own creative 'delight,' and by something resembling the Gnostic 'spark.'

The end of mutability is death. The ancient Chinese sages' gaiety in the face of tragedy recalls Yeats's central mythological figure, Cuchulain. Yeats's ultimate 'Swordsman' and the epitome of tragic joy, Cuchulain, the great warrior of Irish myth, is the hero of several Yeats poems and a cycle of five plays, ending with *The Death of Cuchulain*. Though indebted to the translations of Celtic mythology by Standish O'Grady and Lady Gregory, Yeats's Cuchulain also reflects his reading of Nietzsche, who, though 'exaggerated and violent,' had 'helped me very greatly in building up in my mind an imagination of the heroic life.'[2]

The poet's final encounter with his Celtic Achilles takes place in a ghostly poem completed on 13 January 1939, two weeks before his death. 'One of the greatest ever death-bed utterances,' in the discerning judgment of Seamus Heaney, the eerie and magnificent 'Cuchulain Comforted' is composed, appropriately, in Dante's *terza rima*, Yeats's sole

---

2   In 'The Phases of the Moon,' after eleven phases pass, 'Nietzsche is born,/ Because the hero's crescent is the twelfth.' In a September 1902 letter to John Quinn, who had sent him copies of *Zarathustra*, *On the Genealogy of Morals*, and *The Case of Wagner*, Yeats wrote: 'I don't know how I can thank you too much,' reporting that he and Nietzsche 'had come to the same conclusions on several cardinal matters,' including the 'heroic life.' Cited by William Murphy, *Prodigal Father*, 596n69.

venture into the form Shelley too had chosen for his final masterpiece.[3] Yeats's poem finds the nameless hero, wounded in battle and slain by a blind man, in the Underworld among 'Shrouds that muttered head to head,' and 'Came and were gone.' He 'leant upon a tree/ As though to meditate on wounds and blood.' The newcomer is among his polar opposites—'convicted cowards all,' according to one 'that seemed to have authority/ Among those birdlike things,' and who informs the still armed hero: 'Now must we sing and sing the best we can.' The poem ends with the hero's apotheosis imminent. Having set aside his warrior's sword and taken up a tailor's needle, he has joined these spirits in a communal, almost emasculating sewing-bee, making shrouds, his own included. He is soon to undergo their transfiguration, described in haunting final lines reminiscent of Zarathustra's vision of evil absolved by its own bliss so that all that is 'body' becomes 'dancer, all that is spirit, bird': 'They sang but had nor human tunes nor words,/ Though all was done in common as before./ They had changed their throats and had the throats of birds.'

That uncanny final line (an alexandrine which Conor Cruise O'Brien once remarked to me in conversation seemed to him 'to have been written on the moon') is also a final fusion. Marrying the posthumous continuation, in 'Sailing to Byzantium,' of a bird-like poet's need to sing with the transformation and liberation of the soul, it should thrill Romantics and Gnostics alike. Valentinus insists, 'what liberates us is the *gnosis* of who we were, what we became; where we were, whereunto we have been thrown; whither we hasten, from what we are redeemed; what birth is, and what rebirth.'[4] This formula of salvation, now famous but unknown to Yeats, is cited by Harold Bloom as a 'good motto' for 'Cuchulain Comforted,' which he considers 'Yeats's finest achievement in the Sublime.'[5] The triumph of this mysterious, yet confessional death-poem is that, like 'Man and the Echo,' it discloses—along with an

---

3　Heaney's comment was made in *The Irish Times* on 28 January 1989, the fiftieth anniversary of Yeats's death. The Shelley poem, earlier discussed, is *The Triumph of Life*, interrupted by the poet's drowning while sailing during a storm: a death eerily anticipated on what became the last page of the MS, filled with Shelley's sketches of a sailboat.

4　Valentinus, *Excerpts from Theodotus*. Theodotus was a leading Valentinian of the Eastern school. The second century *Excerpts* were quoted and thus unintentionally preserved by the Christian theologian, Clement of Alexandria.

5　Bloom, *Poetry and Repression*, 230, 228.

unexpected aspect of the solitary Cuchulain, 'a heroic figure because he was creative joy separated from fear' (L, 913)—Yeats himself: the man under the many macho-heroic masks. He is neither fearful 'coward' nor stricken rabbit, but still 'one that,' in yet another bird image, 'ruffled in a manly pose/ For all his timid heart' ('Coole Park, 1929'). No wonder Yeats, shortly before his death, referred to the self-revealing 'Cuchulain Comforted,' a poem in process at the time, as 'strange' and 'something new' (L, 922).[6]

§

In the spring of 1936, not quite three years before that death, Yeats received a request for a 'representative' poem for *The Erasmian*, the magazine of his old Dublin high school. He selected 'What Then?,' which lays out for the Erasmus Smith students a planned life of disciplined labor, aimed at achieving what Yeats's 'chosen comrades' at school believed to be his destiny: the conviction, in which he concurred, that he would 'grow a famous man.' Writing intimately though in the third person, 'he' tells the young students and us that he 'crammed' his twenties 'with toil,' and that, in time, 'Everything he wrote was read.' He attained 'sufficient money for his need,' true 'friends that have been friends indeed,' and that predestined yet industriously sought-after fame. Eventually—fulfilling his deliberate 'plan'—'All his happier dreams came true': house, wife, daughter, son; 'Poets and wits about him drew.'

But this self-satisfied rehearsal of accomplishment has been challenged by the italicized refrain ending each stanza: *'"What then?" sang Plato's ghost, "What then?"'* As in 'Man and the Echo' ('what do we know?'), despite best-laid plans, an ultimate uncertainty attends the certainty of death. In the fourth and final stanza, as the litany of achievement mounts in passionate intensity, the opposing challenge from the world beyond earthly accomplishment also reaches a crescendo:

> 'The work is done,' grown old he thought,

---

6 Unfortunately 'Cuchulain Comforted' was not Yeats's last poem. A week later, he dictated to his wife on his deathbed 'The Black Tower,' in which he resumes the heroic mask shed in 'Cuchulain Comforted' and 'Man and the Echo.' 'The Black Tower,' with its 'oath-bound men' valiantly defending a lost cause, has its own merits, but we are right to regret its place of honor as Yeats's very last poem.

'According to my boyish plan;
Let the fools rage, I swerved in naught,
Something to perfection brought';
But louder sang that ghost, 'What Then?'

In 'The Choice,' written a decade earlier, Yeats had declared that 'the intellect of man is forced to choose/ Perfection of the life, or of the work.' The 'something' brought to 'perfection' in 'What Then?' is clearly the second choice. Must 'he' therefore, as in 'The Choice,' 'refuse/ A heavenly mansion, raging in the dark'? Momentous in import despite its casual tone, 'What Then?' revisits 'A Dialogue of Self and Soul,' with the spiritual spokesman, despite being restricted to two words, at last mounting a potent challenge. The refrain Yeats places in the breathless mouth of that formidable ghost—'What then?'—fuses the Idealism of that 'Plato,' who (in 'Among School Children') 'thought nature but a spume that plays/ Upon a ghostly paradigm of things' with the 'Plato' who, as the principal 'advocate of the "Beyond," the greatest slanderer of life,' Nietzsche said presented 'the complete, the genuine antagonism' to Homer, the 'instinctive deifier, the *golden* nature.' In 'What Then?' the ghost of Plato, linking West and East, reiterates the question raised in the synoptic gospels—what do you profit if you gain the whole world but lose your immortal soul?—and couples it with the Hindu *'tatah kim'*[What's the use?]; to quote the hermit-poet Bhartrihari: 'you may by your good fortune have gathered friends about you: *what further?* You may have gained glory and accomplished all your desires: *what further?'*[7]

What further? What then? That relentless question also tallies with the Gnostic insistence that the liberating spirit within, the 'divine spark,' was the sole agent of salvation. That spark, once ignited, redeems 'inner' spirituality, freeing us from all Archon-imposed limitations, especially enslaving attachment to earthly things. However, powerful though the Otherworldly challenge is in 'What Then?,' here as always—from 'To the Rose upon the Rood of Time' on—dialectical Yeats is not quite succumbing to the spiritual, a realm at once alluring, demanding, and life-denying. 'His' litany of achievements, in the poem Yeats himself chose to represent his life-work to the students of his former high school, are triumphs of the imagination even more than they are flauntings of

---

7   Nietzsche, *On the Genealogy of Morals*, III.25. *The Satakas, or Wise Sayings, of Bhartrahari, Vairagasataka* §71 (italics in original). In 1913, J. M. Kennedy translated both Bhartrihari and Nietzsche's *Die Morgenröte* (*Dawn* or *Daybreak*).

material success; *and*, given the massiveness of the poetic achievement of Yeats, awarded the 1923 Nobel Prize in Literature, 'his' is far from empty boasting.

As Nietzsche concluded after asserting his crucial *agon*, 'Plato versus Homer': to place himself 'in the service' of ascetic Platonism is 'the most destructive *corruption* of an artist that is at all possible.' In 'What Then?' the ghost of Plato gets the last word, but the poem consists of more than its refrain. Taken as a whole, 'What Then?' shows us an artist once again vacillating 'between extremities' ('Vacillation,' I), and, in the process, making poetry of the quarrel with himself. Yeats was reading at this time Nietzsche's *Genealogy* and *Daybreak* (the latter translated by the same man who had, speaking of extremities, translated Bhartrihari), and it was Homeric Nietzsche—Yeats's chosen counterweight to Plato and Christianity, that 'Platonism for the people'—who said, in the *Genealogy* (III.3), 'It is precisely such "contradictions" that seduce us to existence.'

Nietzsche's prophet famously advises us, at the outset of *Thus Spoke Zarathustra*, to '*remain faithful to the earth*, and do not believe those who speak to you of otherworldly hopes.'[8] In 'What Then?,' Yeats seems in part to be following Zarathustra's imperative; but he had not yet been introduced to Nietzsche when, almost a half-century earlier, he wrote 'The Man who Dreamed of Faeryland,' a poem to which 'What Then?' responds almost point for point. As we have seen, in that earlier poem every earthly pleasure and achievement had been spoiled by a repeated, cruel 'singing' whose theme was a golden and silver Fairyland, an Otherworld of immutable, but unattainable beauty. Everything lost in the early poem, including the 'fine angry mood' required to rebut mockers, is re-gained in this late poem, where the speaker, his work done, cries out, 'Let the fools rage, I swerved in naught,/ Something to perfection brought.' The mature, accomplished man has 'succeeded' beyond his dreams, and thus exposed the folly of the man who wasted his life away by fruitlessly dreaming of Fairyland.

And yet, that 'singing' from the Otherworld continues: '"*What then*," *sang Plato's ghost*, "*What then?*"'—an amplified, more insistent 'singing' from the 'Beyond' that grows 'louder' the more the speaker rehearses his accomplishments. Seven years earlier, in his 1930 diary, Yeats had set out 'two conceptions' of reality that 'alternate in our emotion and in history,' and are not reconcilable. 'I am always in all I do, driven to

---

8   'Thus Spoke Zarathustra,' I.3,'Zarathustra's Prologue' (*Portable Nietzsche*, 125).

a moment which is the realization of myself as unique and free, or to a moment which is the surrender to God of all that I am [...] Could these two impulses, one as much a part of truth as the other, be reconciled, or if one could prevail, all life would cease' (Ex, 305). It is hardly unique thematically, but 'What Then?' in its very simplicity as a text suitable for high school students, offers us a late and almost uniquely accessible example of a recurrent phenomenon in Yeats: evidence that the tension between the temporal and the eternal, the pagan and the Christian, the Homeric *antithetical* and the Platonic *primary*, persists, as both challenge and imaginative stimulus, to the very end.

§

On 14 October 2019, Harold Bloom passed away, in his ninetieth year and having just taught two classes at Yale. He was on the verge of completing yet another book, this one exploring 'the figurations we term immortality, resurrection, and redemption' (published posthumously as *Take Arms Against a Sea of Troubles: The Power of the Reader's Mind Over a Universe of Death*, a titular fusion of *Hamlet* and *Paradise Lost*). My own book is dedicated to Bloom, a eulogy for whom may be found at the end. However inadequate as a token of my admiration and personal affection, I add to the present essay this brief coda, commemorating Harold Bloom, but also disagreeing with him.

Having come to half-accept the Gnostic vision he harshly rejected in his 1970 book *Yeats*, as a pessimism alien to the affirmative vision of Blake and Shelley, Bloom ended the essay he wrote a half-dozen years later— 'Yeats, Gnosticism, and the Sacred Void'—by positing Romanticism as allied with, rather than a deviation from, Gnosticism. Indeed, it 'could be argued that a form of Gnosticism is endemic in Romantic tradition without, however, dominating that tradition, or even that Gnosticism is the implicit, inevitable religion that frequently informs aspects of post-Enlightenment poetry.' But he also contrasted Yeats to one of the Irish poet's own formational precursors, Shelley, and to Schopenhauer. Though Bloom doesn't get into the lineage, Schopenhauer, fusing blind 'will' and clear-eyed pessimism, was an 'educator' of Nietzsche, whose 'curious astringent joy' allied him in Yeats's mind with Blake, and so helped transform the Irish poet from a lyricist of the Celtic Twilight into the most powerful poet of the twentieth century. But here is Bloom: 'Shelley and Schopenhauer were questers, in their very different ways, who could journey through the Void without yielding to the temptation of worshiping the Void as itself being sacred. Yeats, like Nietzsche, implicitly decided that he too would rather have the Void as purpose, than be void of purpose.'[9]

Though Bloom does not mention it, Yeats seems to have been thinking of the Gnostic vision when he ended one of his final letters by declaring, 'The last kiss is given to the void' (LTSM, 154). No more a believer in linear progress than Nietzsche (for whom the 'theory of progress' was a 'modern' concept, 'and therefore vulgar'), Yeats, under Indian influence, the Hindu mysticism he first imbibed from Mohini Chatterjee and to which he returned in his final decade, came to consider cultures and civilizations a succession of provisional illusions: that 'manifold illusion' or *maya*, seen through by those who, in 'Meru,' realize that 'man's life is thought,' its ultimate destructive / creative goal to 'come/ Into the desolation of reality.' Such seers as the ascetic hermits caverned on Mount Meru or Everest, 'know/ That day brings round the night, that before dawn/ [Man's] glory and his monuments are gone.'[10]

Those who have, after 'Ravening, raging, and uprooting,' finally 'come/ Into the desolation of reality,' have come far, but—despite the gay farewell to civilizations, 'Egypt and Greece good-bye, and good-bye, Rome!'—they may not have attained the state of 'bliss' achieved by Bhagwan Shri Hamsa, who describes climbing Meru in *The Holy Mountain*, read and introduced by Yeats shortly before writing 'Meru.' In that Introduction, Hamsa is quoted describing his attainment of indescribable 'bliss [...] all merged in the Absolute Brahma!' (E&I, 479, 481). Yeats's sonnet registers the strenuous mental steps to the Absolute, but, reflecting his unwillingness to surrender the individual self to the divine Self of the *Upanishads*, does not culminate in the merging joy expressed by Hamsa. Nevertheless, Yeats's hermits, by coming to 'know' the truth underlying illusions, have achieved a considerable degree of *gnosis*.

In the letter I began with, Yeats insists that there is 'no improvement, only a series of sudden fires,' each fainter than the one before it. 'We free ourselves from delusion that we may be nothing. The last kiss is given to the void.' In early Yeats, lured by Fairyland, it is an apocalyptic 'God'

---

9   Bloom, 'Yeats, Gnosticism, and the Sacred Void,' in *Poetry and Repression*, 234, 212.
10 See Charles I. Armstrong, '"Born Anew": W. B. Yeats's "Eastern" Turn in the 1930s,' in Gibson and Mann.

who is said to 'burn nature with a kiss'; at the end, that divine yet erotic and liberating act becomes human. Glossing this letter, the Irish critic Declan Kiberd, in 'W. B. Yeats—Building Amid Ruins,' perceptively observed that, for Yeats, 'the only hope of humanity was to break out of this diminishing series of cycles by recasting life on an altogether higher plane of consciousness.'[11] Kiberd (whose title echoes that favorite Blake saying of both Yeats and Joyce) does not dwell on the 'void,' or connect this 'higher plane of consciousness' with *gnosis*, but those familiar with Gnosticism well might. I believe Yeats himself did.

The memorable paragraph in *Per Amica Silentia Lunae* that begins, 'We make out of the quarrel with others, rhetoric, but of the quarrel with ourselves, poetry,' ends: 'I shall find the dark grow luminous, the void fruitful, when I understand that I have nothing; that the ringers in the tower have appointed for the hymen of the soul a passing bell' (Myth, 332). Most are committed to the world and to social conventions symbolized by the marriage bell. By contrast, the soul of the poet achieves its 'hymen' or marriage when it forsakes the gratifications of a merely material world, a forsaking symbolized by death's 'passing bell,' though a 'last kiss' is given to the void. A lifelong Seeker, Yeats, though his imagery remains fecund and erotic, seems at times as much a Gnostic Quester as he is a Romantic Poet. In his very last letter, written to Elizabeth Pelham on 4 January 1939, three weeks before his death, Yeats concluded:

> I am happy, and I think full of an energy, an energy I had despaired of. It seems to me that I have found what I wanted. When I try to put all into a phrase I say, 'Man can embody truth but he cannot know it.' I must embody it in the completion of my life. The abstract is not life and everywhere draws out its contradictions. You can refute Hegel but not the Saint or the Song of Sixpence. (L, 922)

It had been thirty-seven years since Yeats, annotating Nietzsche, had scribbled in the margin his polar contrast between 'denial of self,' the soul 'seeking *knowledge*,' and 'affirmation' of a self that energetically 'seeks *life*.' In that diagram, Yeats was, under the auspices of Nietzsche, refuting Plato's Socrates, who, in his advocacy of mind and knowledge, famously insisted, in the face of imminent death, that 'the unexamined

---

11   In Kiberd's *Irish Classics*, 454.

life is not worth living' (*Apology* 38a5–6). Anticipated by others, including Mark Twain and Oscar Wilde, William James responded that, while that was perfectly true, it was equally true that the 'unlived life was not worth examining.' In the October 1938 letter to Ethel Mannin in which he described his 'idea of death' as best depicted by Blake's *Grave* illustration of 'the soul and body embracing,' Yeats immediately added: 'All men with subjective natures move towards a possible ecstasy, all with objective natures towards a possible wisdom' (L, 917). It was the old *antithetical-primary* polarity once again, with Yeats presenting both sides, but making his intuitive preference clear. Happy even on the threshold of his own death, the 'completion of my life,' Yeats had not forgotten the vital affirmation he embraced in his 1902 marginalia; and I for one have no wish to resist let alone refute his gay farewell, celebrating both *primary* and *antithetical*, Saint and Song.

Not so Harold Bloom; in his 2004 book *Where Shall Wisdom Be Found?* Bloom resisted that Yeatsian emphasis on embodiment by choosing, in keeping with his title, to focus on wisdom rather than that 'truth', which Yeats said could not be 'known' but could be embodied. 'Of wisdom,' writes Bloom—who thought his reversal of Yeats important enough to place in splendid isolation on his book's back cover—'I personally would affirm the reverse. We cannot embody it, yet we can be taught how to learn wisdom, whether or not it can be identified with the Truth that might make us free.' His final, skeptical allusion is to the Gospel of John (8:32), but Bloom's emphasis on being taught how to learn wisdom would appeal to all Seekers, certainly Gnostic Seekers. And yet Harold Bloom—critical, as we saw at the outset, of Yeats's emphasis on 'the wisdom of the body'—is not William Butler Yeats, a 'singer born,' whose poetry and vision, however drawn to the spiritual, remains life-affirming and perpetually 'embodied'—a poet who, to 'put all into a phrase,' finds even the 'void fruitful.'

Fig. 1 Maud Gonne, 19 November 1897; inscribed by Maud: 'Onward always till Liberty is won!' Negative: glass. Library of Congress, Prints and Photographs Division, https://commons.wikimedia.org/wiki/File:Maude_Gonne_McBride_nd.jpg.

PART TWO

LOVE'S LABYRINTH: YEATS AS PETRARCHAN POET (THE MAUD GONNE POEMS)

So what do you say? That I invented the name of 'Laura' to give myself something to talk about and to have others talk about me! And that in fact there is no Laura in my mind except that poetic Laurel to which I have aspired with long-continued unwearied zeal, as my labor bears witness; and that concerning the living Laura, by whom I seem to be captured, everything is made-up, that my poems are fictions, my sighs pretended. Well, I wish it were all a joke, a pretense and not a madness! [...] Believe me, to labor to appear mad, to no purpose, is the height of madness.

Petrarch, Familiar Letters, II.ix

Does the imagination dwell the most
Upon a woman won or woman lost?
If on the lost, admit you turned aside
From a great labyrinth out of pride,
Cowardice, some silly over-subtle thought
Or anything called conscience once;
And that if memory recur, the sun's
Under eclipse and the day blotted out.

Yeats, 'The Tower,' II

Preface to Part Two

As noted in the General Prologue, my emphasis in both parts of this book is on the poetry. As for the love poems discussed in Part Two: though I am, of course, aware of the distinction to be made between an author and the 'speaker' of a poem, I refer to 'Yeats' and 'Maud Gonne,' rather than, as the more discreet Yeats does, to a 'Poet' and his 'Beloved'. My justification is that Yeats really wants us, under all the camouflage, to know who he is, as man and poet, along with the identity of the Muse and living woman who inspired him and simultaneously broke his heart

Though I try in what follows to read the poems *as poems*, attending to the variety of lyrical forms deployed by Yeats, in my focus on Maud Gonne I sometimes necessarily fail to do justice to the poems in their entirety. That is most obviously true in the case of four major poems in which Maud figures significantly, but whose presence does not begin to exhaust their richness and complexity. These four are 'The Tower,' 'Among School Children,' 'A Dialogue of Self and Soul,' and 'A Prayer for my Daughter.' My second epigraph, taken from Part II of 'The Tower,' neglects the splendid first and third movements, though both have been discussed earlier. Maud figures in three of the eight stanzas of 'Among School Children,' leaving five stanzas on which I am silent, a barely forgivable omission in the presence of what is one of Yeats's indisputable masterpieces. Of the nine stanzas of Yeats's great debate-poem, 'A Dialogue of Self and Soul,' in many ways the central text in Yeats's canon, Maud's presence is restricted to just two stanzas. But they happen to be the penultimate stanza and, by implication, the rhapsodic finale.

In 'A Prayer for my Daughter,' Maud is implicitly, and almost explicitly, present throughout. But the poem, as its title indicates, is about the poet's infant daughter, with Maud hovering as a counterexample of what he wishes for his child. While no one disputes the aesthetic beauty

https://doi.org/10.11647/OBP.0275.08

of the 'Prayer,' its cultural and sexual politics have stirred controversy. Yeats has been attacked by some readers, feminists in particular, for objectifying, even dehumanizing his daughter. He prays for her to 'become a flourishing hidden tree/ That all her thoughts may like the linnet be,' birds having 'no business but dispensing round/ Their magnanimities of sound.' In his patriarchal, programmed future for his daughter—including being brought by her bridegroom to a house where 'all's accustomed, ceremonious'—thought, certainly 'opinion,' is rejected in favor of 'merriment' and the soul's recovery of 'radical innocence.'

By contemporary standards, even by some standards of 1919 elevating the then New Woman, Yeats's conservatism certainly seems retrograde. But even critics offended by the poet's alleged misogyny or by his obvious neo-Burkean Anglo-Irish reverence for tradition, custom and ceremony, have to acknowledge the exceptional beauty of 'A Prayer for my Daughter,' along with the awkward paradox that the very aspects most likely to offend some readers are precisely the poetic and structural elements that make the poem as beautiful as it is. In addition, the 'Prayer' itself supplies the appalling counterexample to organic stability: the litany of actual (Maud's) and mythological bad marriages, which are the disastrous alternatives to the kind of life and marriage Yeats wishes for Anne. Finally, if a man cannot be paternalistic when he is praying for an infant daughter, born in a time of violence, when *can* he be paternalistic?

I touch on these issues here because I pass over them in my later discussion of the poem as beyond the range of my present Maud-centered subject. Though I hasten to add that I can certainly see why some might find these considerations, here restricted to a father's protective or 'patriarchal' stance toward his infant daughter, relevant to the issue of a male poet's projection rather than accurate portrayal of the adult woman he makes his Muse. Notably, seven years after he'd prayed for his daughter to be 'Rooted in one dear perpetual place,' Yeats 'liberated' her by imaginatively celebrating that daughter's rebellion against social conformity and parental authority. Told by his wife that she had chastised their daughter, then seven, for being seen with a boy with a bad reputation, Yeats was so disturbed yet delighted by Anne's reply—'Yes, but he has such lovely hair and his eyes are as cold as a

March wind'—that he decided to put her reply, aesthetic individualism triumphing over communal ethics, 'into verse' (1926 Diary). The result was the poem 'Father and Child.'

Advancing Anne, for the song's sake, to adolescence, Yeats transforms the threatening 'wind' of the 'Prayer' into the still dangerous but exciting wind of sexual awakening. He also converts his role as scolding father to that of empathetic poet, overturning in the process poet-priest George Herbert's 'The Collar'—which begins, 'I struck the board and cry'd "No more",' and ends with Herbert as 'Childe' submitting to 'My Lord.' Here is 'Father and Child,'

> She hears me strike the board and say
> That she is under ban
> Of all good men and women
> Being mentioned with a man
> Who has the worst of all bad names;
> And thereupon replies
> That his hair is beautiful,
> Cold as the March wind his eyes.

The child's independence and her unanswerable response are reinforced by the fact that 'Father and Child' is the opening poem of Yeats's 'A Woman Young and Old,' a concentrically structured sequence that ends by elegizing 'Oedipus' child,' the archetypal female rebel, Antigone.

8. Poet and Muse

Since my subject is W. B. Yeats's poetry to and about Maud Gonne, I use their names freely, though, as noted above, Yeats himself does not, preferring to cast the relationship as one of a Poet and a Beloved, who also happens to be his Muse. Since I feel some critical guilt about this forwardness in naming names, I'll begin by briefly discussing this issue, setting autobiography—as Yeats did, and as Joseph Hassett demonstrated in *W. B. Yeats and the Muses*—in the context of the Poet–Muse tradition. I'll then unpack my two epigraphs, which I see as intimately related. First, then, the issue of names.

Teaching poetry, we remind students of the difference between the author and the 'speaker' in a poem. There are obvious cases in which speakers are personae quite different from their authors: dramatic monologues, for example; or, a more complicated case, dialogue poems, of which Yeats wrote over thirty, with debates between, say, *Hic* and *Ille*, He and She, Michael Robartes and Owen Aherne, Robartes and the Dancer, Crazy Jane and the Bishop, Self (or Heart) and Soul—parceling out contrasting aspects of the poet himself, the man and his various masks. And there are the two female sequences, 'A Woman Young and Old' and the 'Crazy Jane' poems, lyric experiments in which he explored what he described to Dorothy Wellesley as 'the woman in me.' There can be multilayered distinctions even within a poem. In his book on *The Tower*, discussing 'Among School Children,' David Young writes, 'The smiling public man can maintain his façade masking his wild thought and in the process reflecting the poet who stands outside the poem.'[1] In the case of even the most 'personal' lyrics, there is *some* distinction between author and speaker; as Emily Dickinson warned Thomas Higginson in a letter of July 1862, 'When I state myself, as the

---

1   Young, *Troubled Mirror: A Study of Yeats's The Tower*, 90.

    https://doi.org/10.11647/OBP.0275.09

Representative of the Verse—it does not mean—Me—but a supposed person.' But it is also true that, in such intimate lyrics, we are often invited to attribute the voice we hear, and the thoughts and feelings uttered, to the poet in his or her own person.

In 1937, Yeats began what was intended to be 'A General Introduction' to a projected 1940 *Collected Works*, by making two points: first, that 'a poet writes always of his personal life, in his finest work out of its tragedy, whatever it be, lost love, or mere loneliness'; but, second, that 'he is never the bundle of accident and incoherence that sits down to breakfast; he has been reborn as an idea, something intended, complete' (E&I, 509). So, there are distinctions to be made between that bundle at the breakfast table, the man who lived the life, the maker of the poems, and the poet who appears in them or stands just outside them. Yeats also insisted, in 'Friends of My Youth,' a lecture intended to be delivered on 9 March 1910, that a poet's 'life is an experiment in living and those that come after have a right to know it. Above all, it is necessary that the lyric poet's life be known that we should understand that his poetry is no rootless flower but the speech of a man.' That is the justification for Yeats's own autobiographical texts (shaped for a purpose), and for biographies by others, from the first, by Joseph Hone in 1940, through Richard Ellmann's permanently valuable *Yeats: The Man and the Masks* (1948), A. Norman Jeffares' *W. B. Yeats: A New Biography* (1990, a thoroughly revised version of a volume originally published in 1949), Terence Brown's critically astute *The Life of W. B. Yeats* (1999), and culminating in the completion, in 2003, of the magisterial two-volume study by R. F. Foster, who cites this 'no-rootless-flower' passage as one of two epigraphs to his first volume—a dictum also cited early on in their books by both Ellmann and Hassett.[2]

On the other hand, there is an argument to be made, one brilliantly embodied in Hazard Adams's *The Book of Yeats's Poems*, that what is most 'important is to recognize that the poet's making is *other* than his historically recoverable self,' and that, 'with a great poet like Yeats, it is likely to prove less valuable that we recover what he did and the relationship between what he did and what he made' than that we engage endlessly in the critical study of the *Collected Poems* as an integrated, carefully arranged, progressive text. It is not quite what

---

2   Ellmann, *Yeats: The Man and the Masks*, 5. Hassett, *W. B. Yeats and the Muses*, 2.

Hugh Kenner called (in an early essay Adams rightly praises) a 'sacred book,' but what Adams insists is an 'antithetical and secular' book in which mere autobiography is a 'lower-court' affair to be subordinated to a poetic canon organized by the poet to tell a dramatic-mimetic story (what Wallace Stevens termed a 'Supreme Fiction').[3] In using Yeats's and Gonne's actual names, I am registering the fact that a rooted poet writes always of his personal life, with lost love, remorse, and loneliness present, but capable of being absorbed and transcended. In also recognizing the poet being reborn as an 'idea,' I try in what follows to keep Yeats's supreme if reality-based fiction—the Poet–Muse story—at the vital center.

Demonstrating the intimate relationship between my two epigraphs, especially placing the stanza from 'The Tower' in its full Yeatsian and Muse-tradition context, will take some doing. I hope that in the process, I will not put a dragon at the mouth of the cave by being as garrulous as Yeats seems to be in this section of 'The Tower'—which *appears* to ramble, but is always directed toward that final question: one crucial to Yeats and at the heart of the whole history of love poetry in the Petrarchan tradition.

In the first passage, Petrarch is responding to the charge—by his close friend and confessor, Cardinal Giovanni Colonna—that the 'Laura' of his love poems (destined to become the most influential collection of such poems in the literary history of the West)[4] is a poetic fiction; that the name is a mere pun on the 'poetic Laurel' Petrarch had aspired to and worked so hard and successfully, to achieve; and that 'Laura' herself is no more than an 'invented' symbol for the Muse. Would that it were so, cries Petrarch, who proudly acknowledges his relentless toil as a poetic craftsman, but also insists on an attendant 'madness'; that beneath the artifice of those ornate and endlessly inventive poems (the

---

3   R. F. Foster, *The Apprentice Mage*, vii. Hazard Adams, *The Book of Yeats's Poems*, 11–12, 253–54. The reference to Stevens is mine, but Adams does see the Yeatsian 'Book' as a sustained fictive performance.

4   There is an irony here. Critical of Dante for writing the *Commedia* in the ephemeral vernacular, Petrarch staked his claim to future fame on his epic poem *Africa*, written in immortal Latin. Instead, that fame rests on the lyrics to Laura, written in—the vernacular. The hero of Petrarch's almost unreadable epic was the great Roman general Scipio Africanus, whose admonishing spirit had engaged in dialogue with his grandson, a younger Scipio, in Cicero's famous *Somnium Scipionis* [The Dream of Scipio], which, as we've seen, plays an unexpected but highly significant role in Yeats's pivotal 'A Dialogue of Self and Soul.'

sonnets and *ballatas* that constitute his *Canzoniere*), his ardent though never consummated love of an actual, 'living Laura,' participated in that Corybantic 'madness' said, or conceded, by Plato in the *Ion*, to inspire poets, when they are not merely masters of their art [*techne*], but possessed by the Muse. In fact, Plato-Socrates tells us, there is no genuine 'invention' in the poet 'until he has been inspired and is out of his senses, and the mind is no longer in him.'[5]

This wary view of poetic inspiration is ambivalent, even hostile, as we might expect coming from rational philosophers like Socrates and Plato. Nevertheless, the image persists: that of the enraptured poet, his 'eye in a fine frenzy rolling,' and, like 'lovers and madmen,' able 'to apprehend more than cool reason ever comprehends.' This is, of course, Shakespeare's Duke Theseus, holding forth at the start of the final act of *A Midsummer Night's Dream*. For Theseus—a man as skeptical of the irrational as Socrates and Plato, and therefore dubious of the lovers' reports of enchantment in the moonlit forest—'the lunatic, the lover, and the poet' are alike, their 'seething brains' all fired by 'imagination.'[6] The image of transported poets, their imaginations Muse-maddened, their music attuned to the harmony of the spheres, has proven powerful over the ages.[7] Coleridge, familiar with the *Ion*, gives us, at the climax of his visionary poem 'Kubla Khan,' an iconic image of the vatic bard, with his 'flashing eyes, his floating hair,' who, having 'fed' on 'honey-dew' and 'drunk the milk of paradise,' evokes among rational folk 'holy dread,' knowing that they are in the presence of a poet possessing the power of 'music' and possessed *by* semi-divine inspiration akin to 'madness.'

---

5   Plato, *Ion*, 523–534b. This short dialogue is named for the *rhapsode* with whom Socrates is conversing.

6   *A Midsummer Night's Dream* V.i.4–8. The dismissive skepticism of Theseus is of course memorably refuted by Hippolyta, the woman he is about to marry, who finds 'great constancy' in the lovers' wondrous accounts.

7   But the original harmony of the spheres is often diminished or distorted in the process of transmission, as in the stanza of Yeats's 'Among School Children' that begins, 'Plato thought nature but a spume that plays/ Upon a ghostly paradigm of things.' Within a few lines we are told that Pythagoras 'fingered upon a fiddle-stick or strings/ What a star sang and careless Muses heard.' These casual Muses, carefree but imperfect auditors, pass on a distorted version of the celestial harmony to mortal poets. Spiritually aware of our failure to hear the harmony of the spheres, Shakespeare's Lorenzo directs Jessica's gaze to the star-paved heavens: 'there's not the smallest orb which thou behold'st/ But in his motion like an angel sings,/ Still quiring to the young-eyed cherubins;/ Such harmony is in immortal souls,/ But while this muddy vesture of decay/ Doth grossly close it in, we cannot hear it.' *The Merchant of Venice*, V.i.58–65

The sources of inspiration in 'Kubla Khan' are benign and barbarous, divine and demonic. As it happens, the topography of Coleridge's Xanadu is reproduced and naturalized by Yeats in 'Coole and Ballylee, 1931,' where the waters racing past Yeats's tower, 'Run for a mile undimmed in Heaven's face/ Then darkening through 'dark' Raftery's 'cellar' drop,/ Run underground, rise in a rocky place/ In Coole demesne, and there to finish up/ Spread to a lake and drop into a hole.' In Xanadu, the river meandered for five miles through wood and dale until it 'reached the caverns measureless to man,/ And sank in tumult to a lifeless ocean.' That 'sacred river' had its source in a 'mighty fountain' hidden in 'a deep romantic chasm'—a 'savage place! as holy and enchanted/ As e'er beneath a waning moon was haunted/ By woman wailing for her demon lover!' But there is also a benign Muse in 'Kubla Khan': that 'damsel with a dulcimer' the enraptured speaker once heard and 'saw' in a 'vision,' and whose 'symphony and song,' if he could only 'revive' it 'within' himself, would empower him, 'with music loud and long,' to create a paradise of the imagination superior even to Kubla's Xanadu.

The mad, and maddening, power of Muse-inspired poetry provides the immediate context of my second epigraph: the final and climactic stanza of Part II of 'The Tower,' which had begun with Yeats summoning forth, through the power of imagination, various 'images and memories' of figures from Irish history and myth, associated with the local area surrounding Yeats's Tower. The most important is none other than 'dark' Raftery, the blind nineteenth-century Gaelic poet Anthony Raftery. He is joined by one of Yeats's own creations, Red Hanrahan, whose 'Song about Ireland' was Maud Gonne's favorite Yeats poem, though Hanrahan is presented here with a sexual frankness that would have distressed Maud, who disliked the 'coarseness' of some of Yeats's later poetry. Though the poet 'would ask a question of them all,' we will focus, as Yeats does, on Raftery and Hanrahan, both song makers.

Raftery's Muse, 'a peasant girl commended by a song,' was local beauty Mary Hynes, and 'So great a glory did the song confer' that 'certain men, being maddened by those rhymes,' rose up from their tavern table and set off to 'test their fancy by their sight.' The upshot was tragic for at least one, who 'drowned in the great bog of Cloone.' Their wits driven 'astray' by drink but more by the 'music' of Raftery's Muse-poetry, these Seekers had mistaken 'the brightness of the moon/ For

the prosaic light of day.' Even Yeats, seemingly garrulous but actually
artfully rambling, professes at first to find this local anecdote

> Strange, but the man who made the song was blind;
> Yet, now I have considered it, I find
> That nothing strange; the tragedy began
> With Homer that was a blind man,
> And Helen has all living hearts betrayed.

By 1928, when this poem was published, most readers of poetry were
aware that Nobel Laureate W. B. Yeats had conferred glory on his own
Muse, Maud Gonne, by repeatedly identifying her, most splendidly
in 'No Second Troy,' with Homer's beautiful, destructive and heart-
betraying Helen. That Yeats, despite the camouflage and distancing,
wants us to know who his 'beloved' was in 'real' life, partially excuses
my indiscretion in cutting to the chase by actually naming her, as Yeats
does only once in a poem. Taking the same shortcut, I also refer, for
the most part, to 'Yeats' rather than the 'speaker,' for reasons given in
addressing the issue from the outset.

To return to the passage from 'The Tower': Yeats has other questions
to ask (prominent among them, 'do all in public or in secret rage/ As I
do now against old age?'); but he eventually dismisses everyone from
his phantasmagoria but Hanrahan, left behind because the poet needs
'all his mighty memories.' Yeats has a particular memory in mind,
repressed even in evoking it. It was he who 'drove' Hanrahan 'drunk
or sober through the dawn,' a bewitched man who 'rose in a frenzy,'
led on a strange quest 'towards—//O towards I have forgotten what—
enough!' What Yeats represses is Hanrahan's discovery (related in the
first of six of *Red Hanrahan's Stories*) of a palatial house, lit from within
by sunlight though it is night-time. There he encounters, surrounded by
mystical symbols borne by four grey old women, an enthroned figure,
pale with 'long waiting.' It is a 'woman, the most beautiful in the world':
the fairy queen, Echtge. But Hanrahan, too tongue-tied and 'weak' to
address her, is unable to break the spell she is under. Following her 'very
sad sigh,' the scene dissolves. In the end, Hanrahan, who had (Yeats
later remarked) 'gone into some undiscoverable country' (E&I, 298–99),
loses both Echtge and his earthly sweetheart, Mary Lavelle. When, after
a distraught year's absence, a transformed Hanrahan returns to find her,

Mary is gone; in the final sentence of the story, 'he never met with her or with news of her again.' (Myth, 220–21, 224)

Having abandoned his human sweetheart and lost what fleeting contact he had with the faery queen, blighted Hanrahan 'became a half-mad rhapsodic poet, a seer of visionary women, and a failed seducer of real women.'[8] It is to that 'old lecher'—'lured by a softening eye,/ Or by a touch or a sigh,' to 'plunge' into the 'labyrinth of another's being'— that Yeats poses the crucial question he has been headed toward all along, however casual the journey has seemed: 'Does the imagination dwell the most/ Upon a woman won or woman lost?' The question is answered in the very asking, and not only because 'I myself created Hanrahan.' Centuries of poetry in the Petrarchan tradition, reincarnated in Yeats's own Petrarchan poems of obsessive and unrequited love, make the answer obvious; but not what immediately follows: 'If on the lost, admit you turned aside/ From a great labyrinth' out of 'pride' (usually praised by Yeats but here, a less commendably stubborn independence), or 'cowardice,' or out of 'some silly, over-subtle thought / Or anything called conscience once.' That 'over-subtle thought' probably refers to a difference Yeats specifically acknowledges in the Maud Gonne poem, 'The People': his overly analytical mind, diametrically opposed to Maud Gonne's spontaneous, instinctual nature, that 'purity of a natural force' that attracted *and* profoundly disturbed him.

The middle and related charge, 'cowardice,' would apply not only to Hanrahan, intimidated in the presence of Echtge, but to Yeats as well. When in 1898, Maud opened up to him the secrets of her life, and even kissed him on the mouth, Yeats, who had hitherto avoided any physical advance, may have reacted less with what he called 'high scruple' than from what Deirdre Toomey, in an essay whose title is drawn from this passage of 'The Tower,' has described as 'psychic impotence' brought on by fear of seeing a woman he had idealized as almost supernaturally 'virginal' dragged down into 'sexuality' and even motherhood.[9] That fearful reaction is one form of cowardice. Maud herself had leveled that charge in a *political* context, though she acknowledged that his behavior was intended to protect her.

---

8   This concise and accurate synopsis is by Daniel Albright, in his Notes to *W. B. Yeats: The Poems*, 636.

9   Toomey, 'Labyrinths: Yeats and Maud Gonne,' in *Yeats and Women*, 1–40.

The occasion (more fully described in my discussion of the poem just referred to, 'The People') was her first major public speech, on 22 June 1897, part of a patriotic counter-demonstration protesting Queen Victoria's Diamond Jubilee, which happened to conflict with Ireland's national celebration of the executed heroes of the 1798 United Irishman Rising. When, electrified by Maud's speech, the crowd turned violent, violence exacerbated by a charge of baton-wielding police, Yeats prevented Maud from joining the melee, fearing she would be injured (as hundreds were). In her letter of reprimand, Maud accused him of having 'made me do the most cowardly thing I have ever done in my life,' a charge she turned back on him: 'Do you know that to be a coward for those we love, is only a degree less bad than to be a coward for oneself. The latter I know well you are not, the former you know well you are.'[10]

This was just the most dramatic example of Yeats's protective fear, for he was far more often troubled than he was thrilled by the impassioned political activism of his equivalent of Hanrahan's 'most beautiful woman in the world': Maud, 'the loveliest woman born/ Out of the mouth of Plenty's horn.' Related to that cornucopia (degraded in 'A Prayer for my Daughter' to 'an old bellows full of angry wind'), the fascinating, complex and dangerous 'labyrinth,' the maze of the Muse, through which Yeats must remorsefully wander, rather than heroically 'plunge,' armed only with memory and imagination, is symbolically coterminous with his personal Muse, Maud Gonne. And if *that* 'memory recur, the sun's/ Under eclipse and the day blotted out.' These final two lines of the stanza I chose as epigraph, confusing but explicable, are immediately germane to the Muse-inspired 'madness' to which Plato and Petrarch refer.

Yeats had begun this question-asking movement of 'The Tower' by sending 'imagination forth/ Under the day's declining beam,' anticipating this final day-blotting eclipse. The poetry-intoxicated men riding to compare the actual Mary Hynes with Raftery's glory-conferring praise of his Muse, 'being *maddened* by those rhymes [...] mistook the brightness of the *moon/ for the prosaic light of day—/ Music had driven their wits astray.*' No sooner had Yeats mentioned Homer's heart-betraying 'Helen,' triggering memories of his own Helen, than he had cried out, 'O may *the moon and sunlight seem/ One inextricable beam,/*

---

10   G-YL, 72–73. For details, see discussion below of 'The People.'

For if I triumph I must make men *mad*.' Combining his occult studies in alchemy with his 'excited' reading of 'that strong enchanter, Nietzsche,' Yeats, adopting that enchanter's distinction between the Apollonian and the Dionysian (L, 403), attributed 'to the sun all that came from the high disciplined or individual kingly mind,' while 'to lunar influence belong all thought and emotions that were created by the community, by the common people, by nobody knows who' (Ex, 21–24).

Robert Graves makes a similar contrast: between inferior Apollonian poets of male intellect and order and genuine Muse-poets, who all, whether they know it or not, are in thrall to the lunar Muse he labelled the 'White Goddess.' This does not imply, in Graves any more than in Yeats, an abandonment of Apollonian order and poetic craftsmanship. As the best of Graves's poems, including the 'White Goddess' poems, amply demonstrate, he was obsessed by *techne*, craftsmanship and verbal precision. The sacred duty of the 'true poet' is to tell the Muse-goddess 'the truth about himself and her in his own passionate and peculiar words.'[11]

Though Graves considered himself a poet antithetical to Yeats, they have more than lunar Muse-ship in common. Whatever his attraction to the mysteries and primitivistic rites surrounding his White Goddess, Graves had, like Yeats, a post-Renaissance mind and a skeptical Anglo-Irish temperament that combined to keep his magical-shamanistic tendencies in balance. Concluding his Introduction to the second (1937) edition of *A Vision*, Yeats acknowledges that some may 'ask whether I believe in the actual existence of my circuits of sun and moon.' To such a question, he can only answer that, while 'sometimes overwhelmed by miracle' while in the midst of it, 'my reason has soon recovered.' He realizes, now that 'the system stands out clearly in my imagination,' that his circuits of sun and moon are not to be taken literally but 'regarded as stylistic arrangements of experience' that 'have helped me to hold in a single thought reality and justice' (Vis, 24). This is what Nietzsche meant by simultaneously recognizing the tumult of the actual and the aesthetic need to 'organize the chaos,' with the tension between the Apollonian and Dionysian, as laid out in *The Birth of Tragedy*, resolved in what later Nietzsche called a new and improved Dionysianism: one example of the fusion referred to as 'wild civility', as used in the title of my 1980s

---

11   Graves, *The White Goddess*, 444.

book on Graves. Though I was borrowing the famous oxymoron from the 1630 lyric 'Delight in Disorder' by Robert Herrick, I was conscious of the Nietzschean creative tension between the Apollonian and the Dionysian, and its subsequent merging.[12]

What Yeats wants, yet fears, is the Dionysian poetic power, primordial or Druidic in intensity, exercised by the blind itinerant Raftery, like him, a singer born and a celebrant of the beauty of a woman. Of the 'early poets' Yeats says: 'Instead of learning their craft with paper and pen' (the *techne* Plato and Petrarch agree is necessary but not sufficient for the Muse-inspired poet), 'they would sit still' until 'imagination' brought forth 'images so vivid' and contagious that passers-by became 'part of the imagination of the dreamer, and wept, or laughed, or ran away as he would have them' (E&I, 43). To again quote Seamus Heaney, born in the year his predecessor died, 'true poetry' like Yeats's, tapping into a deep and mysterious consciousness, requires 'more than the artful expression of daylight opinion and conviction.' As Yeats himself says in this section of 'The Tower,' if he succeeds in fusing solar/Apollonian craftsmanship with the imaginative yet maddening power that derives from the lunar influence of the Muse; if he can make sun and moon seem 'one inextricable beam,' his ambiguous triumph, like that of Gaelic Raftery and his ancient predecessors, 'must make men *mad*,' though hopefully in a way more creative than destructive.

§

But when one is actually in love, not merely penning love poems to an 'invented' lady, Muse-inspired madness becomes almost indistinguishable from the near insanity to which one can be driven by love unrequited. To the amused friend who charged him with concocting a poetic fiction and calling it 'Laura,' Petrarch cries out that he wishes it *were* all a joke and a pretense and not what it actually is: 'a

---

12   Yeats was first attracted to Nietzsche by the Apollonian-Dionysian tension, which Yeats connected with two movements: the Dionysian urge 'to transcend forms, the other to create forms' (L, 403). Even in *The Birth of Tragedy*, Nietzsche imagined Dionysus harnessed by Apollo. In his later thought, what he calls the 'Dionysian' subsumes the Apollonian. The Greeks, we're told in *Untimely Meditations* 2.1, 'gradually learned to *organize the chaos*, a parable for each of us.' But the chaos must be organized, not extirpated in what he depicts as Platonic-Christian 'castratism' (*Twilight of the Idols* 5.1). As Zarathustra puts it (*Zarathustra* 1, Prologue 3), 'One must still have chaos within oneself to be able to give birth to a dancing star.'

madness.' Yeats's Muse and Beloved were one and the same, a woman who inspired her devotee to create beautiful lyrics but also left him sex starved and half-mad. In the first draft of his autobiography, completed by the beginning of 1917, but too candid for publication, he looked back twenty years to 1897, when, he says, 'I was tortured by sexual desire and disappointed love. Often as I walked in the woods at Coole, it would have been a relief to have screamed aloud. When desire became an unendurable torture, I would masturbate,' which left him ill. He 'sought no other love,' and, falling back on chivalric Arthurian romance, would repeat to himself 'again and again the last confession of Lancelot, and indeed it was my greatest pride, "I have loved a queen beyond measure and exceeding long." I was never before or since more miserable.'[13] In 1914, he described himself, in 'On Woman,' the first 'Solomon and Sheba' poem focused, not on George but on that 'perverse creature of chance,' Maud Gonne, as so sexually frustrated that he was 'driven mad,/ Sleep driven from my bed.'

Had Yeats's Muse—the extravagantly beautiful, occasionally half-mad and certainly maddeningly elusive Maud Gonne—never existed, Yeats *would* have 'invented' her.[14] But she *did* exist. Maud exploded into the young poet's life in 1889, but even then her future as a Muse was doubly predestined. First, like most love poets in the Romantic and Celtic traditions, Yeats required an enchantress, a destructive yet life-giving lunar goddess and *femme fatale* (the Celtic *Leanhaun Shee*), who also inspires creativity. Second, he was, early on, writing in the erotic-spiritual tradition of obsessive and unrequited love established six centuries earlier: in Dante's mixed-genre *La Vita Nuova* (1294), and in the lyric sequence of Petrarch, its earliest poems dating to 1327, the year he fell in love with 'Laura,' the latest to the final year of his life, 1374.

However idealized, Dante's Beatrice was real, even to the name, Beatrice Portinari. Petrarch's *Rime in vita e morte di Madonna Laura* was also inspired by an actual woman—from Avignon, blond, brilliant-eyed, probably swept away by the Black Death in 1348. There was

---

13 Mem, 125. This misery is recalled in Poem II of 'A Man Young and Old,' where the victim of a lunar Muse thinks, 'I could recover if I shrieked/ My heart's agony/ To passing bird, but I am dumb/ From human dignity.'

14 Lady Gregory confided in her 1898 diary that Yeats once told her that Maud might be 'locked up as mad,' since her political activity was guided by 'visions'—an odd accusation coming from a fellow occultist.

most certainly a 'real' Maud Gonne, well known to be the inspiration of Yeats's love poems. Readers of those poems will find little reason to doubt—though she was as 'unattainable' as Laura and Beatrice—that Yeats was as deeply and painfully in love with Maud as his predecessors had been with *their* Muses. Like Petrarch, Yeats, despite Plato's relative dismissal of *techne* in the *Ion*, devoted sustained labor to perfecting the craftsmanship that produced lyric forms varied enough to allow him to express his love in all its ecstasy and anguish. In fact, I will be arguing, it was the very art she inspired that allowed Yeats (in *this* case, at least, without cowardice or intellectual over subtlety) to 'turn aside' from the 'great labyrinth' that *was* Maud Gonne. Not even *she* could triumph over the poems she helped generate. That would please her since, as we know, she thought of those poems as the 'children' of their otherwise childless union, herself the Father, Yeats the Mother! And, as she added, 'our children' will have 'wings.'

The volatile, recklessly heroic Maud Gonne was wrong in many of her actions and judgments, but not in her assessment of the poetry she had inspired, even co-created. Yeats had other sexual relationships over the years—the liaison with Mabel Dickinson actually flanking his brief physical intimacy with Maud—and his marriage to Georgie Hyde-Lees ('George') was important to him, both personally and esoterically. But it was Maud—'*that* one'—who broke the poet's heart, simultaneously fascinating, obsessing, and inspiring him. One can admire the verse and be dismissive of the Muse. Thomas Flanagan, critic and author of a famed trilogy of Irish historical novels, observed in 1997, casting a cold eye on Maud Gonne: 'Some of Yeats's most magnificent poetry was inspired by this addlepated zealot.' The formidable Harold Bloom, hardly an uncritical admirer, has said of Yeats as a love poet: 'one can wonder if any poet of our century enters into competition here with him.' In *W. B. Yeats and the Muses*, Joseph M. Hassett has pronounced the poetry to and about her 'the most sustained and fully developed tribute to a Muse in the history of literature in English.' Whatever one makes of Maud herself, and it is hard to overlook her flaws, especially her life-long anti-Semitism, those informed literary judgments seem incontrovertible.[15]

---

15   Flanagan, 'A Terrible Beauty is Born,' 10. Bloom, *Yeats*, 459.

9. Maud Gonne, and Yeats as Petrarchan Lover

Like most love poems in the West, Yeats's Maud Gonne lyrics are in the Petrarchan tradition. James Longenbach, who has written on Yeats and, as both practitioner and critic, on poetic form, observed in 2004 that, 'to read love poetry—to speak of the language of love—is to read Petrarch, who is largely responsible for inventing what W. B. Yeats called 'the old high way of love.'[1] He is quoting from one of the pivotal Maud Gonne poems, 'Adam's Curse,' a poem as much about, and beautifully demonstrating, lyric craftsmanship, as it is about the travail of unrequited love. As Longenbach is hardly alone in recognizing, Yeats conceived of Maud, unique though she was, as yet another kind yet inevitably cruel and inaccessible *domina* in the Medieval and Renaissance courtly love tradition:

> I had a thought for no one's but your ears:
> That you were beautiful, and that I strove
> To love you in the old high way of love;
> That it had all seemed happy, and yet we'd grown
> As weary-hearted as that hollow moon.

This elegiac evening scene, with love faded beneath a 'hollow' moon, is gentle; but the Maud Gonne we encounter more often than not in the poems to and about her is a more violent cousin of Petrarch's Laura, and of the even more famously unattainable Beatrice of Dante, a Dante whose iconically gaunt cheek was 'hollowed,' in Yeats's telling (in his

---

1   Longenbach's comment linking Petrarch and Yeats appears as the first of three notes of praise prefacing David Young's 2004 translation of *The Poetry of Petrarch*. I cite the poet from this text.

    https://doi.org/10.11647/OBP.0275.10

1917 dialogue-poem 'Ego Dominus Tuus'), by his 'hunger for the apple on the bough/ Most out of reach'—Sappho's simile, as translated by Dante Gabriel Rossetti ('Like the sweet apple which reddens upon the topmost bough' beyond the reach of pickers, Fragment 105A, titled by Rossetti 'One Girl'). As I will suggest when we return to 'Adam's Curse,' Yeats also has in mind Sir Philip Sidney's sonnet-sequence, *Astrophil and Stella*, whose immortal 'Stella' is based (almost as transparently as Astro*phil* is on Philip Sidney) on the Elizabethan court-'star' Penelope Rich, a beauty engaged, like Maud, in dangerous political intrigue. She was a Muse with whom Sidney, unlike Dante, Petrarch, and Yeats, may not actually have been in love, but who compelled him, as a Petrarchan poet, to adopt the artifice of courtly love 'invention' (a word thrice repeated in the famous opening sonnet), before he is told by his Muse to 'looke in thy heart and write.'[2]

'Beloved, gaze in thine own heart,' Yeats begins and ends the opening movement of the esoteric and yet personal *Rose* poem, 'The Two Trees.' The benign tree, holy, rooted in joy and quiet, is growing in her heart; if she looks therein, her 'eyes grow full of tender care.' But there is also its antithesis, a malignant tree, its 'fatal image' of 'stormy night' and 'barrenness' reflected in her mirror (a looking glass very different from the one in 'Michael Robartes and the Dancer'). She is warned, at the beginning and end of the poem's second and final movement, to 'Gaze no more in the bitter glass,' lest her 'tender eyes grow all unkind.' Beneath the Cabbalistic and Blakean foliage of the poem, and the Muse-stereotypes of a beloved's alternately kind and unkind eyes, Yeats is addressing two opposing aspects of the actual Maud Gonne, who was capable of tender care, and susceptible, politically, to the storm-tossed and ultimately barren abstract hatred that could make her 'tender eyes grow all unkind.' Yeats didn't have to invent a Muse of double and divided aspect. He already *had* one in Maud Gonne. That is obvious from many of Yeats's poems to and about her, culminating in the stern-eyed 'A Bronze Head,' but also from some of the life choices of the 'real' Maud.

---

2   Aside from Shakespeare's, the other great Elizabethan sonnet-sequence, the *Amoretti* by Edmund Spenser, departs from the tradition since Spenser is courting and celebrating the woman, Elizabeth Boyle, soon to become his wife, their marriage immortalized in the rapturous 'Epithalamion.'

Nevertheless, that Maud Gonne, however real, was also, in part, Yeats's 'invention,' is graphically illustrated in two flanking texts of 1903, written before and after she had shocked Yeats by informing him (speaking of bad life choices) that she had decided to wed. She had often told him that she would not marry *him*—for which the world should 'thank me' because 'you make such beautiful poetry out of what you call your unhappiness'—an axiom for denying herself to him, though she happens to have been largely right. But she had also assured him that she would marry no one else. The plan to wed MacBride violated that repeated 'deep-sworn vow,' later immortalized in Yeats's concise, powerful poem of that title. The first of the two texts I referred to is a letter written just before the marriage; the second a poem, 'Old Memory,' written after that debacle. I will return to both; it is enough for now to describe the letter as one of bitter recrimination, written in a desperate attempt to stave off the impending union of Maud with Captain John MacBride, a hero of the Irish Brigade that had fought against the British in the Boer War. It was a marriage, Yeats insisted, 'beneath her' in every way: not only a betrayal of herself and her Anglo-Irish 'class,' but of *him*, personally and in terms of public humiliation.

He had elevated her in his poetry to the heroic status of a Greek or Celtic goddess reborn, and as a modern Helen of Troy; above all, he had presented her to the world as a woman as aloof and unattainable as the worshiped ladies of the courtly love tradition in whose virginal company he had poetically enlisted her. By marrying MacBride—vulgar, violent, and Catholic (from Yeats's Protestant perspective, a religion of censorship and of opposition to the Irish nationalism both he and Maud espoused, he constitutionally, she by whatever means necessary)— Maud was not only throwing *herself* away, he charged, but trashing the image he had labored long and successfully to put before the public.

In 'Old Memory,' the first lyric he could bring himself to write in the numbed aftermath of that marriage, Yeats is even more possessive, an impresario jealously protecting an investment, or a publisher a copyright. Here, Maud's aristocratic and oxymoronic nobility—'Your strength so lofty, fierce and kind,/ It might call up a new age,' evoking 'queens that were imagined long ago'—is, he tells her, only *'half* yours.' Echoing Wordsworth as 'lover' of the 'world of eye, and ear—both what they half create,/ And what perceive' ('Tintern Abbey,' lines

102–7), Yeats claims that the 'Maud Gonne' persona was half-created by *himself*: a suffering unrequited lover and skilled artist who 'kneaded in the dough/ Through the long years of youth,' and, like a secular Yahweh, brought forth the iconic image of a solitary, heroic, and above all, unattainable Muse.

Of course, fourteen years earlier, before she had publicly sullied the image by marriage to 'a drunken, vainglorious lout' (Yeats's accurate depiction of MacBride even in later honoring his memory as one of the executed Easter 1916 leaders), there *was* the seemingly *un*tarnished and instantly idealized Maud: the stunning beauty Yeats fell in love with at first sight when, under the auspices of the old Fenian hero, John O'Leary, she swept exuberantly into the Yeats family home in Bedford Park. Maud had come, bearing an introduction from O'Leary's sister, ostensibly to visit Yeats's artist father; but, as Yeats's wary sister Lolly accurately surmised, 'really to see Willie,' whose just-published *The Wanderings of Oisin* she had read with enthusiasm. He seemed a promising talent to be enlisted in Ireland's cause. Both sisters were annoyed by Maud's 'royal sort of smile,' and, as a family with little cash, noticed that the independently wealthy Maud (heiress to a portion of her grandfather's huge fortune) extravagantly kept her hansom cab waiting for the entirety of her visit.[3]

As for the young poet, he recorded twenty years later in private notes that he 'had never thought to see in a woman so great beauty. It belonged to famous pictures, to poetry, to some legendary past. A complexion like the blossom of apples, and yet face and body had the beauty of lineaments which Blake calls the highest beauty because it changes least from youth to age, and a stature so great that she seemed of a divine race.' That first meeting evoked 'overpowering tumult that had yet many pleasant secondary notes.' On that day, 30 January 1889, the 'troubling of my life began.'[4] With the retrospect of twenty years, in his 1909 essay 'The Tragic Theatre,' Yeats acknowledged an element of self-consciousness in his idealization of Maud. 'When we love,' he asked rhetorically, 'if it be in the excitement of youth, do we not also' exclude

---

3   Foster, *The Apprentice Mage*, 87.
4   Mem, 40. Though Maud thought they had first met in 1887, at John O'Leary's house, Yeats, as the more thunderstruck, is likelier to be right about the place and date: Bedford Park on 30 January 1889.

little 'irrelevancies' of character, in order to emphasize the mysterious, archetypal personality. We do so 'by choosing that beauty which seems unearthly because the individual woman is *lost amid the labyrinth* of its lines as though life were trembling into stillness and silence, or at last folding itself away' (E&I, 243–44).

Given my title and the emphasis already placed on Maud Gonne, that 'woman lost,' as 'a great labyrinth' from which the long-ensnared poet admits having 'turned aside,' a brief turning aside in the form of digression may be in order. The recurrent image of the labyrinth is one of internalization, in which one is self-enfolded, either protected or 'lost.' A year after he made the remarks just quoted from 'The Tragic Theatre,' Yeats described Maud, in the poem 'Against Unworthy Praise,' as being secreted within 'the *labyrinth* of her days/ That *her own strangeness perplexed*.' In the great sequence 'Nineteen Hundred and Nineteen,' we are told that 'A man in his own secret meditation /Is *lost amid the labyrinth* he has made/ In art or politics,' and in that sequence's tumultuous coda, chaos attends the cyclical and occult return of Herodias' crazed daughters, 'their *purpose [lost] in the labyrinth of the wind*.' Perplexity, being lost, caught up in a maze or whirlwind of violence the 'purpose' of which is difficult to discern: all seems concentrated in the image of Maud Gonne. Politely but firmly rejecting the protection Yeats offered in 1898, she wrote that she was 'under the great shield of Lugh,' and 'should not need and could not accept protection from any one,' though she fully realized and understood 'the generous and unselfish thoughts which were in [his] heart.' She continued, 'I love you for them [...]. I am in my whirlwind, but in the midst of that whirlwind is dead quiet calm which is peace too.'[5] In the eye of the storm, Yeats's 'labyrinth of the wind,' Maud also seems a Daedalian 'great labyrinth,' herself anything but peaceful: the devouring minotaur at the center, half-divine, double-gendered, a creature both spiritual and driven by instinct, and with an appetite for violence.

For all its fusion of opposites, the minotaur is a monster, hardly young Yeats's initial impression of Maud Gonne. After that life-changing first meeting, he remained in virginal thrall for a decade, and, despite sexual affairs and his own eventual marriage, stayed connected

---

5   An undated fragment of a letter, quoted by Ward, *Maud Gonne*, 57.

to her—mystically, personally, and of course poetically—essentially for life. They had quarrels, personal and political, some, as we shall see, leading to estrangements. But there were also sustained periods of deep intimacy, of friendship and love, albeit—with a single exception, in December 1908—non-sexual. Maud may not have fully understood him, certainly not his politics nor the more demanding of his poems, though she was always aware of her co-creative role as Muse. And though she never plumbed the depths of his suffering on her account, she was often kind and considerate. Aside from the brief period, in 1908/9, when he was 'beloved,' she addressed her letters to him for decades as 'my dear Willie,' and she meant it. But that is part of the tragedy, what made the situation, like the minotaur, 'monstrous.' I am quoting the eerie but intimately revealing dream-poem, 'Presences,' placed, in *The Wild Swans at Coole,* immediately after 'A Deep-sworn Vow,' in which Maud's face looms up from the subconscious. Of the three presences he imagines of women 'laughing or timid or wild,' one is a 'harlot,' the second, a 'child,' the third, 'it may be, a queen.' The one thing the trinity (perhaps Mabel Dickinson, certainly Iseult Gonne, and Maud herself) have in common was that 'they had read/ All I had rhymed of that monstrous thing,/ Returned and yet unrequited love.'

But that was still in the future. When she erupted into Yeats's life, the twenty-two-year-old Maud was a strikingly beautiful woman radiating energy yet poised, majestically tall, with a stunning hourglass-figure, a glorious head of Pre-Raphaelite bronze hair, heart-melting eyes, and a complexion delicate and translucent as the 'apple-blossom' Yeats associated with her from the epiphanic moment he first laid eyes on her. The poet certainly had promising Muse-material to begin with. A month before Maud descended on Yeats, Douglas Hyde—Fenian, Irish scholar and, a half-century in the future, destined to be the first president of Ireland—recorded in his diary for 16 December 1888: 'I saw the most dazzling woman I have ever seen: Miss Gonne, who drew every male in the room around her [...]. My head was spinning with her beauty.'[6] Among many others, another Irish president (of the post-Treaty Free State), Arthur Griffith, was equally bedazzled. George Bernard Shaw

---

6   Dominic Daly, *The Young Douglas Hyde,* 95. Maud subsequently took Irish lessons
     from Hyde.

was another notable struck by the statuesque Maud. Though he had fallen in love with another of Yeats's Muse-figures, the actress and occultist Florence Farr, Shaw, a man of the world not given to hyperbole, pronounced Maud Gonne 'the most beautiful woman in the British Isles.' For Yeats, her smitten bard, Maud, a study in Contraries, was sweet and childlike, yet also a Virgilian goddess *redivivus* and a Helen of Troy born out of phase, and thus destined to be a destroyer: 'terrible beauty' personified.

Even, then, of course, she was an activist prone to violence. Describing their momentous first meeting back in January 1889, Yeats, though blinded with love at first sight, also recorded, not only that 'she vexed my father with talk of war,' but—and here Maud was reflecting, along with physical-force Irish nationalism, the kind of apocalyptic excitement that was in the air—'war for its own sake, not as the creator of certain values but as if there were some virtue in excitement itself.'[7] When Yeats took Maud's side against his father, it 'vexed him the more, though he might have understood that a man young as I could not have differed from a woman so beautiful and young' (Mem, 40). If, he remarked, she held that 'the world was flat or the moon an old caubeen I would be proud to be of her party.' Her excitement in turn excited Yeats, who was both fascinated and, later, disturbed by her commitment to the cult of blood sacrifice, and appalled by what he saw as the self-destructive virulence of her hatred of the British Empire.

It didn't take long for Yeats to realize that his own love was self-destructive. In explaining to himself why, in 1896, he returned to Maud, throwing away his first sexual relationship (with Olivia Shakespear, disguised as 'Diana Vernon'), Yeats cited a passage from the notebooks of Leonardo: 'All our lives long, as da Vinci says, we long, thinking it is but the moon we long [for], for our destruction, and how, when we

---

7   Addressing Florence Farr (under her Golden Dawn initials, S.S.D.D.), in December 1895, Yeats wondered if the Venezuelan border dispute of that year might initiate 'the magical armageddon' (L, 259–60). Maud, writing to Yeats from Samois on 27 September 1898 (G-YL, 95), told him, 'I believe more than ever in some terrible upheaval in Europe in the near future.' She reports the 'most extraordinary sight I ever witnessed': lights flashing across the night sky, one a seeming 'spear of light.' She was witnessing the aurora borealis, but Maud welcomed the flashing lights as portents of violence: 'It was so wonderful I felt a sort of awe I am sure it presaged terrible events.'

meet [it] in the shape of a most fair woman, can we do less than leave all others for her. Do we not seek our dissolution upon her lips?'[8]

§

Given her fame as a great poet's Muse, it is easy for enthralled readers of the poetry to forget, or simply never care to know (and there's a case to be made for both perspectives) that Maud Gonne was a woman of considerable if obsessive achievement in her own right: an impressive if eccentric woman not only of remarkable beauty but of great physical courage, and indefatigable commitment to the Irish cause. The label, 'Ireland's Joan of Arc,' first proposed by her secret French lover, was put in print in late 1897 by the *New York Herald* during her tour of the United States to raise money for a Wolfe Tone memorial. Since it is an aspect of her heroic myth, most readers of the poetry know, or else should know, that Maud Gonne was an Anglo-Irish English-born revolutionary nationalist, more Irish than the Irish, committed, by any means necessary—violence very much included—to the cause of Irish independence. Quite aside from her role in Yeats's poetry, Maud Gonne had her own life, though even the most personal aspects of that life were mingled with the political and the excessive, the 'overflowing abundance' (Mem, 41) and self-destructive 'wildness' Yeats had seen in her from the outset. 'But even at the starting-post, all sleek-and new,' he claims in 'A Bronze Head' (1938), 'I saw the wildness in her and I thought / A vision of terror that it must live through/ Had shattered her soul.'

At the time of their first meeting, Maud's instant worshiper had no idea that across the Channel she was in the midst of a clandestine sexual relationship with the French Boulangist Lucien Millevoye, the father-to-be of Maud's daughter, Iseult. An embodiment of Maud's spiritual and political credo, 'life out of death, life out of death, always,' Iseult was conceived in the tomb of an earlier child by Millevoye, Georges, who had

---

8   Yeats, (Mem, 88). In the passage Yeats paraphrases (turned a quarter-century later into a poem, 'The Wheel'), da Vinci describes a 'return to primal chaos, like that of the moth to the light.' The 'man with perpetual longing' for (for instance) too-slow seasonal change is actually 'longing for his own destruction.' *Notebooks of Leonardo da Vinci*, 1:80–81.

died of meningitis in 1892, at just nineteen months old.[9] Inconsolable and obsessed by the thought of reincarnation, Maud, encouraged by Yeats's friend George Russell (AE) to believe the myth that a dead child might be reborn within a family, persuaded Millevoye to have intercourse with her in Georges' tomb, a vault under the memorial chapel in the Samois graveyard.

Yeats, who had heard stories of a French lover, stories he naively 'disbelieved,' and thought 'twisted awry by scandal,' was finally trusted by Maud with at least most of the truth. Writing in 1915/16, in an account unpublished until 1972 (Mem, 132–33), Yeats recorded the story told him by Maud 'bit by bit.' It was a story too bizarre *not* to be believed, though she had been lying to him for years, even as he defended her, at least once at her request, against those who maligned her as either a French or a British spy, or as 'a vile abandoned woman who has had more than one illegitimate child.' The latter accusation was made by Charles MacCarthy Teeling, a violent man already despised by Yeats for having thrown a chair at the venerable John O'Leary, causing Teeling to be ousted from London's Young Ireland Society, of which Yeats was president.[10] As for the occult experiment in the graveyard vault: it worked. Iseult, passed off by Maud as her niece or as a 'child I adopted,' was born on 6 August 1894. All of this—the liaison with Millevoye and the sex among the tombstones—was a secret unknown to Yeats, until Maud, trusting him with the key to 'the labyrinth of her days,' finally confided in him. That was in 1897, a full eight years after they had first met; and yet, a year later, Yeats was still willing to champion Maud in poetry as well as prose, most notably in the poem 'He Thinks of Those Who Have Spoken Evil of His Beloved.' His song, made 'out of a mouthful of air,' would, he assured her, outweigh their slander:

> Half close your eyelids, loosen your hair,
> And dream about the great and their pride;

---

9   The same archetypal belief was intoned by Padraic Pearse over the grave of O'Donovan Rossa in 1915 and put to the test a year later at, inevitably, Easter, feast of the Resurrection.

10   Yeats also spoke out publicly against Frank Hugh O'Donnell, the Irish nationalist who had accused Maud of being a French spy. See Bendheim, 98.

> They have spoken against you everywhere,
> But weigh this song with the great and their pride;
> I made it out of a mouthful of air,
> Their children's children shall say they have lied.

No matter that, at least when it came to such vicious but accurate charges as those of Teeling, it was Yeats who was fabricating. Nevertheless, through the power of his poetry he will, he assures his beloved, turn the tables on her enemies, persuading their posterity to believe *them* the liars.

But then, as public as the earlier liaison was private, there was her later troubled marriage to MacBride, another 'physical-force' political revolutionary: a marriage a devastated Yeats had tried, as we've just seen, to prevent. The penchant for violence in MacBride, that 'drunken, vainglorious lout,' was exercised domestically as well as politically, as Yeats discovered in later working to extricate Maud from that short-lived but disastrous marriage. In 1905, he confided to Lady Gregory that MacBride's drunken violence and sexual abuse extended ('the blackest thing you can imagine') to ten-year-old Iseult. Ironically, it was her wish to give Iseult a conventional home that had motivated Maud to marry; now her husband's molestation of that child led her to seek a legal separation.

She had from the outset been more tolerant of MacBride's penchant for *political* violence. Planning their honeymoon in Gibraltar in 1903, MacBride conceived of a plot to assassinate King Edward VII, a plot that fizzled out because of his drinking. But Maud, as she tells us in one of the more revealing moments in her unrevealing autobiography, acquiesced in the plan.[11] Their union did, however, produce a son, Séan, at first an IRA revolutionary, but later President of the International Peace Bureau, co-founder of Amnesty International, and, in 1974, fulfilling his mother's most commendable advocacy, recipient of the Nobel Peace Prize for 'his efforts to secure and develop human rights throughout the world.'

---

11   For Maud's account of the abortive plot, see *A Servant of the Queen*, 282–85.

Fig. 2 Maud Gonne, three-quarter length oval portrait wearing Celtic brooch, by J. E. Purdy, January 1900, during Maud's second American tour. Wikipedia, https://commons.wikimedia.org/wiki/File:Maud_Gonne,_as_photographed_by_J.E._Purdy_circa_1890_to_1910.jpg.

By the time long-pining Yeats was himself finally admitted into Maud's bed, briefly and inconsequentially except in terms of poetry, twenty years had passed since their first meeting in 1889. By the time they finally physically consummated their strange union, in Paris, in December 1908, Maud had mothered three children, two of whom survived; converted to Catholicism; was in the midst of a legal separation from MacBride (though divorce was refused or postponed by the court); and was, at 42, still attractive but no longer the stunner that had once taken men's breath away. She had told Yeats as early as 1898 that she had a 'horror of physical love.' At the time, given her circumstances, it may have been a ploy to keep their relationship non-sexual. But the confession also seems accurate, despite her history. She reiterated her dread of physical intimacy following their one night in Paris, informing Yeats, in what amounted to a loving but firm morning-after note (G-YL, 258), that she had triumphed over her physical desire for him, was now 'praying' that he could overcome *his* for *her* (easier said than done), and wished to return to their intimate but sexless 'mystical marriage,' which they had recently renewed, in Paris in June 1908. Now, to Yeats's immediate grief, though it triggered a mature reassessment on his part, Maud quickly reverted to the old arrangement—an *amitié amoureuse.*

Yeats adhered to Maud's decree, though he *did* make one last try, a final marriage proposal in 1917, after MacBride had been executed by the British as one of the Easter Rising leaders. It should be mentioned that Maud seemed willing to forgive all in that tragic but redemptive light. Speaking of those who were 'executed in cold blood,' her 'husband among' them, she noted, in a letter of 16 August 1916, to John Quinn (who knew all about Maud's earlier domestic situation, Yeats having consulted him as attorney): 'He has died for Ireland and his son will bear an honoured name. I remember nothing else,' his 'fine heroic end' having 'atoned for all.' After citing the account of the Franciscan friar who was with MacBride during his final hours, she concluded, 'he is with his comrades and England is powerless to dishonor their memories.'[12]

That was left to Yeats. Though, in 'Easter 1916,' he included MacBride by name among the honored dead, he did not refrain from violating

---

12   John Quinn Papers, Berg Collection, NYC Library; cited in Cardozo, 309, n444–45.

elegiac decorum by labeling him 'a drunken, vainglorious lout' who 'had done most bitter wrong/ To some who are near my heart.'

> Yet I number him in the song;
> He, too, has resigned his part
> In the casual comedy;
> He, too, has been changed in his turn,
> Transformed utterly;
> A terrible beauty is born.

Just as in his poems to and about Maud Gonne, Yeats here transcends political reservations and personal bitterness to celebrate a role played in a larger, heroic drama. His transformative love for his own 'terrible beauty,' which changed Yeats utterly, was also celebrated in 'song.' Much of the history I have just synopsized does not seem the biographical material out of which great love poetry is to be made. But it *was*; and it is primarily Maud Gonne's role as Yeats's Muse that concerns me here. Since, as the poet declares (in Part III of 'The Tower'), 'only an aching heart/ Conceives a changeless work of art,' Maud may be said— to adapt Auden's phrase, 'Mad Ireland hurt you into poetry'—to have 'hurt' Yeats into great love poetry. She was fully aware of her status as a Muse-figure, and, as an active agent in the collaboration, is not to be thought of as a mere projection, a passive recipient of male adoration— an understandable feminist charge regarding Muses, but in Maud's case somewhat off the mark. That Maud, a political activist and lifelong advocate of human rights, was more than a great poet's Muse, is clear from the biographies by Nancy Cardozo (1978), Margaret Ward (1990), and Trish Ferguson (2019). Maud Gonne's complexity is suggested by the titles of the two other recent biographies: Adrian Frazier's good if gossipy *The Adulterous Muse* (2016) and the latest, with the title lifted from the Yeats poem, Kim Bendheim's engaging though overly personal *The Fascination of What's Difficult* (2021).

But Maud's complexity extends to her function as Muse, assuming a masculine role, as Yeats had assumed a female role, in his elegy for the Easter 1916 martyrs. In that remarkable letter written to Yeats on 15 September 1911, Maud strangely anticipates Yeats's taking on, along with the role of national elegist and eulogist, of a specifically maternal role in the final stanza of 'Easter 1916.' Answering his own question as to when Ireland's long 'sacrifice' may finally 'suffice,' he responds as choral commemorator of what Michael Collins called 'a Greek tragedy': 'That is Heaven's part, our part/ To murmur name upon name/ As a mother names her child.' In that 1911 letter, Maud assumed the role of *domina*, but, like her devotee, reversing genders. 'Our children were your poems,' she informs Yeats, 'of which I was the Father sowing the unrest & storm which made them possible & you the mother who brought them forth in suffering & in the highest beauty & our children had wings—' (G-YL, 302).[13]

---

13   Maud added that Yeats and Lady Gregory also had a 'child,' in the form of the Abbey Theatre Company. She was 'the Father who holds you to your duty of motherhood,' with a child that 'requires much feeding & looking after.' There is a parallel in Yeats's later personal and poetic relationship with Lady Dorothy Wellesley, who was lesbian. Yeats admired in her poetry 'its masculine element amid so much feminine charm,' a mixture reminiscent of Maud Gonne. His own creativity, he'd told her earlier, arose out of 'the woman in me,' artistically demonstrated in his 'Woman Young and Old' and 'Crazy Jane' poems. Yeats saw his collaboration with Wellesley on a sequence of explicit ballads on a sexual triangle, as a marriage of her masculine rhythms with his feminine Muse (L, 875).

10. The Poems: A Sampling

There are many Maud poems, in all but one of which ('Beautiful Lofty Things,' 1937) she is un-named; and some, perhaps including the short lyric Yeats intended to be his final word, in which she is a covert presence. She figures importantly in 'A Prayer for my Daughter,' 'Among School Children,' and 'A Dialogue of Self and Soul,' in which the battered Self affirms the most painful yet 'most fecund' experience of Yeats's life: his unrequited but poetically fertile love for that 'proud woman not kindred of his soul.' Concluding Part II of 'The Tower,' Yeats, insistent that only an aching heart conceives a changeless work of art, asks if the imagination dwells 'the most/ Upon a woman won or woman lost?' In Yeats's case, we know the answer, but, as we have seen, he at first surprises us by adding, 'If on the lost, admit you turned aside/ From a great labyrinth.' The path through that fascinating but troubling labyrinth is primarily poetic.

I intend to say something about almost all of the poems written to and about Maud Gonne, placing most of them in biographical and thematic context. After discussing a few representative poems, beginning with 'The Song of Wandering Aengus' and 'The Cap and Bells,' and ending with 'A Prayer for my Daughter' (three beautiful Maud Gonne poems clothed in Celtic and Greek myth), I will discuss, in Yeats's own thematic order, several specific 'clusters' of lyrics to or about her, including the splendid 'No Second Troy' and the enigmatic 'The Cold Heaven.' After paying particular attention to the last and most somber of the Maud poems, 'A Bronze Head,' I'll devote time to 'The Circus Animals' Desertion' and 'Man and the Echo,' and end, like Yeats himself, with 'Politics,' the little poem he chose as his final word, the culmination of his *Collected Poems*, and which, I will suggest, may be a Maud Gonne lyric in disguise.

 https://doi.org/10.11647/OBP.0275.11

§

Since, as Maud Gonne herself demonstrates, beauty has its privileges, we may begin with the meticulously crafted yet almost miraculously beautiful 'The Song of Wandering Aengus' (1897), an early mythological poem in which Maud's not-so-covert presence is revealed by the reference to 'apple blossom.'

The poem (three 8-line stanzas of fused *abcb* quatrains) is cast in the old Irish lyric-form of an *aisling*, in which a seeker is granted a magical vision of a beautiful woman. In this case, the Muse-possessed seeker, impelled 'because a fire was in my head' (the poem was originally titled 'A Mad Song'), is the Celtic god of poetry, love, and youth. Here, however, he ages in his quest of the transfigured beauty, fleetingly visible but elusive, he had once glimpsed in the evanescent form of one of the shape-changing women of the Celtic *Sidhe*. We begin with Aengus preparing to fish in a stream in flickering pre-dawn starlight:

> I went out to the hazel wood,
> Because a fire was in my head,
> And cut and peeled a hazel wand,
> And hooked a berry to a thread;
> And when white moths were on the wing,
> And moth-like stars were flickering out,
> I dropped the berry in a stream
> And caught a little silver trout.

Maud has not yet come into the poem, but her entrance has been prepared for by 'The Fish,' a self-pitying poem which precedes the Aengus poem in *The Wind Among the Reeds*. The fish-woman of that poem may 'hide in the ebb and flow' of the tide, but people in time to come will know how the poet cast his net, 'And how you have leaped times out of mind/ Over the little silver cords,/ And think that you were hard and unkind,/ And blame you with many bitter words.' In the Aengus poem, the magical transformation is about to take place. Once he had laid the little silver trout on the ground,

> I went to blow the fire a-flame,
> But something rustled on the floor,
> And someone called me by my name:
> It had become a glimmering girl,
> With apple blossom in her hair

> Who called me by my name and ran
> And faded through the brightening air.

The stages of transformation are as delicately handled as everything else in this exquisite poem: some*thing* rustled, some*one* called him by name; before we know it, the 'little silver trout' has 'become a glimmering girl' who again calls him by his name, but runs and fades in dawn's 'brightening air.'

She had become not merely a 'glimmering girl,' but, with that telltale 'apple blossom in her hair,' had metamorphosed into *that* one, as Maud Gonne herself recognized. A third of a century after he first laid eyes on Maud, he described her complexion as 'luminous, like that of apple-blossom through which the light falls, and I remember her standing that first day by a great heap of such blossoms in the window.'[1] Given that it was January in London, they must have been almond rather than apple blossoms. But the latter had occult as well as poetic significance for Yeats. In July 1899, he described a dream invoked by thinking of apple blossoms, adding, 'The apple-blossoms are symbols of dawn and of the air and of the east and of resurrection in my system and in the poem.'[2] Though referring to the dramatic poem he was working on at the time, *The Shadowy Waters*, in which Dectora imagines a stream that disappeared when 'a kingfisher/ Shook the pale apple-blossom over it' (274–5), he may also have been glancing back two years, to Aengus's glimmering girl. And two or three years *on* from 1899, he would describe Maud in a poem, 'The Arrow,' as 'Tall and noble but with face and bosom/ Delicate in colour as apple blossom.'

In 'The Song of Wandering Aengus,' the glimmering girl with apple blossom in her hair is no sooner glimpsed than she vanishes 'through the brightening air.' No less predictably, Aengus, a remarkably human god, pursues her, even envisioning, after much wandering, a projected reunion in an earthly paradise, its sexuality celestially sublimated:

---

1   Au, 123. Maud's daughter inherited her mother's beauty, including that lovely apple-blossom coloring. On meeting Iseult in 1917, Lady Cunard pressed Yeats as to who she was, adding, 'Never in my life have I seen such a complexion.' Meeting her at the same time at Stone Cottage, Ezra Pound, who later had a brief affair with Iseult, pronounced the young beauty worthy of a troubadour's romance. See Cardozo, 310.

2   Yeats, '*Vision Notebook*,' transcribed by Warwick Gould and Deirdre Toomey; cited by Foster, *The Apprentice Mage*, 219, 575n70.

Though I am old with wandering
Through hollow lands and hilly lands,
I will find out where she has gone,
And kiss her lips and take her hands;
And walk among long dappled grass,
And pluck till time and times are done,
The silver apples of the moon,
The golden apples of the sun.

In the passage in which he associates Maud with the luminousness of apple blossom through which the light falls, Yeats also described her—in keeping with his symbolic association of apple blossoms with renewal (dawn, the east, and resurrection)—as seeming to be 'a classical impersonation of "the Spring," the Virgilian commendation "She walks like a goddess" made for her alone' (Au, 123). This image is not only Virgilian since Dante, in *La Vita Nuova*, echoed his Master in having Love himself tell the poet of his beloved: 'She is Spring [*Primavera*], who springs first, bearing herself the name of Love [*Amor*].'[3]

Despite these Celtic and courtly love connections with Maud Gonne, the enchanting 'Song of Wandering Aengus' remains cloaked in mythology, and those final lunar and solar images—'The silver apples of the moon,/ The golden apples of the sun'—drawn from Deuteronomy and alchemy, would seem to transcend any projection of a fruitful union between Yeats and his vernal goddess. Still, those final celestial images *do* seem to deliberately echo the evolution of the longed for woman— from a little '*silver* trout' to that Maud-like 'glimmering girl,/ With *apple* blossom in her hair.'

An earlier, even more covert Maud poem, 'The Cap and Bells' (1893), was accompanied by an evasive note when it was published in *The Wind Among the Reeds*. Describing it (as Coleridge had described the genesis of 'Kubla Khan') as coming to him in a dream or vision, Yeats concludes, 'The poem has always meant a great deal to me, though as is the way with symbolic poems, it has not always meant quite the same thing.

---

3   Dante, *La Vita Nuova*, chapter XXIV, describes, to cite the chapter title, how 'I felt my Heart Awaken' [*lo mi senti' svegliar dentro a la core*]. The final stanza of the poem I am quoting begins, '*Amor mi disse; quelle Primavera.*' Yeats read *La Vita Nuova* as translated by Dante Gabriel Rossetti. Another major modern poet, Wallace Stevens, also admired Dante's account of his 'new life.'

Blake would have said, "The authors are in eternity," and I am quite sure they can only be questioned in dreams.'[4]

He had reason to deflect the curious. For him, 'The Cap and Bells' was, in retrospect, a counter-poem to the beautiful but abject 'He wishes for the Cloths of Heaven,' which he described as 'the way to lose a woman.' Being 'poor' (the nonce word in this poem 'Enwrought with golden and silver light'), he cannot afford 'the heavens' embroidered cloths,' and so says, 'I have spread my dreams under your feet;/ Tread softly because you tread on my dreams.' This is to invite the female response threatened a half-century ago by Nancy Sinatra, whose boots were made for walking, 'and that's just what they'll do./ One of these days these boots are gonna walk all over you.' If he was not engaging in massive repression or sardonic irony in describing the no less beautiful *and* even more masochistic 'The Cap and Bells' as 'the way to win a woman,' Yeats must have believed that Maud Gonne was to be won only through total sacrifice.

In a chivalric scenario set in the evening in a garden beneath the palace window of a young, beautiful, and aloof queen, a lovelorn jester bids his blue-garmented soul, 'grown wise-tongued by thinking' of her 'light footfall,' to rise upward to her windowsill. Unresponsive, she decisively 'drew in the heavy casement/ And pushed the latches down.' He then sends her, in a 'red and quivering garment,' his heart, 'grown sweet-tongued by dreaming/ Of a flutter of flower-like hair.' It 'sang to her through the door.' But the dismissal of the heart is even more painful because so nonchalant: 'she took up her fan from the table/ And waved it off on the air.' With soul and heart, thought and dream, both rejected, he sends the young queen what is at once the symbol of his occupation, of his role in the Poet–Muse drama, and (at the risk of invoking reductive Freudianism) of his manhood: '"I have cap and bells," he pondered,/"I will send them to her and die."'

> And when the morning whitened
> He left them where she went by.
> She laid them upon her bosom,

---

4   For Yeats's note on 'The Cap and Bells,' see VP, 808. In a letter of 6 July 1803 to his friend Thomas Butts, Blake said he was able to praise his epic poem *Milton*, 'since I dare not pretend to be any other than the Secretary; the Authors are in Eternity.' *The Letters of William Blake*, 69.

> Under a cloud of her hair,
> And her red lips sang them a love-song
> Till stars grew out of the air.

In the original draft, 'She took them into her chamber/ Her breast began to heave,' less in grief than triumph. Though Yeats deleted these tone-disturbing lines, their morbid eroticism (which would flower perversely in his late dance plays where lowly fools are decapitated to appease haughty queens) offers a glimpse into the poem's psychological origins. When, at last, the queen lets in soul and heart, they set up a 'chattering wise and sweet,/ And her hair was a folded flower/ And the quiet of love in her feet.' But it seems too little too late. Soul and heart had *grown* through suffering. Now her 'red lips' sang his final offering 'a love-song/ Till stars *grew out of the air.' Grew,* because, in a variation on the mythic origin of the constellation Coma Berenices, *her* star-making song's genesis lies in *his* lethal self-sacrifice. Here as 'always' in Yeats, a 'personal emotion' has been 'woven into a general pattern of myth and symbol.'[5] But on the 'personal' level of this medieval Poet–Muse drama, the *belle dame sans merci* to whom the lowly jester gives 'all' is unmistakably Maud, 'that one' who (in 'Friends') 'took/ All till my youth was gone/ With scarce a pitying look.' Though 'The Cap and Bells' ends with 'the quiet of love in her feet,' they are the very feet under which he had 'spread my dreams' in the subservient poem supposedly rebutted in this ballad of terrible beauty, lyrically lovely but psychologically rooted in a symbolic act of self-castration.

Positioned between 'The Cap and Bells' and 'He wishes for the Cloths of Heaven' in *The Wind Among the Reeds* we find 'The Lover pleads with his Friend for Old Friends' and 'He wishes his Beloved were Dead,' a poem as strange as its title. The first poem was written in 1897, when Maud was at the height of her public fame, giving speeches and working with Yeats, whom she'd enlisted in the cause, on what would be the Centennial celebration of the 1798 United Irishman rebellion led

---

5   Yeats, Au, 151. These 'stars,' like the 'disheveled' stars of 'Who Goes with Fergus?,' play on the Berenice-myth via Milton and Pope. The myth is adopted by name in a much later Yeats poem in *Words for Music Perhaps,* in the 1933 *Winding Stair.* A woman dreams 'That I had shorn my locks away/ And laid them on Love's lettered tomb:/ But something bore them out of sight/ In a great tumult of the air,/ And after nailed upon the night/ Berenice's burning hair' ('Her Dream,' 1929).

by Wolfe Tone, Lord Edward Fitzgerald, and others. The lover's plea, a petition that, at this zenith of her fame, she not forget such old friends as himself, is mingled with a reminder of the transience of beauty, which will be remembered and recorded only by her devotee, *her* loyalty rewarded by *his*. The usual paradox, of course, is that memory of Maud will *not* perish because of poetry as unforgettable as this poem's final three lines, with that wonderful repetition of 'eyes,' ensuring the opposite of what is asserted, since what Yeats saw is now seen by 'all' of us:

> Though you are in your shining days,
> Voices among the crowd
> And new friends busy with your praise,
> Be not unkind or proud,
> But think about old friends the most:
> Time's bitter flood will rise,
> Your beauty perish and be lost
> For all eyes but these eyes.

In the second poem, it is not only her 'beauty' that will perish; he imagines the beloved herself 'lying cold and dead,' yet mysteriously able, while 'lights were paling out of the West,' to 'come hither, and bend your head,'

> And I would lay my head on your breast;
> And you would murmur tender words,
> Forgiving me, because you were dead:
> Nor would you rise and hasten away,
> Though you have the will of the wild birds,
> But know your hair was bound and wound
> About the stars and moon and sun:
> O would, beloved, that you lay
> Under the dock-leaves in the ground,
> While lights were paling one by one.

Whatever her reaction to this morbid-ecstatic poem, Maud would have been in a better position than most readers to *understand* it, having attended, in Paris with Yeats, a five-hour 1894 production of Villiers de l'Isle-Adam's *Axël*, in the final scene of which the heroine, Sarah, comes to the Black Forest castle of Count Axël, described by Yeats as 'a wizard ascetic of the Rosy Cross.' Together they drink poison, the ultimate renunciation of the common world of action, thought, and temporal love itself. Yeats, who was, like many major modernists affected by *Axël*, approved of this combination of spiritual renunciation and a Romantic voluptuousness that summons up Keats, who remarks in one of his letters (25 July 1819) to his beloved, Fanny Brawne: 'I hate the world...would I could take a sweet poison from your lips to send me out of it.'[6]

In his 1894 review, 'A Symbolical Drama in Paris,' Yeats observes of this 'marvelous scene' in *Axël* that 'the infinite alone is worth attaining, and the infinite is the possession of the dead. Such appears to be the moral. Seldom has the utmost pessimism found a more magnificent expression.'[7] Many of Yeats's love poems, early and late, envisage reunion beyond the grave; hence his fascination, early and late, with Blake's illustration of 'The Reunion of the Soul & the Body.' At the conclusion of *The Shadowy Waters*, a dramatic poem largely completed by 1899 (though not staged till 1906), Dectora puts her arms around Forgael, and says, in final lines combining Yeats's desire for extraterrestrial consummation and his obsession with his beloved's Pre-Raphaelite mane of tenting hair: 'Bend low, that I may cover you with my hair,/ For we will gaze upon this world no longer.'[8]

§

These poems and others like them, in which the beloved is anonymous and the speaker either a figure from Celtic myth or a nameless 'He,' are, however transparent to the informed reader, more or less covert Maud poems. The most *overt*, the only poem in which Yeats claims, in

---

6   *Letters of John Keats*, 2:133.
7   For the Paris viewing of the play by Yeats and Maud, see Hassett, *W. B. Yeats and the Muses*, 75. For his praise, and criticism, of *Axël*, see Yeats's April 1894 *Bookman* review, in *Uncollected Prose*, 1:323–24. Yeats was not alone in being affected by this play. Edmund Wilson's first book—his 1931 study of English and French literature from 1870–1930, covering Yeats, Valery, T. S. Eliot, Proust, Joyce, and Gertrude Stein—is titled *Axël's Castle*.
8   *The Shadowy Waters*, lines 429–30. The hair-tent image recurs in two mid-nineties back-to-back poems in *The Wind Among Reeds*: 'Let your eyes half close, and your heart beat/ Over my heart, and your hair fall over my breast' ('He bids his Beloved be at Peace'); and in 'He reproves the Curlew,' he bids the bird to cry no more, 'Because your crying brings to my mind/ Passion-dimmed eyes and long heavy hair/That was shaken out over my breast.'

his own name, that his passion for Maud (un-named, of course) was reciprocated, is 'To a Young Girl,' written in 1915 but not published until *The Wild Swans at Coole* (1917, 1919). The girl addressed is Maud's then twenty-year-old daughter, Iseult, the fruit of the old liaison with Lucien Millevoye, one aspect of which was, as we've seen, as weirdly morbid as anything in 'He wishes his Beloved were Dead.' Like many of Yeats's middle poems, 'To a Young Girl' consists of a single syntactical unit spun out over eleven mostly 3-beat lines. Ironically, Iseult had come to Yeats for advice in love! His response, presumably accurate if boastful, contains perhaps more than Iseult needed to know—unless her mother had already confided in her that she and Yeats had finally, seven years before this poem was written, physically consummated their then- two-decade-long Muse and Poet relationship:

> My dear, my dear, I know
> More than another
> What makes your heart beat so;
> Not even your own mother
> Can know it as I know,
> Who broke my heart for her
> When the wild thought,
> That she denies
> And has forgot,
> Set all her blood astir
> And glittered in her eyes.

He acknowledges his own intensity in 'Friends,' written four years earlier. 'Now must I these three praise—/ Three women that have wrought/ What joy is in my days.' He names no names, but we know who the three are, even if, from their depictions, the order is uncertain; plausible cases can be made that Olivia Shakespear, his first lover, comes first, Lady Gregory, his friend and patron, second – or vice versa. Whatever the 'correct' order, the first friend (Olivia?) is praised because, over fifteen often 'troubled years,' no thought 'Could ever come between/ Mind and delighted mind'; the second because her steady 'hand' (suggesting Augusta Gregory) had the strength to unbind (as Augusta had practically and Olivia sexually) 'Youth's dreamy load, till she/ So changed me that I live/ Labouring in ecstasy.'

Yeats may have *intended* ambiguity in his depictions of the first two friends, in order to emphasize, as he always does, the uniqueness of the third and climactic figure to be praised, who promptly proceeds to take over the poem. There is of course no question as to *her* identity, even though the double challenge she presents is introduced by the posing of two questions: 'And what of her that took/ All till my youth was gone/ With scarce a pitying look?/ How could I praise that one?' His answer, as so often in the Maud poems, incorporates and transcends pity for himself and accusation of the woman who both tormented and inspired him, all resolved in bittersweet affirmation:

> When day begins to break
> I count my good and bad,
> Being wakeful for her sake,
> Remembering what she had,
> What eagle look still shows,
> While up from my heart's root
> So great a sweetness flows
> I shake from head to foot.

Writing sixty years ago, the acute but too severely scrupulous poet-critic Yvor Winters, notoriously hostile to Yeats, found in these final lines behavior unseemly for a grown man. He may have a point, but it is not one likely to catch on with admirers of the poem responsive to its compression and syntactical momentum, *and* to its emotion. Ezra Pound realized that Yeats knew 'what violent emotion is really like' and could see and write 'from the centre of it.' Samuel Beckett 'would read "Friends" aloud and stand up as he repeated the three final lines in amazement, exclaiming, "Imagine such feeling".'[9] And the final image of 'Friends' would not be forgotten by Yeats. That sweet flow associated with Maud Gonne was to be memorably and even more movingly reprised a decade and a half later in the major poem, 'A Dialogue of Self and Soul,' which culminates in an ecstatic affirmation that 'we are blest by everything' precisely because 'So great a sweetness flows into the breast' of the lover who has plunged into 'that most fecund ditch of all,/ The folly that man does/ Or must suffer if he woos/ A proud woman not kindred of his soul.'

---

9   Winters, *The Poetry of W. B. Yeats*. Pound, December 1915 letter to Harriet Monroe, cited in Longenbach, *Stone Cottage: Pound, Yeats, & Modernism*, 183. For the Beckett anecdote, see Hassett, *Yeats Now: Echoing Into Life*, 60.

Maud serves as warning and counterexample in the conservative but too facilely criticized 'A Prayer for my Daughter.' Alternately casual and ceremonious, and always beautiful, this poem is composed in a stanza (eight lines, pentameters with an unusually effective embedded tetrameter couplet), adapted from Abraham Cowley, and previously employed in Yeats's elegy, 'In Memory of Major Robert Gregory,' another sustained poem centered, as is this 'Prayer,' on 'courtesy,' the virtue in which Yeats would have his daughter 'chiefly learned.'

We begin with the poet's infant, Anne, 'half-hid/ Under this cradle-hood and coverlid,' and so necessarily still half-*exposed*, born as she is into the violent world and 'rocking cradle' evoked in the immediately preceding, apocalyptic poem, 'The Second Coming,' destined to become the most frequently cited poem of the century to come. Pacing the battlements of the Tower while his child 'sleeps on,' the anxious father listens to the 'sea-wind' bred on the Atlantic, at once an actual storm and a politically 'levelling wind' that 'scream[s] upon the tower,' under 'the arches of the bridge,' and in 'the elms above the flooded stream.' He imagines 'in excited reverie/ That the future years had come,/ Dancing to a frenzied drum,/ Out of the murderous innocence of the sea': lines of terrible beauty preparing us for the silent entrance of Maud, a woman Anne's protective father prays his daughter will not emulate:

> May she be granted beauty and yet not
> Beauty to make a stranger's eye distraught,
> Or hers before a looking-glass, for such,
> Being made beautiful overmuch,
> Consider beauty a sufficient end,
> Lose natural kindness and maybe
> The heart-revealing intimacy
> That chooses right, and never find a friend.

As he emphasizes at the end of the poem, projecting her happily 'rooted' future, 'in one dear perpetual place,' the poet-father wants his daughter's eventual bridegroom to 'bring her to a house/Where all's accustomed, ceremonious,' a conservative but hardly misogynistic wish in 1919, and given the alternative: 'For arrogance and hatred are the wares/ Peddled in the thoroughfares.' This Anglo-Irish conservatism, however snobbish, is to be understood rather than glibly condemned, especially in light of the examples of bad marriages Yeats had summoned up earlier in the poem. Thinking of Maud's catastrophic marriage to the boorish John MacBride, Yeats camouflages biography, however transparently, by repairing to Greek mythology; to Maud's precursor, Helen (and her boorish husband Menelaus, along with Paris, her loving but foolish abductor), and to foam-born Aphrodite, who could pick for husband anyone she wished, having no father to please, yet chose Hephaestus, lame weapon-maker to the gods:

> Helen being chosen found life flat and dull
> And later had much trouble from a fool,
> While that great Queen, that rose out of the spray,
> Being fatherless, could have her way
> Yet chose a bandy-leggèd smith for man.
> It's certain that fine women eat
> A crazy salad with their meat
> Whereby the Horn of Plenty is undone.

The father prays that his daughter be granted, along with moderate rather than excessive (troubled and troubling) beauty, a 'natural kindness' free of rancor, the 'worst' form of which is 'intellectual hatred,' attended by 'opinion,' always in Yeats, as here, 'accursed' because mechanical and political rather than organic and autonomous.

> Have I not seen the loveliest woman born
> Out of the mouth of Plenty's horn,
> Because of her opinionated mind
> Barter that horn and every good
> By quiet natures understood
> For an old bellows full of angry wind?

Here as so often, Maud is front and center, in all but name, though there may be another, more deeply hidden female presence in this poem.[10] The degeneration of life's overflowing cornucopia into an old bellows 'full' only of 'angry wind' parallels other images conveying Yeats's

---

10 Uncharacteristically departing from the text, Helen Vendler has argued that the truly hidden presence here is Yeats's mother, another victim of a bad marriage and improvident husband. While 'Maud Gonne is the chief overt exemplum of a woman making a wrong marital choice, her disastrous marriage to John MacBride was public and could be commented on, as Yeats's mother's marriage could not.' Vendler's five moving pages on the subject have convinced me that, were it not for the tragic examples of *both* his mother and Maud Gonne, Yeats's 'prayer for his daughter might have been different.' *Our Secret Discipline*, 297–302.

hatred of life-destroying political abstraction. It anticipates Maud's voracious yet famished image in old age, 'Hollow of cheek as though it drank the wind/ And took a mess of shadows for its meat' ('Among School Children'), as well as the 'dark tomb-haunter' of 'A Bronze Head,' reduced—by abstract politics, and by a sculptor who read those passions well and stamped them on a lifeless bust—to 'a bird's round eye,/ Everything else withered and mummy-dead.' In 'In Memory of Eva Gore-Booth and Con Markiewicz,' an elegy as beautiful as those aristocratic and revolutionary sisters themselves, Eva, dreaming of 'some vague Utopia,' seemed, 'When withered old and skeleton-gaunt,/ An image of such politics.'[11]

And then there is Constance (Con) herself, a commandant in the Rising, whose activist days had been 'spent/ In ignorant good-will,/ Her nights in argument/ Until her voice grew shrill.' That judgmental misogyny occurs in the group-elegy, 'Easter, 1916.' We also have, written like 'A Prayer for my Daughter' in 1919, the splendid 'On a Political Prisoner.' With time to be uncharacteristically 'patient,' Con drew to her cell a grey gull, who 'endured her fingers' touch/ And from her fingers ate its bit.' Yeats wonders if, in 'touching that lone wing,' she recalled the years when—'The beauty of her country-side/ With all youth's lonely wildness stirred'—she herself 'seemed to have grown clean and sweet/ Like any rock-bred, sea-borne bird,'

> before her mind
> Became a bitter, an abstract thing,
> Her thought some popular enmity:
> Blind and leader of the blind
> Drinking the foul ditch where they lie?

Reading 'On a Political Prisoner,' we can hardly avoid thinking of Maud Gonne, who was also imprisoned at this time. In fact, Yeats had intended to write a poem about Maud, but instead wrote 'one on Con,' as he told his wife, precisely 'to avoid writing one on Maud.'[12] Con was, said Maud, 'like a sister to me,' and Yeats himself always associated the two

---

11 Yeats chose this haunted and haunting elegy to open both editions (1929, 1933) of *The Winding Stair*. Back in the mid-nineties, he had briefly considered proposing to the beautiful Eva, before realizing that the aristocratic Gore-Booths of Lissadell House 'would never accept so penniless a suitor.'

12 Jeffares, *A New Commentary on The Poems of W. B. Yeats*, 195.

women: both beautiful and both political revolutionaries who had long devoted themselves to the Irish poor, the starving and evicted. While he admired their heroism, from his conservative perspective, they had traded their Anglo-Irish birthright and palpable life itself—symbolized in his secular prayer for his daughter by the cornucopia and the Tree of Life in the form of 'the spreading laurel tree'—for a mess of shadows in the unceremonious form of often vague, hate-choked, embittering political abstractions. Patronizing and judgmental, to be sure; and yet the harshness of his political critiques of both women, and of Eva, are usually tempered by tenderness. He contemplated what he perceived as their tragic fates with compassion and love as well as condemnation: a mixture, elevated and intensified, at the heart of almost all the Maud Gonne poems.

I have been ranging freely among a number of illustrative poems, most with special appeal to me. But it seems time, at this point, to step back and browse through, in roughly chronological but primarily thematic order, a fairly full sample of the earlier Maud poems. I will begin with a discussion of two lyrics from the poetry grouping later published separately (in *Poems*, 1895), as *The Rose*. A third—'Who Goes with Fergus?,' excerpted from a play and subsequently added to *The Rose*—has already been discussed in Part One, though it should be mentioned that the final stanza seems to evoke that 'troubling' of his life that began in 1889. The other two, 'When You are Old' and 'The White Birds,' are directly addressed to Maud Gonne.

I will then focus on those earlier-mentioned clusters of poems to and about Maud Gonne in *In the Seven Woods* (1904) and *The Green Helmet and Other Poems* (1910); then turn to poems about Maud in *Responsibilities* (1914) and *The Wild Swans at Coole* (1917, 1919). When I get to those clusters, I will discuss them sequentially, since Yeats wanted his poems read, not in the order he wrote them but in the mutually illuminating order in which he arranged them.

11. Rose, Wind, and the Seven Woods

Beautiful as many of them are, most of the poems to his 'Beloved' in *The Rose* (1895) and even in *The Wind Among the Reeds* (1899), are too 'heavy' with dream and dew, too perfumed with *fin-de-siècle* 'lilies of death-pale hope, roses of passionate dream' ('The Travail of Passion,' 1896), too filled with languor and dim hair, to move most modern readers; or, at least, *this* reader. My favorite poem in *The Rose*—an enthusiasm shared by James Joyce—is 'Who Goes with Fergus?', discussed in Part One. A year after writing the Fergus poem, which ends with those 'disheveled wandering stars,' Yeats had his young queen, a medieval version of Maud, place her lovelorn jester's cap and bells under 'a cloud of her hair,' while 'her red lips' would, as we just saw, sing 'them a love song/ Till *stars grew out of the air.*'

Stars reappear in the most familiar poem in *The Rose*, 'When You Are Old' (1891), a Muse-poem echoing the opening of a well-known sixteenth-century sonnet by Pierre Ronsard, which also reminds the beautiful woman (in Ronsard's case, his mistress, Hélène de Surgerès) that she will not always be so. Ronsard's opening line, *Quand vous serez bien vielle, au soir à la chandelle* [When you are very old, in the evening by candle-light], is duplicated by Yeats: 'When you are old and grey and full of sleep,/ And nodding by the fire.' As Maud grew older, Yeats, in poem after poem, obsessively summoned up her youthful beauty; here, conversely, he imagines her old, though Maud was only twenty-five when the poem was written. He is following Ronsard; but only up to a point, and the divergence is worth emphasizing, not least because of the way these obviously intimately related sonnets play tonal variations on both the Petrarchan and *carpe diem* traditions.

 https://doi.org/10.11647/OBP.0275.12

Now a spirit 'beneath the earth,' the French poet imagines the old woman 'singing his verses' while saying to herself in amazement: 'Ronsard used to celebrate me when I was young.' Yeats, too, wants his beloved to read his poems; but Ronsard says of his aged woman, 'hunched at the fireplace,' that she will then feel regret regarding his love and her proud disdain (*'Regrettant mon amour et vestre fier desdain'*). So, abruptly reverting to the present, he urges her to live now, 'gathering the roses' of her 'life.' Ronsard's direct if derivative invocation of the *carpe diem* theme is softened and romanticized by Yeats. When his woman is old and nodding by the fire, he gently urges her to take down 'this book,' written by the 'one man' who, seeing beneath the beautiful surface to her inner, spiritual being, 'loved the pilgrim soul in you.' And yet, even in that projection into the future, we are left with nostalgia for an elusive love that was never to be fully, physically and spiritually, consummated. 'Bending down beside' the fireplace's 'glowing bars,' she will have no choice, in Yeats's beautiful but decidedly Celtic-Twilight rhetoric and personification, but to 'Murmur, a little sadly, how Love fled/ And paced upon the mountains overhead/ And hid his face amid a crowd of stars.'

The poem immediately following, 'The White Birds,' was inspired by a specific incident. As Yeats and Maud Gonne were resting after walking on the cliffs at Howth, two seagulls flew over and out to sea, prompting Maud to casually remark that if she had a choice to be any bird, it would be her favorite, a seagull: 'in three days, he sent me the poem with its gentle theme, I would we were my beloved white birds on the foam of the sea.'[1] She is quoting the poem's opening line; Yeats goes on to describe himself as 'haunted by numberless islands, and many a Danaan shore/ Where Time would surely forget us, and Sorrow come near us no more.' He depicts Maud as sharing in his own weariness and sorrow: *'We* tire of the flame of the meteor,' and 'the flame of the blue star at twilight, hung low on the rim of the sky,/ Has awakened *in our hearts*, my beloved, a sadness that may not die.'

But Maud is unlikely to have shared, anywhere nearly as intensely as he, the feelings he attributes to her. *He* certainly was sorrowful, having,

---

1   For Maud's remark, see Jeffares, *A New Commentary on the Poems of W. B. Yeats*, 32. When, eleven years later, in 1903, Maud purchased a summer home in Normandy, she named it *Les Mouettes*, 'The Seagulls.'

just the day before, made his first marriage proposal, and been rejected. It's not surprising that he would contrast transient seafoam and flaming meteor to the dream of a permanent haven for lovers on the shore of the Celtic paradise, Tir na nOg. If we are reminded of *The Wanderings of Oisin*, so was Yeats; the anapestic hexameter meter employed in Part III of that epic poem is repeated in 'The White Birds.' And Yeats appends to the poem a note emphasizing, despite its natural setting at Howth, a place loved by Yeats and Maud, his immersion in Celtic mythology: 'The birds of fairyland are white as snow. The "Danaan Shore" is, of course, Tier-nan-oge' (VP, 799).

It wasn't until 1912, at the end of *Responsibilities*, that Yeats announced the casting off of his early poetry's myth-embroidered Celtic 'coat': 'Song, let them take it,/ For there's more enterprise/ In walking naked.' The first poem celebrating his Muse's beauty in a stripped rhetoric less languid than lean came three years earlier, epitomized in his revision of lines 5–6 of 'The Arrow.' The original, 1901, version of these lines read, 'Blossom pale, she pulled down the pale blossom/ At the moth hour and hid it in her bosom.' This Celtic Twilight imagery was hardened in the revised version, which now opens the Maud Gonne cluster in *In the Seven Woods*, launching a series of love poems addressed to a Muse now in her thirties. Spare as it is, the poem is based on a traditional image with an elaborate poetic lineage. Cupid's arrow is a metaphor for the potent glance of the unattainable lady of the courtly love and *dolce stil novo* tradition, a shaft that pierces the lover's heart, inspiring him to sing even as he suffers.

The enjambed lines of 'The Arrow,' in tension with its taut couplets, end in 'feminine' or double rhyme, a stressed followed by an unstressed syllable. This falling pattern is established with the title itself. That 'arrow' is forged in part by the beloved's beauty (in the revised version, she is heroically 'Tall and noble,' though her flesh is, as always, the color of apple blossom), and in part by the 'wild thought' that now-fading loveliness continues to engender in her worshiper, who still laments the loss of her original if less gentle beauty:

> I thought of your beauty, and this arrow,
> Made out of a wild thought, is in my marrow.
> There's no man may look upon her, no man,
> As when newly grown to be a woman,

> Tall and noble but with face and bosom
> Delicate in colour as apple blossom.
> This beauty's kinder, yet for a reason
> I could weep that the old is out of season.

In the next poem, 'The Folly of Being Comforted,' written not long after, and a companion to 'The Arrow,' a 'kind' friend (in fact, Lady Gregory), sounding like Petrarch speculating that Laura's aging might diminish her beauty and thereby alleviate his pain, suggests that 'time' and the diminution of Maud's extravagant youthful beauty should 'make it easier to be wise.' Yeats was well aware of that diminution, much of which he attributed to Maud's exhaustive activism as a political agitator. But the lover, far from being a patient man guided by common sense, is not only a poet, but a poet committed to the Platonic or Neoplatonic belief that, beneath surface appearance, Maud possessed a permanent beauty, archetypal and unalterable. Furthermore, like the Shakespeare who writes, in Sonnet 116, of an abiding love that 'alters not' with the passage of time, Yeats reinforces his Muse's immortality through the very poems in which he celebrates her beauty and nobility of spirit.

Petrarch imagined his lady in her 'later years,' the 'light extinguished from your lovely eyes,/ your head of fine gold hair transformed to silver' (Sonnet 12). The 'ever kind' friend in Yeats's poem, offering well-intended but misplaced consolation, may be accurate in pointing out that 'Your well-belovéd's hair has threads of grey,/ And little shadows come about her eyes.' (Yeats originally had the friend refer to 'crowsfeet,' to which Maud objected; this was 'the first time,' Yeats claims, that he 'realised that she was human.') 'Though now it seems impossible,' counsels the friend, 'Time can but make it easier to be wise,' and so 'All that you need is patience.' But reason is no match for emotion. Recalling Shakespeare's insistence, in Sonnet 116, that 'Love's not Time's fool, though rosy lips and cheeks/ Within his bending sickle's compass come,' the lovelorn poet adamantly dismisses his friend's proffered patience and practical if pedestrian wisdom:

> Heart cries, 'No,
> I have not a crumb of comfort, not a grain.
> Time can but make her beauty over again:
> Because of that great nobleness of hers
> The fire that stirs about her when she stirs,

Burns but more clearly. O she had not these ways
When all the wild summer was in her gaze.'

O heart! O heart! If she'd but turn her head,
You'd know the folly of being comforted.

In Yeats we always return to the heart. As Pascal says in the *Pensées*, 'the heart has reasons of which reason knows nothing.' Focused on how we perceive God, Pascal was speaking of a spiritual, not a temporal love. The two often merge in Yeats's Muse-poems, where Maud's phoenix-like beauty incorporates but transcends the physical and the temporal, burning spiritually and thus even 'more clearly' on emerging from the re-creative 'fire that stirs about her when she stirs.' The poet ends by telling his Heart what the Heart already knows: that wisdom would be exposed as folly if his beloved would 'but turn her head.' That minute but momentous gesture recalls a similar 'turn' in Petrarch, when 'Love' made Laura 'pause her foot/ and turn those holy lights in my direction,' a gaze and 'gracious turn' enshrined in his heart: 'a solid diamond statue would wear out/ before I could forget her deed, so sweet/ that it has filled my mind till now/ and never will desert my memory.'[2]

The Maud Gonne cluster in *In the Seven Woods* continues, speaking of memory, with 'Old Memory.' Though not a particularly distinguished lyric, it is notable as the first poem that Yeats—who had escaped to America for what became a profitable and confidence-restoring lecture tour—found himself able to write after the tongue-numbing despair he fell into in the immediate wake of Maud's marriage. I have already referred to this poem in terms of Yeats laying claim to at least partial ownership of the 'Maud Gonne' image, which he described to her in a letter as only 'half yours,' with the other half created by himself, the product of both his suffering and skill as a poet. This is the one letter, rather shocking in itself, that has survived of the three he wrote to

---

2   Sonnet 108. Laura also turns her eyes to him in the three sonnets that follow. In 110, those 'rays that melt me were unleashed in full;/ the way that thunder comes along with lightning/ that's how those eyes, so brilliant, hit me.' If we think the imagery hyperbolic and out of date, consider 'the fireworks that go off' in Chrissie Hynde's 'Don't Get Me Wrong,' the hit song recorded by The Pretenders in 1986. Her best lines, sung with mounting excitement, recreate Petrarch: 'Once in a while two people meet,/ Seemingly for no reason, they just pass on the street;/ Suddenly thunder, showers everywhere;/ Who can explain the thunder and rain,/ But there's something in the air.'

Maud after recovering from the initial shock of learning of her intended marriage to MacBride.

In that letter, the possessive and class-conscious poet seems less disturbed by losing Maud as the woman he loved than as his carefully curated and very public Muse: a 'proud haughty' woman resembling not only a Greek goddess, but, crossing genders, 'one of the Golden Gods.' Though a populist revolutionary, Maud was also representative of the Anglo-Irish Ascendancy. Now she was *de*scending, spiritually and socially, into the gutter. As he would later record in bitter, unpublished lines echoing Tennyson's 'Locksley Hall': 'My dear is angry that of late,/ I cry all base blood down/ As if she had not taught me hate/ By kisses to a clown' (Mem, 145). In the letter, Yeats does not state the obvious: that she was not only violating their 'mystical' or 'spiritual marriage,' but removing any chance that they might *actually* wed. Worse yet, by choosing instead the vulgar John MacBride she was desecrating the image he had created: 'Maud Gonne is about to pass away.'[3]

Now, in 'Old Memory,' having suffered during those long years as an unrequited lover, and having labored, far more successfully, as a Muse-poet, he is writing in the immediate aftermath of that appalling 1903 marriage. Rhetorically and understandably, he asks, 'who would have thought' it would all have 'come to naught,/ And that dear words meant nothing?' Yet he ends by blaming no one: 'But enough,/ For when we have blamed the wind we can blame love;/ Or, if there needs be more, be nothing said/ That would be harsh for children that have strayed.' He might admonish Maud in a letter, but not in the poetry, where she is worthy of blame, yet never blamed. As for the 'children' remark: MacBride was no child; but Maud, in Yeats's poems, was always 'half child,' even if the other half was alternately eagle or lion or even identified, as in 'A Bronze Head,' with the Celtic death-crow, the Morrigu.

---

3   G-YL, 164–65. Yeats's lines about 'crying base blood down' because Maud had taught him 'hate/ By kisses to a clown,' recall those in which Tennyson's jilted Locksley rebukes his cousin Amy not only for not marrying *him* but for degrading herself in the process: 'As the husband is, the wife is; thou art mated with a clown,/ And the grossness of his nature will have weight to drag thee down' (lines 47–48). Though the preceding couplet ('thou shalt lower to his level day by day,/ What is fine within thee growing coarse to sympathize with clay') might also seem apropos, the full forecast does not apply to Maud Gonne, saddened but not coarsened by her mating with MacBride.

The poem immediately following, 'Never give all the Heart,' written while Yeats was in New York City visiting John Quinn, who had arranged his 1903 American tour, combines Quinn's worldly advice about women with recollection of a poignant little lyric from William Blake's 1791–92 Notebook, 'Never pain to tell thy love,' in the central stanza of which the speaker laments, 'I told my love, I told my love,/ I told her all my heart;/ Trembling cold, in ghastly fears—/Ah, she doth depart!' In Yeats's poem both parties 'give their hearts,' but in very different ways. Aware of play-acting on the stage and in affairs of the heart, Yeats, also reflecting the attitude toward women of the sexually sophisticated bachelor Quinn (who kept a copy of the poem for life), advises us to 'never give the heart outright' to passionate women of a theatrical bent, for they

> Have given their hearts up to the play.
> And who could play it well enough
> If deaf and dumb and blind with love?
> He that made this knows all the cost,
> For he gave all his heart and lost.

The next poem, 'The Withering of the Boughs,' breaks away from direct focus on Maud, reverting to a moonlit Celtic fairyland. Asleep beneath a 'honey-pale moon,' the dreamer, hearing the sound of coupled swans flying (referring to the coupled swans, Baile and Aillinn, in Yeats's narrative poem of that title) as well as the cry of peewit and curlew, longs for their 'tender and pitiful words.' The thrice-repeated italicized refrain echoes the warning against sincerity in 'Never give All the Heart' (and in the related poem a few pages later, 'O Do Not Love Too Long,' which also advises against emotional openness): the boughs have not withered because of the wintry wind; '*The boughs have withered because I have told them my dreams.*'

Next comes the plangent and justly celebrated 'Adam's Curse,' revealing a passion more obliquely disclosed but no less unrequited, with the 'withered' boughs replaced by a 'hollow' moon, again reflecting the weary-heartedness of a beautiful but frustrated love. The two speakers and the auditor are nameless; but we know who they are, not only intuitively but because Maud provided in her autobiography her own account of this conversation, which followed another of Yeats's marriage proposals. She repeated what she had told him a decade earlier: that 'poets should never marry,' once again asserting her indispensable role as unattainable Muse: 'you make beautiful poetry out of what you call your unhappiness.'[4]

In the poem, written in the conversationally enjambed heroic couplets Browning perfected in 'My Last Duchess,' Maud sits silently by while, on a late summer evening, her sister Kathleen and the poet discuss various forms of 'labour,' which is, after all, the bitter fruit of God's curse against a disobedient Adam and Eve. There is, to begin with, the labor involved in the poet's quest, even if a line 'takes hours,' to 'make it seem a moment's thought,' an illustration of *sprezzatura* followed by the insistence that 'to articulate sweet sounds together' is 'to work harder' than kitchen-scrubbers and stone-breakers 'and yet/ Be thought an idler.' Kathleen, her voice 'sweet and low' as Cordelia's, adds her intuitive knowledge that a woman 'must labour to be beautiful.' It's certain, he responds, that 'there is no fine thing/ Since Adam's fall but needs much labouring.' There have been, he continues—invoking the elaborate decorum of the courtly love tradition of Dante's *La Vita Nuova* and Petrarch's *Canzoniere*—

> lovers who thought love should be
> So much compounded of high courtesy
> That they would sigh and quote with learned looks
> Precedents out of beautiful old books;
> Yet now it seems an idle trade enough.

So, the poet turns out to be an 'idler' after all! Familiar with the art-of-love tradition from his reading of D. G. Rossetti on Dante and his circle, and of Dante's own *La Vita Nuova*, Yeats was aware, like all love poets in English, of Petrarch's inventive sonnets and songs of obsessed and unrequited love, at once erotic and spiritual. He was also familiar with the English Petrarchan sonneteers from Spenser to Shakespeare, including Sir Thomas Wyatt and, especially, Sir Philip Sidney, to whom Yeats, in 'In Memory of Major Robert Gregory,' would later compare Lady Gregory's airman son, shot down over Italy (by friendly fire, as it ironically turned out). By then, having been introduced to the book by Augusta Gregory, Yeats could draw on his enthralled immersion in Castiglione's *The Courtier* to present a highly refined setting in which Lady Gregory's Coole Park, which Robert Gregory would have

---

4   *A Servant of the Queen*, 328–30.

inherited, was an Irish version of the Duchess's Urbino. Yeats had, he says in the poem, grown accustomed to the 'lack of breath' of the other friends memorialized in this decorous group-elegy, 'but not that my dear friend's dear son,/ Our Sidney and our perfect man,/ Could share in that discourtesy of death.'

Reading the lines in 'Adam's Curse' about love 'compounded of high courtesy,' it is hard not to think, as Yeats doubtless did, of the famous opening poem (written in rare hexameters) of Sidney's sonnet sequence, *Astrophil and Stella.* 'Loving in truth' and hoping to show his love in 'verse,' so that the beloved 'might take some pleasure of my paine,' win her pity, 'and pitie grace obtaine,' he sought, Philip / Astrophil tells us, 'fit words' to depict his woe. Though his emotion was sincere, he found himself 'Studying inventions fine, her wits to entertaine,' often 'turning others' leaves, to see if thence would flow/ Some fresh and fruitful showers upon my sunne-burn'd braine.' His fevered brain is burnt by light beams streaming from his lady's eyes, a courtly and recurrent Petrarchan metaphor played on by Yeats in 'The Arrow.' That particular stereotype had been brilliantly mocked by Shakespeare in Sonnet 130, 'My mistress' eyes are nothing like the sun,' but even Shakespeare, though he ridiculed some now-hackneyed courtly imagery, absorbed and continued, if less overtly than Sidney, the resilient Petrarchan tradition.

Like Yeats, laboring over precedents, Sidney, too, had set himself to 'studying' old books, Italian and French, in the courtly love tradition of worshiping devotee and distant lady. Finally, emulating woman's biological labor, 'great with child to speake' but helplessly burdened with the derivative rhetoric of the 'art' of love rather than pregnant with 'Nature's child,' and biting his idle 'pen,' he stops reading and ranting and listens: '"Foole," said my Muse to me, "looke in thy heart and write".' Yeats will echo and intensify that emotional imperative a quarter-century later, in the final line of 'The Circus Animals' Desertion,' with high artifice, at once concealing and revealing his love of Maud Gonne, yielding to the passionate origin of all art: 'the foul rag and bone shop of the heart.'

But in 'Adam's Curse,' the very mention of 'love,' ideally but idly 'compounded of high courtesy,' puts an end to all conversation, which yields, like the dying daylight, to a beautiful but elegiac moon:

> We sat grown quiet at the name of love;
> We saw the last embers of daylight die,
> And in the trembling blue-green of the sky
> A moon, worn as if it had been a shell
> Washed by time's waters as they rose and fell
> About the stars and broke in days and years.
>
> I had a thought for no one's but your ears:
> That you were beautiful, and that I strove
> To love you in the old high way of love;
> That it had all seemed happy, and yet we'd grown
> As weary-hearted as that hollow moon.

So much for the exalting and yet humiliatingly painful travails of the courtly love tradition: that 'old high way of love' Yeats had pursued on the chivalric and virginal high-road leading from Petrarch to Sidney and beyond—beginning with Dante, that love-famished 'hollow face of his' in 'Ego Dominus Tuus' anticipated by 'that hollow moon' symbolic of Yeats's own frustrated, desolate love in 'Adam's Curse.'

In the same year he wrote 'Adam's Curse,' Yeats put Maud on stage as Ireland herself in *Cathleen ni Houlihan*. That 'Red Hanrahan's Song about Ireland' was Maud's favorite Yeats poem is unsurprising. Written in 1894 but now incorporated in this sequence, it makes Maud indistinguishable from Cathleen *as* Ireland. We may be thrilled by the couplet on one queen's mountain cairn: 'The wind has bundled up the clouds high over Knocknarea,/ And thrown the thunder on the stones for all that Maeve can say.' But it was surely this stanza's final lines— echoing 'the quiet of love in her feet' from the finale of 'The Cap and Bells,' written a year earlier—that appealed to Maud, servant of another queen: angers like 'noisy clouds' may have 'set our hearts abeat;/ But we have all bent low and low and kissed the quiet feet/ Of Cathleen, the daughter of Houlihan.' While Maud relished the poem, Yeats must have had mixed feelings, perhaps in writing it in the first place, but certainly in including it *here*, where it emphasized the self-abasing politics he hated yet succumbed to under the intense influence of Maud Gonne. Five years later, in 'He wishes for the Cloths of Heaven' (the more abject lyric supposedly countered by 'The Cap and Bells'), a submissively foot-conscious Yeatsian speaker, addressing his beloved, says, 'I have spread my dreams under your feet;/ Tread softly because you tread on my dreams.'

§

Between *In the Seven Woods* and his next collection of lyric poetry, *The Green Helmet and Other Poems* (1910), there was a six-year hiatus, during which Yeats, for the most part stunned into poetic silence by Maud's marriage, was also, as a co-manager of the Abbey, preoccupied by 'theatre business, management of men.'[5] But much else had happened in the interim. The tragic death, in March 1909, of Yeats's friend and the Abbey's greatest early playwright, John Millington Synge, had been preceded by the long-delayed, briefly ecstatic, and ultimately unsatisfactory physical union of Poet and Muse, in December 1908.[6] After that night of lovemaking in Paris, Maud had quickly put the relationship back on its old non-physical basis. Earlier synopsized, Maud's letter should be quoted more fully. Though reflecting genuine tenderness, it is firm in its conviction:

> Beloved I am glad & proud beyond measure of your love, & that it is strong enough & high enough to accept the spiritual love & union I offer—
>
> I have prayed so hard to have all earthly desire taken from my love for you & dearest, loving you as I do, I have prayed & I am praying still that the bodily desire for me may be taken from you too. I know how hard & rare a thing it is for a man to hold spiritual love when the bodily desire is gone & I have not made these prayers without a terrible struggle—a struggle that shook my life though I do not speak much of it & generally manage to laugh.

---

5   Such business, and cursed 'plays/ That have to be set up in fifty ways,' has 'rent/ Spontaneous joy and natural content / Out of my heart,' and made Pegasus 'shiver under the lash, strain, sweat and jolt/ As though it dragged road metal.' (The title of the poem in which he registered these complaints, 'The Fascination of What's Difficult,' was employed by Kim Bendheim as the title of her 2021 biography of Maud Gonne.) While she didn't want to 'under rate' the Abbey, Maud (writing in the summer of 1911) considered it 'as NOTHING in comparison with your poems & while you are absorbed in the management of the theatre, you won't write a line of poetry' (G-YL, 301).

6   Sworn to secrecy during her husband's lifetime, George Yeats revealed the facts in 1947, confiding in Richard Ellmann, during his visits when he was working on *Yeats: The Man and the Masks*. The date when Yeats and Maud became physical lovers has been confirmed by Elizabeth Heine, 'Yeats and Maud Gonne: Marriage and the Astrological Record, 1908–09,' 3–33.

> That struggle is over & I have found peace. I think today I could let you
> marry another without losing it—for I know the spiritual union between
> us will outlive this life, even if we never see each other in this world again
> (G-YL, 258–59).

In a journal entry the following month (21 January 1909), Yeats referred
despairingly but realistically to the 'return' of Maud's 'old dread of
physical love,' which has 'probably spoiled her life [...] I was never more
deeply in love, but my desires must go elsewhere if I would escape their
poison.' They did.

Maud had anticipated her letter of spiritual renunciation of the body
with an earlier account, sent to him in late July 1908 (G-YL, 257), of
a 'wonderful' dream she had had, an astral projection resulting in a
'union' in which, suspended in space between 'starlight' and 'the sea,'
she and a serpentine Yeats 'melted into one another till we formed only
one being, greater than ourselves [italics in original] who felt all & knew
all with double intensity'—a vision, she says, 'like in the picture of
Blake the soul leaving the body.' Blake's 'The Soul Hovering over the
Body Reluctantly Parting with Life' is the second most-striking of his
illustrations to Robert Blair's *The Grave* (1808). The most vivid of the
Grave illustrations, 'The Reunion of the Soul & the Body,' notable for
the passionate intensity of the embrace of the (female) soul and (male)
body, was chosen by Yeats for all three covers of his and Edwin Ellis's
1893 three-volume edition of Blake, and it was still vivid in Yeats's
imagination when he described it as the image of 'true death' in a 1938
letter to Ethel Mannin (L, 917). A dozen years earlier he had verbalized
Blake's design in 'A Last Confession,' the ninth and most ecstatic poem
in his sequence, 'A Woman Young and Old.' The old woman who is the
speaker of 'A Last Confession' also recaptures Maud's spiritual yet erotic
vision of lovers 'who felt all & knew all with double intensity.'

> when this soul, its body off,
> Naked to naked goes,
> He it has found shall find therein
> What none other knows,
>
> And give his own and take his own
> And rule in his own right;
> And though it loved in misery
> Close and cling so tight,

There's not a bird of day that dare
Extinguish that delight.

But when Yeats, in Maud's 1908 dream, understandably interpreted her vision as intensifying rather than diminishing 'physical desire,' she predictably, even in the dream, responded: 'this troubles me a little, for there was nothing physical in that union—Material union is but a pale shadow compared to it' (G-YL, 257). As demonstrated by her insistence on a spiritual or mystical marriage with Yeats, and by much else, Maud Gonne combined her dread of physical intimacy with a serious attraction to spiritualism. Maud's interest in mysticism, developed in London in 1890, had been encouraged by Yeats, who brought her to meet the celebrated Madame Blavatsky, and arranged for her initiation into his esoteric Order, the Golden Dawn, in November 1891. Predictably bored by what she called the 'British middle-class dullness' of its members, she stayed for just three years, leaving the Order in December 1894. But that she remained engaged by spiritualism and occultism is evident in the mystical marriage and in many of her letters to Yeats.[7]

In any case, after that December in Paris, Yeats's own position was hopeless. He must have intuited in advance the truth of what, as we have seen, he would later call the 'finest description of sexual intercourse ever written,' introduced, in John Dryden's translation of Lucretius, 'to illustrate the difficulty of two becoming a unity': 'The tragedy of sexual intercourse is the perpetual virginity of the soul.' Copulation was an 'attempt to solve the eternal antinomy, doomed to failure because it takes place only on one side of the gulf.'[8] That gulf, between spirit and flesh, would forever frustrate Yeats's desire for a full union with Maud Gonne.

---

7   On the Gonne-Yeats spiritual / sexual correspondence, Blake's illustrations for Blair's *Grave*, and 'A Last Confession,' see my 'The Human Entrails and the Starry Heavens,' 366–91.

8   As earlier discussed in connection with the 'Woman Young and Old' and 'Crazy Jane' sequences, Yeats was referring to Lucretius' long passage on sexual love, the conclusion of Book IV of *De rerum natura*.

12. Maud as Helen:
The *Green Helmet* Poems

But if sexual intercourse could not resolve the eternal antinomy, it still had its consolations. Tired of Maud's 'bond of the spirit only,' Yeats, escaping the 'poison' of sexual repression, returned to the less mystical arms of his clandestine 'visiting' mistress at the time, the attractive Mabel Dickinson, who had become infatuated with him. He was no longer, he told Mabel, satisfied with a 'twilight of religious mystery'; he wanted instead to 'take pleasure in clear light, strong bodies.' He had come, temporarily at least, to the right place. His secret, 'purely amatory' relationship with Mabel, which began in April 1908 and lasted sporadically until 1913 when it ended in 'relief' after a pregnancy scare, was with a woman who practiced as 'a medical gymnast and masseuse.'[1]

Nevertheless, when he put clarity and strength into words, he was back to his true Muse, opening the *Green Helmet* volume with a cluster (originally grouped under the title 'Raymond Lully to his wife Pernella') celebrating Maud as a newborn Helen of Troy. Though it did not keep her from correcting his medieval occult scholarship (it was not Raymond Lully but, as she reminded him, Nicholas Flamel who was married to Pernella), Maud responded with great enthusiasm to the 'music' of the poems in which Yeats had compared her to Homer's Helen. After acknowledging 'a danger of my growing very vain when I think of these beautiful things created for me,' she added a penetrating comment, contrasting the political 'hatred' that drove her fierce activism to the deep 'love' Yeats had given so 'generously and unselfishly.'

---

1   For Yeats's 1908 correspondence with Dickinson, see Cardozo, 259–61. For details on the ending of the affair, including the 'relief' of both Yeats and Lady Gregory (who thought it all 'unworthy,' of him and thanked God he was 'free'), see Foster, *The Apprentice Mage*, 488–89.

   https://doi.org/10.11647/OBP.0275.13

Referring to the greatest of the poems in which he had compared her to Homer's Helen, 'No Second Troy,' Maud said she thought that 'of all my work & all my effort little will remain because I worked on the ray of Hate, & the demons of hate which possessed me are not eternal—what you have written for me will live because our love has always been high & pure' (G-YL, 294).

Maud evidently liked Yeats's comparison of her to Helen of Troy, though, thinking of 'The Arrow' and the best of these new poems, 'No Second Troy,' in which he compares her 'beauty' to 'a tightened bow,' she remarked, 'You are hard on poor Bow and Arrows!' (G-YL, 294). As early as 1891, Yeats had, in 'The Rose of the World,' associated his beloved with Homer's Helen, for whose red lips, 'Troy passed away in one high funeral gleam.' For Maud, Yeats tells us in that same poem, God himself 'made the world to be a grassy road/ Before her wandering feet,' those same feet beneath which he would later (in 'He wishes for the Cloths of Heaven') abjectly spread his dreams, hoping she would 'tread softly.' Thus, by April 1910, when he wrote 'A Woman Homer Sung,' in which he has her proudly treading as on a cloud, he could proudly but accurately claim that he has evoked so powerful an image

> That coming time can say,
> 'He shadowed in a glass
> What thing her body was.'
>
> For she had fiery blood
> When I was young,
> And trod so sweetly proud
> As 'twere upon a cloud,
> A woman Homer sung,
> That life and letters seem
> But an heroic dream.

Maud's palpable 'body' and 'fiery blood' are balanced by her role as a cloud-treading Virgilian goddess and the Helen Homer sang. But the dream, however heroic, had not, as the 'seem' suggests, quite extinguished 'life and letters.' The next poem in the sequence, 'Words,' composed closer to events in Paris, was sketched out in prose in a January 1909 diary entry. The thought had 'occurred' to him, says Yeats, that Maud never really understood his 'plans, or nature or ideas.' He continues: 'Then came the thought—what matter? How much of the best I have done and still do is but the attempt to explain myself to her? If she understood I should lack a reason for writing and one can never have too many reasons for doing what is so laborious' (Mem, 141–42).

'Words,' the poem that resulted, consists of four iambic tetrameter *abab* quatrains, with every fourth line a more insistent trimeter. Yeats at first adheres to the emphasis in his diary entry regarding Maud's incomprehension of his work, but adds a confident claim that his rhetorical mastery had overcome even her politically obsessed resistance to poetry she felt was not propagandistic enough, poetry that he was not willing, after *Cathleen ni Houlihan*, to provide; and concludes with a dramatic but dubious assertion, an assertion that Yeats, as artist, wants us to challenge:

> I had this thought a while ago,
> 'My darling cannot understand
> What I have done, or what would do
> In this blind bitter land.'
>
> And I grew weary of the sun
> Until my thoughts cleared up again,
> Remembering that the best I have done
> Was done to make it plain;
>
> That every year I have cried, 'At length
> My darling understands it all,
> Because I have come into my strength,
> And words obey my call';
>
> That had she done so who can say
> What would have shaken from the sieve?
> I might have thrown poor words away
> And been content to live.

Having come into his strength, with 'words' at his command, he briefly hopes that Maud at last 'understands it all.' But what if she had? He 'might' have 'thrown poor words away/ And been content to live.' But Yeats does not really believe that the poetry was a mere substitute for life and sex. Even if it *is* in part sublimation, the poetry itself matters. As Helen Vendler remarks, in concluding her exhaustive study of Yeats and lyric form, and in direct reference to the final lines of 'Words': 'But of course it was not only to explain himself that Yeats composed poetry; it was to satisfy his ardor for the permutations and combinations of shaped and musical language, the desire [as he says in 'Adam's Curse'] to "articulate sweet sounds together." The resulting strong and decisive poems of formal mastery appeared and kept appearing, throughout his fifty years of writing.'[2]

In the specific case of 'Words,' what is obvious but needs to be said is that it is *in a poem*, after all, that he speculates that, had his love been requited, he 'might' have 'thrown poor words away' and been 'content' to 'live.' It wasn't, he didn't. But the alternative is not between a lyric poet's 'poor words' and rich, vital life. He speaks of being 'content' to live, and mere contentment is hardly an aspiration of Romantic poets. In any case, Maud did *not* fully understand what Yeats wanted to do in Ireland. Gradually, the poet in him 'turned aside' from Maud and back to 'words.' Of course, given the letter she had sent him following the physical consummation of their love the previous month, he may have had little choice. Physically at least, Maud had preceded Yeats in 'turning aside.'

§

'Words' is followed by the more famous 'No Second Troy,' composed within days of Maud's letter, and probably the signature Maud Gonne poem. With the exception of the magnificent opening movement of his sequence, 'Nineteen Hundred and Nineteen,' juxtaposing ancient and modern barbaric assaults on civilization, there is no better example than 'No Second Troy' of Yeats's deployment of what T. S. Eliot called (in his 1923 *Dial* review, '*Ulysses*, Order and Myth') 'the mythical method.' Though perfected by Joyce in *Ulysses*, the method had been 'adumbrated by Mr. Yeats,' the first modern poet, Eliot thought, to be 'conscious' of the need to parallel 'contemporaneity and antiquity.' Implicit in the title, the parallel in 'No Second Troy' is not completed until the final explosive line.

A masterpiece of form writhing with power, 'No Second Troy'— three *abab* iambic pentameter quatrains fused into a single 12-line unit— consists of two 5-line rhetorical questions, followed by two more, each distilled to a single line. We are initially seduced into sharing the poet's complaint; he had abundant reason to 'blame' her, she having 'filled' his days less with joy than 'with misery.' But Yeats is setting us up; his

---

2   Vendler, *Our Secret Discipline*, 376.

rhetorical strategy reveals *our own* pettiness faced with a Helen born out of phase, a Homeric figure living in a modern age unworthy of her.

> Why should I blame her that she filled my days
> With misery, or that she would of late
> Have taught to ignorant men most violent ways,
> Or hurled the little streets upon the great,
> Had they but courage equal to desire?
> What could have made her peaceful with a mind
> That nobleness made simple as a fire,
> With beauty like a tightened bow, a kind
> That is not natural in an age like this,
> Being high and solitary and most stern?
> Why, what could she have done, being what she is?
> Was there another Troy for her to burn?

There is empathy but no sentimentality; the heroine's path may be destined, but she is, despite this poem of questioning, unquestionably destructive. That her nobility made her 'mind [...] simple as a fire,' seems both compliment and criticism. As we know from such major poems as 'Byzantium' and 'Vacillation,' the 'simplicity' of fire is opposed to and spiritually superior to the 'complexity' of mere mire and blood. But it is hard to simply dismiss the secondary implication, that Maud was also somewhat simple-minded. While, as we have seen, some British journalists in the 'nineties' thought Maud's 'mysterious eye' foreshadowed 'battles yet to come,' Yeats was uncertain whether her mysteriously vague eyes suggested 'wisdom' to accompany her 'beauty,' or simple 'lack of any thought' (Mem, 60). Fire is not always attended by light; and there is a certain irony in Maud Gonne's Golden Dawn pseudonym, P.I.A.L., often used by Yeats. It stands for the Latin *Per Ignem ad Lucem*, but Maud's own progress was seldom 'Through Fire to Light.' Still, such quibbles, though registered, seem beside the principal poetic point. As Yeats asks in the prose note that evolved into 'Words,' a rhetorical question repeated in 'The Mask' (discussed below), 'What matter?' In the case of the masked woman, 'What matter, so there is but fire/ In you, in me?'

Yeats had earlier, and peripherally, associated Maud with Helen, for whose beauty 'Troy passed away in one high funeral gleam.' In 'No Second Troy,' with no ancient city to burn, Maud's incendiary energy had to be directed to what was at hand in the local, contemporary world: whether the all-talk, no-action Irish, or Yeats himself, both, perhaps, lacking 'courage equal to desire.' Despite some later theatrical, loose and semi-Fascist talk about 'war,' the poet who wrote 'No Second Troy' would himself hardly condone inciting the 'ignorant' to violence, especially against the 'great' streets of Ascendancy Dublin. But Maud was not Yeats; and even she, for Yeats, was not only Maud but Helen as well, and even more destructive since Maud was a physical-force activist while Homer's Helen was a passive and contrite witness of the violence she had caused. But Maud, like Martin Luther, could do no other. In *acting* as she did, she was, Yeats insists, being true to her quintessential being: 'what she *is*.'

What is to 'blame,' outrageously enough, is not the terrible beauty of Yeats's magnificent and fiery heroine, 'high and solitary and most stern,' but the low, gregarious, and ignoble modern world itself, for not being (as Richard Ellmann once wittily remarked) 'heroically inflammable.' In 1917, looking back with the judgment of a perceptive critic backed by the experience gained in having shared Stone Cottage with Yeats, Ezra Pound said of his friend around the time he wrote 'No Second Troy,' that he was in transit from the *'dolce stile'* to the *'stile grande'*.[3] Having wearied of Yeats's nostalgic, romanticized celebrations of his Muse as she had been, Pound made an exception for *this* Maud Gonne poem. A tough-mindedly realistic poem filled with feeling but stripped of sentimentality, its syntax taut as that tightened bow, 'No Second Troy' embodied the transition from the sweet style of the Italian sonneteers to the style of later, greater Yeats. From the lofty height of the grand style, to assign 'blame' would be to lower oneself from the noble to the level of the proletarian, all-too-censorious 'little streets.'

'Blame' recurs in the opening line of the next poem in the sequence, but shifted to others. During a public lecture in 1903, Yeats had been suddenly informed of Maud's marriage. The news struck him like a

---

3   Pound, 'The Later Yeats,' 66. Ellmann's remark that the modern world lacked heroic inflammability (*Identity of Yeats*, 112), is matched by his equally witty remark on the final lines of the final poem in *Responsibilities*. Various attacks, especially the mischievous and unforgettable deflations of Yeats's new chinchilla-coated aristocratic pomposity by George Moore, had made him 'Notorious/ Till all my priceless things/ Are but a post the passing dogs defile.' Pound was delighted that Yeats had finally become a 'modern' poet. In Ellmann's summation (*Eminent Domain*, 67), 'An image of urination had finally brought Pound to his knees.' For his part, Yeats was gratified to have made it to modernism, even if he *was* adapting an old metaphor, from Erasmus.

thunderbolt. 'Reconciliation,' the poem immediately following 'No Second Troy,' records that reaction. The background includes her subsequent separation from MacBride, and the reunion of Maud and Yeats, at long last sexual. Like 'No Second Troy,' 'Reconciliation' is twelve lines of iambic pentameter, though this time in conversationally enjambed couplets:

> Some may have blamed you that you took away
> The verses that could move them on the day
> When, the ears being deafened, the sight of the eyes blind
> With lightning, you went from me, and I could find
> Nothing to make a song about but kings,
> Helmets, and swords, and half-forgotten things
> That were like memories of you—

Almost thirty years later, in 'The Circus Animals' Desertion,' Yeats would flesh out the admission here that his early mythological plays were sublimations, 'emblems of' his unrequited love for Maud Gonne. 'Reconciliation' ends with the breach healed between Maud and Yeats, the two 'out' publicly and the poet himself out of hiding behind his archaic-heroic props, theatrical trappings camouflaging his cold and 'barren thoughts' in her absence:

> but now
> We'll out, for the world lives as long ago;
> And while we're in our laughing, weeping fit,
> Hurl helmets, crowns, and swords into the pit.
> But, dear, cling close to me; since you were gone,
> My barren thoughts have chilled me to the bone.

The world of the theater illuminates the curious title of the next poem, 'King and No King,' which begins by rehearsing the brother-sister incest theme in Beaumont and Fletcher's play of that title. Halfway through its sixteen *abba* lines, the congested poem comes to emotional life with the application of that theme to the hopeless love of Yeats and Maud: a union supposedly 'defeated by that pledge' Maud gave 'long ago' never to marry, and even now (December 1909), though she was separated from MacBride, barred from divorce by her Catholicism. Yeats has a poignant question, unresolved by the promise of a Catholic heaven, a Swedenborgian vision of an incandescent reunion in eternity, or the glimpse of domestic bliss, a never-to-be-attained conventional happy ending here on earth:

And I that have not your faith, how shall I know
That in the blinding light beyond the grave
We'll find so good a thing as that we have lost?
The hourly kindness, the day's common speech,
The habitual content of each with each
When neither soul nor body has been crossed.

That celestial light 'beyond the grave' was reserved for other poems, and no contented domestic idyll was ever on offer from the mercurial Maud. We seem left with a negative answer to the question: these star-crossed lovers would never 'find so good a thing as that we have lost'—unless, of course, we count the poetry that loss produced—as Maud Gonne most definitely did in that remarkable acknowledgement that 'what you have written for me will live because our love has always been high & pure' (G-YL, 294).

The sequence ends with 'Peace,' 'Against Unworthy Praise,' and, given the context in which they were deliberately placed by Yeats, who thought of his lyrics as tiles in a mosaic, 'A Drinking Song' and 'The Mask.' In the first poem, 'Peace,' Yeats describes, yet again, Maud's fascinating and oxymoronic mixture of 'charm' and 'sternness.' His reference to 'all that sweetness amid strength' alludes, as he will more momentously in the climactic lines of 'Vacillation' (1933), to Samson's riddle (Judges 14:14) of the lion and the honeycomb. He concludes by acknowledging something he had been reluctant to concede in 'The Folly of Being Comforted': 'Ah, but peace that comes at length,/ Came when Time had touched her form.'

Picking up on the word 'peace,' the poem that follows, 'Against Unworthy Praise,' begins, 'O heart, be at peace.' No matter if his work as poet and playwright is misconstrued by the public: 'Nor knave nor dolt can break/ What's not for their applause,/ Being for a woman's sake.' It is all a strength-renewing 'dream' and 'secret between' Maud and himself, between 'the proud and the proud.' The second and final stanza moves from the artist to his Muse, from self-chastisement for stubbornly seeking applause from the unworthy ('What, still you would have their praise!'), to 'a haughtier text': a celebration of that proud woman who, in the aftermath of her legal separation from Boer War hero MacBride, endured 'slander, ingratitude,' and even 'worse wrong,' from 'self-same dolt and knave.' Yeats is no doubt recalling how Maud, an activist who 'gave' all to the people, had been hissed at when he escorted her one evening from the Abbey Theatre. Yet this most public woman, internally secreted in a mental 'labyrinth' that 'her own strangeness perplexed,' persists, achieving the 'peace' Yeats sought in his own heart. That calm may be beyond his grasp; but, though, in 'No Second Troy' he had famously wondered 'what,' given her nature, 'could have made her peaceful,' in this poem at least tempestuous Maud, 'singing upon her road,/ Half lion, half child, is at peace.'

Though written to be sung by an innkeeper in Lady Gregory's adaptation of *La Locandiera*, a play by Italy's great eighteenth-century comic dramatist, Carlo Goldoni, 'A Drinking Song' (based on Goldoni's '*Viva Bacco, e Viva Amore*') inserted by Yeats at this point in *The Green Helmet*, becomes another tile in the Maud Gonne mosaic. In fact, it introduces the six-line form employed (though with a different rhyme-scheme) five years later for two Maud poems, 'A Deep-sworn Vow' and 'Memory.' The 'Drinking Song' is both charming and poignant:

> Wine comes in at the mouth
> And love comes in at the eye;
> That's all we shall know for truth
> Before we grow old and die.
> I lift the glass to my mouth,
> I look at you, and I sigh.

Similarly, 'The Mask,' though at first apparently unrelated to Maud, by its very placement in this sequence, enters the Maud Gonne orbit. Originally titled 'A Lyric from an Unpublished Play,' it was retitled 'A Mask' three years later, first in the Cuala Press publication *A Selection from the Love Poetry of William Butler Yeats*, then in *The Green Helmet and Other Poems*. This marks Yeats's first *public* use of what will become in his lexicon a crucial term. His concept of the mask is derived not only from his esoteric thoughts about Daimon and anti-self, but, in large part, from his reading of Wilde and Nietzsche, and his agreement with the theories of anti-naturalistic theater innovator and mask-enthusiast, Edgar Gordon Craig, who had designed several of Yeats's own mask-plays at the Abbey Theatre.[4]

The first speaker in this three-stanza dialogue is anxious to discover whether his beloved's dazzling 'mask of burning gold/ With emerald

---

4   For details, see my essay 'Blake, Nietzsche, Wilde, and Yeats: Contraries, Anti-Selves, and the Truth of Masks.'

eyes' conceals 'love' or the 'deceit' of an 'enemy.' Her reply is firm: 'It was the mask engaged your mind,/ And after set your heart to beat,/ Not what's behind.' First worn by Decima in Yeats's *The Player Queen*, this mask was initially inspired by his amatory visitor at the time, Mabel Dickinson. But since the poem appears in the Cuala Press edition of his 'Love Poetry'and, in *The Green Helmet*, deliberately placed among lyrics to and about Maud Gonne, Yeats seems to want us to identify the masked figure with his Muse. To the male speaker's anxious inquiry as to whether she *is* his enemy, the woman responds, 'What matter, so there is but fire/ In you, in me?' Playing with fire is exciting but dangerous, especially if we are dealing with Maud Gonne, political activist, actress, and *femme fatale*.

The *Green Helmet* volume ends with two poems, originally coupled under the rubric 'Momentary Thoughts,' that glance at Maud. The first, in iambic pentameter couplets, takes its title from the opening line:

> All things can tempt me from this craft of verse:
> One time it was a woman's face, or worse—
> The seeming needs of my fool-driven land;
> Now nothing but comes easier to the hand
> Than this accustomed toil.

In reasserting the priority—over politics, even over love—of his proper labor, the 'craft' of poetry, Yeats seems to turn aside, at least momentarily, from Maud Gonne, whose beautiful 'face' tempted him from his 'toil.' The poem's original title, 'Distraction,' highlights the underlying paradox: the very 'things' that, when he 'was young,' supposedly hindered his poetry—the needs of Ireland, the beauty of Maud Gonne—were, and in fact remain, the major subjects of that poetry.

I will not lay a thematic burden on the final poem of *The Green Helmet*, the light and charming 'Brown Penny.' But when the poet (in a lyric originally titled 'Young Man's Song') describes himself as 'looped in the loops of her hair,' and as 'thinking of love/ Till the stars had run away/ And the shadows eaten the moon,' we find ourselves, again momentarily, back in the Celtic Twilight and the Maud Gonne poetry of *The Wind Among the Reeds*, with the beloved's Pre-Raphaelite hair falling over her passive lover's breast.

13. *Responsibilities* and *The Wild Swans at Coole*

Yeats's next collection, *Responsibilities* (1914), far more focused on public issues, contains only a handful of Maud-related poems toward the end, with the dominant tone less heroic than elegiac. This pivotal volume is prefaced by intimately personal untitled lines directed to his ancestors, asking their 'Pardon that for a barren passion's sake,' he has no child, 'nothing but a book,/ Nothing but that to prove your blood and mine.' If asked, Maud would have responded that while, in 1914, Yeats had no human offspring, 'our children were your poems,' spiritual-imaginative 'children' that she had fathered and that he had brought forth out of his suffering and creativity. And, unlike offspring of mere flesh and blood, 'our children had wings' (G-YL, 302). To counter Yeats's apologetic 'nothing but a book,' Maud might have cited the axiom of Hippocrates as famously translated by Seneca: *'ars longa, vita brevis'* [Art is long, life is short.] The Muse and her poet are gone; but as Yeats knew and Maud predicted, their poetic children would live forever.

The little cluster of Maud poems begins with 'A Memory of Youth,' reminiscent of 'Adam's Curse,' but with a strikingly different final 'moon.' Yeats records moments of play and wit, until 'A cloud blown from the cut-throat north/ Suddenly hid love's moon away.' Praise of his beloved's 'body and her mind' brightened her eyes and brought a blush to her cheek. 'Yet we, for all that praise, could find/ Nothing but darkness overhead.' They sit in stony silence, knowing, 'though she'd not said a word,/ That even the best of love must die.' They had been 'savagely undone,' but for a sudden burst of emotion-revivifying illumination, when 'Love upon the cry/ Of a most ridiculous little bird/ Tore from the clouds his marvelous moon.' The re-emergence of Love's moon, violently torn (by Eros himself) from clouds formed by the 'cut-throat'

 https://doi.org/10.11647/OBP.0275.14

north wind, is heralded, not by one of Yeats's numinous annunciatory birds, a peacock or that 'miraculous strange bird' that shrieks at the couple discovering true love in 'Her Triumph' (Poem IV of 'A Woman Young and Old'), but by an unlikely, even laughable herald, well down in the hierarchy. That 'ridiculous little bird' almost turns tragedy into comedy, or tragi-comedy.

In the next poem, 'Fallen Majesty,' the poet sees *himself* as ridiculous. As an aging Petrarchan poet, he is an inappropriate man in an unpropitious place: 'some last courtier at a gypsy camping place/ Babbling of fallen majesty.' But the fallen majesty itself is recorded with elegiac pathos and pride. In the heyday of Maud Gonne's youthful beauty and fiery political activism, when mesmerized 'crowds gathered' if she merely showed her face, 'even old men's eyes grew dim'—like those of the elders of Troy who might disapprove of Helen but had to concede her beauty (in Ezra Pound's wonderful rendering, 'Moves, yes she moves like a goddess/ And has the face of a god,' though 'doom goes with her in walking').[1] Maud's Homer, writing in hexameters a decade or more after her political apogee, memorializes 'what's gone':

> The lineaments, a heart that laughter has made sweet,
> These, these remain, but I record what's gone. A crowd
> Will gather, and not know it walks the very street
> Whereon a thing once walked that seemed a burning cloud.

Following 'Friends,' discussed earlier, come two mysterious, almost apocalyptic poems, 'The Cold Heaven' and 'That the Night Come.' The latter presents a woman who so 'lived in storm and strife,' that her soul, desiring what 'proud death may bring,' could 'not endure/ The common good of life,' seeming—like a king packing his 'marriage day' with banner, trumpet, kettledrum and 'the outrageous cannon'—'To bundle time away/ That the night come.'

The memorable and mysterious 'The Cold Heaven,' a visionary poem that has deeply affected other poets, including (by his own acknowledgement) Seamus Heaney, is thrilling but notoriously enigmatic. Maud Gonne herself wondered what it meant. Yeats told her it was his attempt to describe feelings evoked by a cold winter sky, a sense that he was alone and somehow 'responsible in that loneliness

---

1   Canto II, in *The Cantos of Ezra Pound* 6. Cf. *Iliad* III.160–63.

for all the past mistakes that tortured his peace of mind.' Revisiting the poem as late as 2015, Denis Donoghue found it as unforgettable as ever but, despite an acute close reading, ultimately inexplicable. Though its ultimate question involves the afterlife, 'The Cold Heaven' is also a Muse-poem, pivotal, Hassett argues, in marking Yeats's shift from his 'acceptance of the failure of his relationship with Gonne,' to a new kind of poetry: a 'celebration or interrogation of the past rather than the work of a poet pursuing his Muse.'[2]

'The Cold Heaven,' like 'No Second Troy' and 'Reconciliation,' is a twelve-line poem, but decidedly *not* written in familiar iambic pentameters. It begins, jarringly, with a metrically irregular, enjambed, obliquely-rhymed *abab* quatrain, and with a visionary abruptness anticipating both the opening eruption ('A sudden blow, the great wings beating still') of 'Leda and the Swan' and lines written a quarter-century after 'The Cold Heaven,' in which Yeats records a moment when the 'wildness' he saw in what he perceived to be Maud's 'vision of terror,' brought his own 'imagination' to such a 'pitch' that he had himself 'grown wild' ('A Bronze Head'). We begin staring at a winter sky, galactically cold yet exhilarating:

> Suddenly I saw the cold and rook-delighting heaven
> That seemed as though ice burned and was but the more ice,
> And thereupon imagination and heart were driven
> So wild that every casual thought of that and this
> Vanished, and left but memories.

Going beyond Yeats's desire to write a poem 'cold and passionate as the dawn,' these lines recall the oxymoronic opening lines of the Thomas Wyatt sonnet in which the conflicted Petrarchan lover cries out, 'I burn and freeze in ice.'[3] Yeats's lines also forecast, along with that moment in 'A Bronze Head,' the moment in 'Among School Children' when Yeats conjures up an image of Maud, 'and thereupon' his 'heart is driven wild.' As we would expect from everything we have read thus far, and from

---

2   For Yeats's remark to Maud, see Hassett, *Yeats Now: Echoing into Life*, 111. Donoghue, 'Reading "The Cold Heaven",' in *Yeats 150*, 171–88. Hassett, *Yeats and the Muses*, 95–98.

3   Yeats borrowed (for his poem 'The Fisherman') his father's 'cold-and-passionate' oxymoron. Wyatt's oxymoronic sonnet begins, 'I find no peace,' and ends 'And my delight is causer of this strife.'

the resemblance to the later lines cited from 'Among School Children,' and 'A Bronze Head,' the vision fusing ice and fire, driving heart and imagination wild, issues in a painful looking-back leaving behind only memories

> that should be out of season
> With the hot blood of youth, of love crossed long ago;
> And I took all the blame out of all sense and reason,
> Until I cried and trembled and rocked to and fro,
> Riddled with light.

The reaction is extreme; the speaker is left crying, trembling, rocking back and forth, pierced with light, either lacerated with remorse or 'riddled' with bullet-like shafts of epiphanic illumination. Making its sole appearance in Yeats's poetry and plays, the violent participle 'riddled' seems both contextually and punningly appropriate to 'The Cold Heaven,' itself 'a riddle wrapped in a mystery inside an enigma' (to recall Churchill's definition of Stalin's Russia). Unlike the nonce 'riddled,' 'blame' shows up repeatedly in the Maud poems. Here, coupled with a doubled appearance of 'all' (Yeats's most frequently used word), 'blame' for what he described to Maud as 'all the past mistakes' is accepted as his sole 'responsibility.' He claims the failure of that 'love crossed long ago' is his fault exclusively, even as he simultaneously acknowledges that to 'take *all* the blame' is extreme, an emotional over-reaction, '*out* of *all* sense and reason.'

The poem's extraordinary energy is sustained throughout. The final lines, though they also seem 'out of all sense and reason,' are undeniably powerful—and appropriately haunting, coming from a ghost-haunted man:

> Ah! When the ghost begins to quicken,
> Confusion of the death-bed over, is it sent
> Out naked on the roads, as the books say, and stricken
> By the injustice of the skies for punishment?

Roy Foster ends the chapter of his biography covering the years 1911–13, a chapter he titles 'Ghosts,' by printing the poem in full, as it happens, the only words on the page. He does preface the poem by observing that here, 'the lacerating memory of his failure with Gonne and his theories of death, ghosts and dreams come together in a passionate fusion.'

He relegates these theories to a lengthy endnote, gathering together what Yeats had to say (in commentary he supplied to the stories Lady Gregory and he compiled in *Visions and Beliefs in the West of Ireland*) about what Ovid and Cornelius Agrippa had to say about the fate of ghosts, depending on whether the person had done 'good' or 'ill' on earth, with the speculations of the Roman poet and the German occultist buttressed by the Indian theosophist Rama Prasad's ideas about posthumous punishment.[4]

I may seem to be making fun of that long note (which also directs us to a relevant November 1898 letter Yeats sent to Edward Clodd on the subject of ghosts) as obscurantist pedantry, justifying its semi-burial among some eighty pages of closely printed endnotes. But, in fact, that note is genuinely illuminating. The problem is that it makes for a heavy lift in trying to explicate four lines of poetry. In fact, these concluding lines have struck many commentators as requiring such glosses, especially from *A Vision*, in order to be fully unpacked. In particular, there has been much ado about the posthumous 'Dreaming Back' stage of the 'Spirit'—which would seem anachronistic since *A Vision* was, when this poem was written, still a dozen years in the future, though Yeats may have sensed what he would later say about the life after death.

In the poem itself, to return to *that*, even the poet falls back—a characteristic ploy, as in 'For Anne Gregory'—on 'what the books say.' They must be paradoxical tomes since what they say (despite the terminal question mark, the final line seems less query than declaration) is that the naked ghost *is* 'stricken/ By the injustice of the skies for punishment.' *In*justice, defying commonsense in this world or the next, returns us to that self-contradictory line where Yeats 'took all the blame out of all sense and reason.' If he deserved to take all the blame for the failed relationship with Maud, if he did 'ill,' then he might well expect, especially in a book titled *Responsibilities*, to be stricken by the '*justice* of the skies for punishment.' But if he did 'good,' or if he did not deserve to bear *total* responsibility (if that would be 'out of all sense and reason'), then his posthumous fate—to be, as the poem says, 'stricken/ By the *in*justice of the skies for punishment'—would be a fate both wrong and, in any moral calculus, *un*-reasonable.

---

4   Foster, *The Apprentice Mage*, 491, 490, 620n159.

In the end, Yeats seems to be saying that, while he momentarily thought that, in chivalrously or masochistically shouldering *all* the blame, he was being just, he was actually being doubly extreme; and (to cite a Roman of my own) Cicero reminds us, in his compendium of moral obligations, that *'Summum ius summa iniuria,'* [Extreme justice is extreme injustice.][5] Yeats acknowledges responsibility for the failure of the relationship with that 'woman lost,' only to immediately retract it as being excessive, as 'all' almost always is. His admission here is significant, but his acceptance of responsibility is more plausible in the stanza from 'The Tower' excerpted as my second epigraph, where he acknowledges his own over-intellectualized 'conscience' and 'cowardice' in 'turning aside' from the 'great labyrinth' that was Maud Gonne.

§

In 'The Cold Heaven,' Yeats was haunted by 'memories' of that 'love crossed long ago.' The volume following *Responsibilities*, the autumnal *The Wild Swans at Coole* (1917, 1919), is again haunted by memories, now of a man in his fifties, but feeling older. He is thinking of Iseult in 'The Living Beauty' ('O heart, we are old;/ The living beauty is for younger men:/ We cannot pay its tribute of wild tears'); but the heartache in the volume's beautifully elegiac title poem mingles thematically apt echoes of Wordsworth's 'Tintern Abbey' and Keats's 'Ode to a Nightingale' with memories of Maud and of his own lost youth. In autumn, at twilight, he has looked on the swans, paired lovers, 'And now my heart is sore.'

> Unwearied still, lover by lover,
> They paddle in the cold
> Companionable streams or climb the air;
> Their hearts have not grown old;
> Passion or conquest, wander where they will,
> Attend upon them still.

Like the Wye landscape in 'Tintern Abbey' and the 'immortal Bird' not 'born for death' in the 'Nightingale' ode, the swans are unchanged. But, as with mutable Wordsworth and Keats, 'All's changed' with the poet— in Yeats's case not only because the 'nineteenth autumn has come upon'

---

5   Book I of *De officiis*, Cicero's gathering together of many venerable examples of moral wisdom.

him since he first counted those wild and 'brilliant creatures,' but because he is writing in the immediate aftermath of Maud's recent rejection of yet another (and his final) proposal of marriage. Perhaps that is why (more counting) there are 'nine-and-fifty swans,' one unpaired and solitary.[6] Despite this one last marital attempt, these Maud-poems are, as Hassett remarks, less about Yeats's continued pursuit of an unattainable woman than a celebration of his Muse, and a recording, and interrogation, of his memories.

Five poems in *The Wild Swans at Coole* focus on Maud herself: 'Her Praise,' 'The People,' 'His Phoenix,' 'A Thought from Propertius,' and 'Broken Dreams.' And the 'Solomon and Sheba' poem preceding them, 'On Woman'—despite seeming to be associated with Yeats's wife, as are the other two 'Solomon and Sheba' poems—is a Maud Gonne poem in biblical disguise.

The first two honor her work on behalf of the Irish people. In 'the old days,' we are told in 'Her Praise,' because of her beauty and revolutionary energy, 'she had young men's praise and old men's blame,' an extension of the contrast between wary parent and smitten son on the momentous occasion of Willie's and John Butler Yeats's first encounter with Maud Gonne, when 'she vexed' his 'father by praise of war.' Now, writing in 1915, and wanting 'to talk no more of [...] the long war' actually in progress, a war condemned by Yeats and Maud alike, he returns to the past, concluding with an exception to 'old men's blame': 'Among the *poor* both old and young gave her praise.'

In the second poem, 'The People,' for Yeats a relatively rare (aside from 'The Second Coming' and his narrative poems) exercise in blank verse, the poet / playwright, defending art from philistine attacks and wishing he lived in Castiglione's courtly Urbino rather than 'unmannerly' Dublin, complains of being unappreciated by the Irish people. But then he recalls a 1906 conversation in which Maud had told him, after her 'luck changed' (referring to the hostile public response

---

6   From the time of his first visit to Coole Park, in 1897, Yeats had associated Maud with swans. He told her in an unpublished poem written that year, 'it is/ of you I sing when I tell/ of the swan in the water.' In this volume, even a creature of change—the charming replicator of the lunar phases who, in 'The Cat and the Moon,' creeps through the grass, 'Alone, important and wise,/ And lifts to the changing moon/ His changing eyes'—is related to Yeats's lunar Muse. Referred to by name, Minnaloushe was Maud's black male Persian cat.

to her legal separation from MacBride), that even when the 'dishonest crowd' she 'had driven away' set upon her those she had 'served' and sometimes 'fed,' she had 'never [...] now nor any time,/ Complained of the people.' He responds (in appropriately taut diction) that she has 'not lived in thought but deed,' and so has 'the purity of a natural force,' while he, a man of words rather than action, finds it hard to keep his critical 'tongue from speech.'

Maud had made a related point back in June 1897, in that earlier-mentioned letter to Yeats combining reprimand and recognition. The occasion of her reprimand was the memorable moment of conflict when Yeats had locked Maud inside the National Club, preventing her from joining the crowd during a particularly violent demonstration. That episode and Maud's response are sufficiently crucial to warrant stepping back from the poem for a few moments.

It was Maud, invited to speak by James Connolly himself, who had incited the crowd. The day before—Wolfe Tone's anniversary and the national day set aside for the decoration of patriot graves—Maud had sent a wreath to Tone's grave in Bodenstown, Co. Kildare, and gone herself to the cemetery adjoining St. Michan's Church in Dublin to lay a wreath in honor of Robert Emmet. But the 'great tomb-haunter' (as Yeats later called her in 'A Bronze Head') had been denied admission by the cemetery's custodian 'because it was Queen Victoria's Jubilee.' The next day, the crucial day, she roused the crowd: 'Must the graves of our dead go undecorated' because of the Jubilee of a queen during whose reign many Irish rebels were 'hanged for treason?' She then followed Connolly in a mock funeral procession down Dame Street behind a coffin labelled 'The British Empire' and festooned with black flags with the names of the martyrs on them. Unsurprisingly, as Yeats reports, 'the whole crowd went wild.' Maud's face, he adds, was 'joyous'; she was in her element. No sooner had she and Yeats paused for tea at the National Club than the protest turned into a full-scale riot, with an assault on window-breaking protesters by baton-wielding police. Maud was about to join the crowd, when Yeats, fearing she would be 'hurt' (some two hundred people *were*, according to the next day's *Irish Times*), insisted that, unless she explained what her intentions were, the door would be locked 'to keep her in.' His anything-but-fragile Muse bitterly resented his protective interference as she made clear in a letter written from London a few days later:

Our friendship must indeed be strong for me not to hate you, for you made me do the most cowardly thing I have ever done in my life. It is quite absurd to say I should have reasoned & given explanations. Do you ask a soldier for explanations on the battlefield of course it is only a very small thing a riot & a police charge but the same need for immediate action is there—there is no time to give explanations [...] I less than any others, would be capable of giving lengthy explanations of what I want and I intend to do, as my rule in life is to obey inspirations which come to me & which always guide me right.

Yeats would have been moved by the Romantic appeal to intuitive inspiration, and he might have been recalling this paragraph of Maud's letter and her rhetorical questions when, later and repeatedly, he singled out as his favorite saying of Nietzsche's Zarathustra: 'Am I a barrel of memories that I can give you my reasons?'[7] But Maud is not finished. 'For a long time,' she continues,

I had a feeling that I should not encourage you to mix yourself up in the *outer* [Maud's emphasis] side of politics & you know I have never asked you to do so. I see now that I was wrong in not obeying this feeling more completely & probably you were allowed to hinder me on that comparatively unimportant occasion to show me that it is necessary you should not mix in what is really not in your line of action. You have a higher work to do—With me it is different I was born to be in the midst of a crowd.

Those who did not 'go out to the rescue of the people' being beaten by the police 'ought to feel ashamed' of their 'inaction.' And she seems really to have believed that the worst incident, the death of 'that poor old woman Mrs. Fitzsimmons' who was 'allowed to fall' from the car

---

7   L, 650. The context has its own interest. In this June 1918 letter to his father, Yeats distinguishes between mere 'pietists' like Bunyan and the genuine seventeenth-century 'mystics,' who have also 'been great in intellect.' He was referring to Pascal and, especially, Spinoza, whose intellect he ranked even above 'the more merely professional intellect of the Victorians, even that of Mill.' Having demoted the favored thinkers of his positivist father, Yeats tells him: 'You should not conclude that if a man does not give his reasons he has none. Remember Zarathustra's 'Am I a barrel of memories that I can give you my reasons?' The passage Yeats is recalling is from Part II, §17 ('On Poets'). Asked by a disciple why he had said that 'poets lie too much,' Zarathustra responds: 'Why? You ask, why? I am not one of those whom one may ask about their why. Is my experience but of yesterday? It was long ago that I experienced the reasons for my opinions. Would I not have to be a barrel of memory if I wanted to carry my reasons around with me?' *Thus Spoke Zarathustra,* in *The Portable Nietzsche,* 238–39.

taking her to the hospital 'would not have happened if I had been able to do my duty.' Having, in effect, accused Yeats of complicity in a police murder, she levels that charge mentioned earlier in connection with Yeats's admission that one of the reasons he 'turned aside' from labyrinthine Maud was 'cowardice.' Maud herself mitigates the charge with a distinction: 'Do you know that to be a coward for those we love is only a degree less bad than to be a coward for oneself. The latter I know well you are not, the former you know well you are' (G-YL, 72–73).

There could not be a more dramatic example of her realization that their natures were antithetical; but that was hardly news to Yeats. Maud was, as she said, 'born to be in the midst of a crowd,' while he had 'a higher work to do,' and, as she added, whatever his nationalist commitment, he should not become involved 'in the *outer* side of politics.' She ended her letter by saying that, while they should not work together again 'where there is likely to be excitement or physical danger,' his speech to the Convention gathered together that June 22 (Yeats proposed that the Convention should declare 'its beliefs in the right of the freedom of Ireland' [G-YL, 466n]), was 'quite the best I have ever heard you make, it was magnificent,' capping his 'splendid work' during the centennial celebration of the 1798 Rising. In short, *his* medium was 'words,' not physical action. Though Yeats conceded that 'she was perhaps right to be angry when I refused to let her out unless she explained what she meant to do,' he also knew that, on 'principle,' she would not 'interfere' to stop the violence, in fact, would be far likelier to exacerbate it. 'She had taken all those people into her heart.'[8]

And these were the very people who, within a decade, in the wake of her legal separation from MacBride, had turned on her. In 'The People,' to return to the poem itself (an example of that 'higher work' he had to do), after recording Maud's insistence that, even after they had abandoned and attacked her, she never 'Complained of the people,' Yeats responds, at first and at some length, self-defensively, only to end in humbled yet excited silence:

---

8   Maud devoted much of chapter 10 of *A Servant of the Queen* (272–77) to these events. For Yeats's vivid remembrances, see Mem, 111–14, and Au, 366–68. When, in 'He wishes his Beloved were Dead,' Yeats depicts Maud 'murmur[ing] tender words,' and 'forgiving me,' it is to his intervention and Maud's reprimand that he refers.

> All I could reply
> Was: 'You that have not lived in thought but deed,
> Can have the purity of a natural force,
> But I, whose virtues are the definitions
> Of the analytic mind, can neither close
> The eye of the mind nor keep my tongue from speech.'
> And yet, because my heart leaped at her words,
> I was abashed, and now they come to mind
> After nine years, I sink my head abashed.

Like 'Her Praise,' this poem reassesses Yeats's resistance to, or condemnation of, Maud's fierce political activism, which he always considered his 'one visible rival' (Mem, 63) for her love. In 'The People,' though his position is articulated in a lucid syntax worthy of an analytic mind, there is still that 'And yet,' compelling the man of disciplined *intellect* to bow, abashed, because, as a reluctant admirer and last Romantic, his '*heart* leaped at her words.'

The next poem, the lengthy but lighthearted 'His Phoenix,' ticks off, in jaunty hexameters, a procession of stunning women, starting with an unnamed 'queen in China, or maybe it's in Spain,' whose beauty rivaled that of Leda, 'that sprightly girl trodden by a bird.' He goes through 'a score of duchesses, surpassing womankind,/ Or who have found a painter to make them so for pay,' and dancers, including the famed performers Ruth St. Denis and Pavlova, all 'breakers of men's hearts or engines of delight.' Maud was, as she herself said, 'born to be in the midst of a crowd.' So, too, with these acclaimed performers, though his 'heart denies' exact resemblance:

> There'll be that crowd, that barbarous crowd, through all the
>   centuries,
> And who can say but some young belle may walk and talk men wild
> Who is my beauty's equal, though that my heart denies,
> But not the exact likeness, the simplicity of a child,
> And that proud look as though she had gazed into the burning sun,
> And all that shapely body no tittle gone astray.
> I mourn for that most lonely thing; and yet God's will be done:
> I knew a phoenix in my youth, so let them have their day.

The celebration of the unique beauty of his phoenix is followed by 'A Thought from Propertius.' Echoing one of the Love Elegies of Sextus

Propertius (Book II, 'Her Beauty'), Yeats imagines Maud 'fit spoil for a centaur/ Drunk with the unmixed wine,' yet 'so noble from head' to foot that she might have 'walked to the altar/ Through the holy images/ At Pallas Athena's side.' (In the 1937 'Beautiful Lofty Things,' listing momentary images of 'Olympian' nobility permanently impressed on his memory, Yeats concludes with 'Maud Gonne at Howth station waiting a train,/ Pallas Athena in that straight back and arrogant head'—the single reference to her by name in his poetry.)

The short, tight Propertius poem is followed by 'Broken Dreams,' forty-one lines of artfully rambling reverie, rhymed but loose, to match its free associations. Maud was now fifty, a fact registered in the poem's opening lines: 'There is grey in your hair./ Young men no longer suddenly catch their breath when you are passing.' Yet

> For your sole sake—that all heart's ache have known,
> And given to others all heart's ache,
> From meager girlhood's putting on
> Burdensome beauty—for your sole sake
> Heaven has put away the stroke of her doom,
> So great her portion in that peace you make
> By merely walking in a room.

He imagines some young man asking an old man, 'Tell me of that lady/ The poet stubborn with his passion sang us/ When age might well have chilled his blood.' In a desperate certainty reflecting his reading of Plotinus and Swedenborg, he is confident, as he was *not* in 'King and No King,' that 'in the grave all, all, shall be renewed,' and that he would 'see that lady/ Leaning or standing or walking/ In the first loveliness of womanhood,/ And with the fervor of my youthful eyes.' Though 'more beautiful than anyone,' Maud Gonne had a flaw, her small hands, and he is afraid that she will run, and 'paddle to the wrist' in 'that mysterious, always brimming lake' where the blessed 'Paddle and are perfect.' A true lover, he has a final plea: 'leave unchanged/ The hands that I have kissed,/ For old sake's sake.' The 'last stroke of midnight dies,' ending a day in which he has 'ranged' from 'dream to dream and rhyme to rhyme,' in 'rambling talk with an image of air:/ Vague memories, nothing but memories.'

This Maud-cluster is preceded by 'On Woman' and framed by two short lyrics, 'Memory' and 'A Deep-sworn Vow,' to be discussed in a moment. 'On Woman' (1914) anticipates the 1918 'Solomon to Sheba' and 'Solomon and the Witch,' post-marital poems addressed to his wife. But the Sheba in this poem is allied with Maud. Solomon 'never could,' although 'he counted grass,/ Count all the praises due/ When Sheba was his lass.' If the sexual 'shudder that made them one' anticipates the 'shudder in the loins' in 'Leda and the Swan,' the concluding lines anticipate Self's choice, in 'A Dialogue of Self and Soul,' of eternal recurrence, with its 'fecund' intermingling of joy and pain. The question posed by Nietzsche's demon, introducing the thought-experiment or ordeal of Eternal Recurrence in *The Gay Science* §341, is a weighty one: 'Do you want this once more and innumerable times more?' The very thought, Nietzsche claims, might make you 'throw yourself down and gnash your teeth.' But, he continues, have you, 'even *once*,' experienced a 'moment' so 'tremendous' that you 'fervently craved' it 'once more' and 'eternally'? The speaker in 'On Woman' prays that God grant him, not 'here,' for he is 'not so bold as to 'hope a thing so dear/ Now I am growing old,'

> But when, if the tale's true,
> The Pestle of the moon
> That pounds up all anew
> Brings me to birth again—
> To find what once I had
> And know what once I have known,
> Until I am driven mad,
> Sleep driven from my bed,
> By tenderness and care,
> Pity, an aching head,
> Gnashing of teeth, despair;
> And all because of some one
> Perverse creature of chance,
> And live like Solomon
> That Sheba led a dance.

Here, as in 'Broken Dreams' and, a decade and a half later, in 'Quarrel in Old Age,' Yeats invokes renewal beyond the grave. 'All lives that has lived,' he announces in 'Quarrel' (1931); 'Old sages were not deceived:/ Somewhere beyond the curtain/ Of distorting days/ Lives that lonely thing/ That shone before these eyes': Maud Gonne, who seemed armed like a goddess and 'trod like Spring.' It is a recurrent hope, compounded of Plotinus, Swedenborg's vision of frustrated lovers posthumously united, and the embrace, by Nietzsche's Zarathustra, of the eternal recurrence of passion and joy, no matter the attendant and inevitable suffering. And, as in 'On Woman,' 'all because of some *one*/ Perverse creature'—'*that* one.'

The two short framing lyrics I referred to both consist of six trimeter lines rhymed *abcabc*, and both emphasize the indelible imprint of the unique among the many. There are all the 'others,' and then there is Maud. The title of the mini-lyric, 'Memory,' could refer to all the Maud Gonne poems:

> One had a lovely face,
> And two or three had charm.
> But charm and face were in vain
> Because the mountain grass
> Cannot but keep the form
> Where the mountain hare has lain.

What better image for the impress of memory than the crushed grass where the elusive mountain hare has lain, a hollow enshrining an absent presence? She is gone, but the 'form,' at once palpable and Platonic, remains forever.

Maud had told Yeats she would never marry him, and that he should be 'glad,' since 'you make beautiful poetry' out of what you call your 'unhappiness.' But she also swore she would marry no one else. She did. 'A Deep-sworn Vow' registers that broken oath and its sexual consequences for him. Yet he has been faithful in his fashion; for 'always,' at intense moments of truth—the imagining of one's death, at the height of visionary dream, in the *veritas* of wine—when the defense mechanisms are down, there is a sudden return of the repressed:

> Others because you did not keep
> That deep-sworn vow have been friends of mine;
> Yet always when I look death in the face,
> When I clamber to the heights of sleep,
> Or when I grow excited with wine,
> Suddenly I meet your face.

The opening 'others,' the ostensible subject of this sestet, are swiftly dismissed as of no intrinsic value; they exist solely to be differentiated from 'you,' the vow-breaker. This is typical of the much-admired economy and mounting excitement of the poem. That astute close reader, R. P. Blackmur, memorably observed that 'possibly all poetry should be read as this poem is read, and no poetry greatly valued that cannot be so read. Such is one ideal standard toward which reading tends.'[9] He added that 'to apply that standard of judgment one should first have to assume for the poetic intelligence absolute autonomy and self-perfection for all its works.' I'm tempted to quibble with that 'absolute autonomy' by suggesting that this poem, like 'Her Triumph,' in 'A Woman Young and Old,' has a precursor in the break-out poem that first revealed the genius of John Keats: 'On First Looking into Chapman's Homer.'

In 'A Deep-sworn Vow,' though expected ('always'), the revelation is *sudden*. As in the discovery of true love in 'Her Triumph' ('And now we stare astonished at the sea'), Yeats seems to me, thematically and phonetically, to be recalling the sestet of the sonnet in which Keats compared his discovery of Homer to the awed moment when the ocean's Spanish discoverers 'star'd at the Pacific,' and the conquistador and his men looked at each other 'with a wild surmise—/ Silent, upon a peak in Darien.' In 'A Deep-sworn Vow,' Yeats does not *fall* asleep; he vigorously 'clambers' to its visionary 'heights.' He repeats ('heights,' 'excited,' 'wine') the long *i* of Keats's 'wild,' 'surmise,' 'silent.' And both poems end with a double caesura preceding the abrupt revelation. When Maud's 'face' looms up from the subconscious, it is a chthonic apparition, the rare exact rhyme making *her* 'face' indistinguishable from the 'face' of *death*, as befits a *femme fatale*. It took the subconscious breakthrough of a poem for Yeats to acknowledge the revelation that had come to Lady Gregory intuitively on first being introduced by Yeats to the object of his obsession. Maud was ill at the time, which may explain in part why that first meeting, Lady Gregory reports, was a 'shock' to her, continuing that: 'instead of beauty I saw a death's head.'[10]

In the next chapter we will begin with Maud Gonne, in her own name, depicted as a death's-head. In both Byzantium poems and 'Lapis Lazuli,' Yeats, like Shelley in 'Ozymandias' and Keats in the 'Ode on a Grecian Urn,' wrote about sculpted art; but his most terrifying exercise in *ekphrasis* is his sustained contemplation of the bust of Maud Gonne in 'A Bronze Head.'

---

9   Blackmur, 'The Later Poetry of W. B. Yeats,' 48.
10   *Lady Gregory's Diaries, 1892–1902*, 197. Though wary of her besotted friend's Muse, the 'ever-kind' Lady Gregory was legally of great help to Maud, protecting her money during her marriage to MacBride.

14. 'A Bronze Head' and Beyond

Since the death's-head image of 'A Deep-sworn Vow' culminates in the last and most somberly impressive of the Maud Gonne poems, 'A Bronze Head' (1938), I will move directly to that poem, deferring comment on two Maud-related poems ('An Image from a Past Life' and 'Under Saturn') from *Michael Robartes and the Dancer* (1921), the volume that follows *The Wild Swans at Coole.* I have already noted the presence of Maud in the 1921 volume's 'A Prayer for my Daughter.'

'A Bronze Head' is curiously related to 'Among School Children.' Just as the late play *Purgatory* is the nightmare twin of 'A Dialogue of Self and Soul,' animating the terror implicit in Nietzschean Eternal Recurrence (the enactment 'again, and yet again,' ultimately embraced in the 'Dialogue'), so 'A Bronze Head' seems a darker re-examination of the relationships explored in 'Among School Children' between unity and division, the One and the Many, underlying substance and its various manifestations. The crucial philosophic question and speculation in the later poem is restricted to Maud, ever a shape-shifter: 'who can tell/ Which of her forms has shown her substance right?/ Or maybe substance can be composite.' In a poem riddled with Shakespearean echoes, Yeats is here recalling Sonnet 53, where Shakespeare wonders about the beloved's Platonic essence and its relationship to her accidental attributes, her external appearances: 'What is your substance, whereof are you made,/ That millions of strange shadows on you tend?' Such speculations would be no less at home in the poem in which the Yeatsian old man walks through the long schoolroom 'questioning,' dreaming of a 'Ledaean body,' Maud's, and what came before and after: the beloved as 'child' and in her 'present' form, feeding on the insubstantial, her image (visually Dantesque, verbally Shakespearean

 https://doi.org/10.11647/OBP.0275.15

and Miltonic) 'Hollow of cheek as though it drank the wind/ And took a mess of shadows for its meat.'[1]

That is the image, though even further time-ravaged, sculpted in the plaster of Lawrence Campbell's bronze-painted bust in the Municipal Gallery. Though that bust is at the right of the entrance, Yeats chose not to mention it in 'The Municipal Gallery Revisited,' written shortly after an emotional visit to the Gallery in August 1937. The many artworks he describes in that poem were all paintings, and all stirred memories of lost friends and co-workers. Was the bust of Maud, her beauty now a magnificent ruin, too painful to contemplate? Or was it that, as usual, she was not to be included among 'others,' and had to have a poem devoted to herself alone? 'A Bronze Head' is certainly unique in its form: Yeats's sole venture in rime royal, a seven-line iambic pentameter stanza rhyming *ababbcc*.

The *hysterica passio* Yeats, borrowing from *King Lear*, attributes to Maud Gonne in 'A Bronze Head' anticipates a 2003 ekphrastic poem on Edvard Munch's famous 1910 painting 'The Scream.' In 'Stealing the Scream,' Monica Youn emphasizes 'the figure's fixed hysteria.' But not even the titular sculpture in the Municipal Gallery could permanently fix the protean image of his beloved for Yeats. She is an artifact, but also something 'Human, superhuman, a bird's round eye,/ Everything else withered and mummy-dead.' Though now a 'great tomb-haunter' sweeping the 'distant sky' and terrified by the '*hysterica passio*' of her 'own emptiness,' she was 'once' a 'form all full/ As though with magnanimity of light.' Yet she is also 'a most gentle woman.' And there is more. As the poet first saw her, she was an unmanageable filly—'even at the starting post, all sleek and new,/ I saw the wildness in her'—and a vulnerable human creature, her animal wildness transferred by empathy to the protective poet-lover, who 'had grown wild/ And wandered

---

1   Yeats is fusing images from *Hamlet*, *King Lear*, and Milton's 'Lycidas.' 'How fares our cousin Hamlet?' asks Claudius. 'Excellent, i' faith, of the chameleon's dish,' quips Hamlet; 'I eat the air, promise crammed. You cannot feed capons so.' In 'Lycidas,' St. Peter refers to 'hungry sheep [...] not fed,/ But swoln with wind' (125–26). In addition to imbibing air and wind, the voracious image of Maud 'took a *mess* of shadows for its *meat*.' When he foolishly casts Cordelia from him, Lear makes his 'sometime daughter' as alien to him as 'he that makes his generations *messes*/ To gorge his *appetite*.' The 'propinquity' disclaimed by Lear, is echoed in 'A Bronze Head,' which not only borrows from *Lear* that rare word, but, obviously, transfers to Maud Lear's '*hysterica passio*.'

murmuring everywhere, "My child, my child!"' Finally, returning to the 'bird's round eye' of the opening stanza, Yeats describes her in her anything but vulnerable aspect, possessing a supernatural 'sterner eye.'

Dispensing round his magnanimity of images, Yeats goes beyond the triads of 'Among School Children'—though there too Maud had been evoked as child, beautiful woman, and aged crone, even as bird (a Ledaean 'daughter of the swan') and animal (a wind-drinking chameleon). The poet of 'Among School Children' questions the chestnut tree of the final stanza: 'Are you the leaf, the blossom or the bole?' It is of course all three since we can no more break down the organic unity of that 'great rooted blossomer' than we can 'know the dancer from the dance,' or isolate Maud as child from Maud as 'Ledaean body,' or from her 'present image' as hollow-cheeked but still voracious crone. Yet it is as a crone that Yeats compels us to envisage Maud Gonne in 'A Bronze Head'—compels us by ending his poem in a repetition and intensification of that 'present image.' In the final eugenically tainted movement, he imagines her as if 'a sterner eye looked through her eye/ On this foul world in its decline and fall,/ On gangling stocks grown great, great stocks run dry,/ Ancestral pearls all pitched into a sty.'

The bird-like 'sterner eye' looking through Maud's eye—that 'mysterious eye' that, Yeats reports with fascination and dread, at least one British journalist felt, at the height of her anti-British activism, 'contained the shadow of battles yet to come' (Mem, 60)—seems both a projection of Yeats's own clairvoyant and apocalyptic eye, and that of the Morrigu, the one-eyed 'woman with the head of a crow.' It seems to be that Celtic war-goddess who presides here, her 'sterner eye' looking through the 'eye' of Maud, that 'dark tomb-haunter,' on a corrupt world in decline, and wondering 'what was left for massacre to save.'

The Morrigu, the Celtic demoniac bird of the dead who haunts corpse-strewn battlefields, is the dark side of the Old Woman who demands 'all' of her devotees in the 1902 play, written for Maud's nationalist organization, The Daughters of Ireland, in which Maud herself, playing Cathleen ni Houlihan, personified the oppression and resurrection of Ireland: the old crone transfigured into 'a young girl' with 'the walk of a queen,' rejuvenated by blood sacrifice.

That climax was anticipated, reports Stephen Gwynn, present on opening night, when Maud's Cathleen rose, 'still bent and weighed down with years or centuries; but for one instant, before she went out at the half-door, she drew herself up to her superb height; change was manifest; *patuit dea.*'[2] Written twenty years after Easter 1916, Gwynn's description of the electrifying impact of the play's climax, 'Change was manifest,' echoes Yeats's 'all changed, changed utterly.' Gwynn is also echoing the passage of the *Aeneid* Yeats had cited in recalling his first glimpse of Maud. Both of their Virgilian allusions are apt; though she is disguised as a Spartan huntress, Venus was revealed to Aeneus as she walked away, '*vera incessu patuit dea*,' [the true goddess revealed in her step] (*Aeneid* 1.405). But Gwynn, like Yeats a Protestant constitutional nationalist, also 'went home asking myself if such plays should be produced unless one was prepared for people to go out to shoot and be shot.' As we will see, echoing his echoer, Yeats asked himself that very question preparing for his own death. Maud, too, comes full circle: from the beautiful woman bent and hidden under the rags of the Old Woman of *Cathleen ni Houlihan*, to an actual old woman: the literal terrible beauty of 'A Bronze Head.'

§

No wonder there were 'others,' pre- and post-marital minor Muses, even the poet's wife: important but none of them as magnetic as Maud, who intrudes even into those relationships and the poems celebrating them. Thanks to the work of Joseph Hassett there is no need to deal with these women in more than a peripheral way. In his lucid study of Yeats and his Muses, Hassett captures the essence of the poet's relationships with, not only Maud and her daughter Iseult, but with seven other inspiring women, beginning with Olivia Shakespear and Florence Farr; including the poet's wife, George Hyde-Lees; and ending with Margot Ruddock, Ethel Mannin, Dorothy Wellesley, and Edith Shackleton Heald. I will limit myself to saying a few things about the poetry involving the lovely Olivia, and about poems having to do, essentially, with the occult interests of the poet's wife, with whom he collaborated.

Olivia Shakespear introduced Yeats to sexual love in 1896, and they shared 'many days of happiness.' Olivia took his virginity, but could not uproot Maud, who remained an obsession. 'I had a beautiful friend,'

---

2   For Gwynn's description of the impact of *Cathleen ni Houlihan*, see his *Irish Literature and Drama*, 158–60.

he mourns in an 1898 poem addressed to Maud, 'And dreamed that the old despair/ Would end in love in the end:/ She looked in my heart one day,/ And saw your image was there.' Despite the tearful parting that followed, Olivia remained his lifelong friend and most intimate correspondent. In December 1929, Yeats, who wrote to her of their love as a 'cup left half tasted,' sent her the poignant 'After Long Silence,' a meeting of minds rather than of now-decrepit bodies, love's heartache distilled in the single word 'young,' hovering at the end of the penultimate line. The poem is an *abbacddc* octave, a semi-Petrarchan sonnet truncated because there was no more to say:

> Speech after long silence; it is right,
> All other lovers being estranged or dead,
> Unfriendly lamplight hid under its shade,
> The curtains drawn upon unfriendly night,
> That we descant and yet again descant
> Upon the supreme theme of Art and Song:
> Bodily decrepitude is wisdom; young
> We loved each other and were ignorant.[3]

The late marriage to his wife, Georgie Hyde-Lees, in 1917 (he was 52, she half his age) ushered in Yeats's most creative period. Her interest in the occult matched his: her gift co-creating *A Vision*. While the 'learning' they share is stressed in 'Solomon to Sheba' (the third and final 'Solomon and Sheba' poem), the playful but serious 'Solomon and the Witch' fuses the erotic and occult in almost world-ending sexual ecstasy. But since 'the world stays,' Sheba cries out in the final lines: 'the moon is wilder every minute./ O! Solomon! Let us try again.' Yet the poem also acknowledges that the 'bride-bed' can bring 'despair,/ For each an imagined image brings/ And finds a real image there.' This candid reflection of biography—the couple's Maud- and Iseult-haunted

---

3   The end of their love affair was publicly, though anonymously, recorded in 'The Lover mourns for the Loss of Love' (1898), in *The Wind Among the Reeds*. Privately, Yeats quoted Olivia directly: 'There is someone else in your heart" (Mem, 88–89). In December 1926, thirty years after their love affair, Yeats wrote to Olivia, with whom he maintained a deep friendship until her death in 1938, a death that devastated him: 'One looks back to one's youth as to a cup that a mad man dying of thirst left half tasted. I wonder if you feel like that' (L, 721; cf. 'The Empty Cup,' poem V in 'A Man Young and Old'). She may well have; if so, it was a shared feeling movingly expressed in the final heartbreaking lines of 'After Long Silence.'

honeymoon—is fleshed out in the two poems that immediately follow (though written a year later).

In the second, 'Under Saturn,' the poet asks how he should 'forget the wisdom that you brought,/ The comfort that you made?' But he has to ask the question in the first place because, having 'grown saturnine,' he fears she might 'Imagine that lost love, inseparable from my thought/ Because I have no other youth, can make me pine.' Like Olivia, George saw Maud's image there. In 'An Image from a Past Life,' the immediately preceding dialogue-poem, *She,* possessed like George of occult powers, senses that

> A sweetheart from another life floats there
> As though she had been forced to linger
> From vague distress
> Or arrogant loveliness,
> Merely to loosen out a tress
> Among the starry eddies of her hair
> Upon the paleness of a finger.

He reassures her that any such image, 'even to eyes that beauty had driven mad,' can only make him 'fonder.' Unconvinced, *She* does not know whether the uplifted arms of the spectral figure intend to 'flout' her, or (in another hauntingly exquisite tress-centered tercet) 'to find,/ Now that no fingers bind,/ That her hair streams upon the wind.' Given these glimpses of Pre-Raphaelite beauty, what *She* definitely *does* know is: 'I am afraid/ Of the hovering thing night brought me.'

Given the mysterious wisdom brought to the poet as the wedding gift of his wife's occult 'Communicators,' it is less surprising than it might otherwise be that Yeats's most direct love poem to George should occur in the Browningesque dramatic monologue, 'The Gift of Harun Al-Rashid' (1924). The 'gift' the great caliph gives to his friend and learned treasurer Kusta Ben Luka is a woman who shares his 'thirst' for 'old crabbed mysteries,' yet 'herself can seem youth's very fountain,/ Being all brimmed with life' (85–90). Whatever the source of the 'Voice' of the Djinn she heard, Kusta comes to realize that his young wife is not simply a conduit. He now knows, instead, that that mysterious voice has drawn 'A quality of wisdom from her love's/ Particular quality.' The signs, shapes, and abstractions, 'All, all those gyres and cubes and midnight things/ Are but a new expression of her body/ Drunk with the bitter sweetness of her youth./ And now my utmost mystery is out' (179–87).

But this 'embodied' revelation is followed immediately by the poem's concluding lines, in which Kusta-Yeats insists that, while 'A woman's beauty is a storm-tossed banner,' he is neither 'dazzled by the embroidery, nor lost/ In the confusion of its night-dark folds.' This imagery echoes the poem's opening 'banners of the Caliphs,' hanging 'night-coloured/ But brilliant as the night's embroidery' (6–7); but in the *full context* of Yeats's love poetry, the image inevitably recalls 'the heaven's embroidered cloths'—'Enwrought with golden and silver light,/ The blue and the dim and the dark cloths/ Of night and light and the half-light'—the young, Maud-dazzled poet wished to 'spread' under her 'feet.' Now, a quarter-century later, he is no longer 'dazzled' by the storm-tossed and night-dark but brilliant embroidery because, ostensibly, he is choosing wisdom over beauty—autobiographically, George over Maud. That is what he had actually done a decade earlier when he turned Maud, illegally in Ireland to celebrate the December 1918 Sinn Fein victory, away from the door of her own house (which she had made available to the Yeatses) in order to protect his wife— pregnant and ill with the influenza that would take far more lives than the Great War itself—from a potential police raid. This literal 'turning aside' from the 'great labyrinth' was the cause of much gossip in Dublin, and created a wound between Yeats and Maud that took long to heal.

§

'The Gift of Harun Al-Rashid' is the penultimate poem in *The Tower*, preceded by 'A Man Young and Old.' In this eleven-poem sequence, Yeats, masked as Everyman, gives us symbolic autobiography, with anonymous appearances by Maud and Iseult. The emotional / erotic tensions involving Yeats, George (his new wife), Maud, and Iseult, also play out in *The Only Jealousy of Emer* (1919), the most lyrical of the Cuchulain plays. That play opens with the First Musician's 'Song for the folding and unfolding of the cloth,' in which the 'loveliness' of 'a woman's beauty' is compared to that of a 'white sea-bird alone/ At daybreak after a stormy night,' and to an 'exquisite' seashell the 'vast troubled waters bring/ To the loud sands before day has broken': a beauty-producing violence 'imagined within/ The labyrinth of the mind,' an autobiographical maze intricate enough to enfold three women barely detectable beneath the otherworldly mythology.

In 'First Love,' the opening poem of 'A Man Young and Old,' Yeats's mask as Everyman slips from the outset, and the lunar figure is clearly based on Maud. 'Though nurtured like the sailing moon/ In beauty's murderous brood,' she walked and blushed awhile and 'on my pathway stood/ Until I thought her body bore/ A heart of flesh and blood.' But since he 'laid a hand thereon,/ And found a heart of stone,' he realizes that 'every hand is lunatic./ That travels on the moon.' She 'smiled and that transfigured me/ And left me but a lout,' wandering aimlessly, 'Emptier of thought/ Than the heavenly circuit of its stars/ When the moon sails out.' And this painful but lyrically beautiful final stanza of the first poem leads directly to the lunar opening of the next in the sequence: 'Like the moon her kindness is/ If kindness I may call' what has no 'comprehension' in it, 'But is the same for all/ As though my sorrow were a scene/ Upon a painted wall.'

It should be mentioned that, in contrast to this otherwise man-centered sequence, poem IV, 'The Death of the Hare,' expresses unexpected empathy for the *female* in the love-hunt. The Man's 'heart is wrung,' when he remembers her 'wildness lost.' He empathetically feels the 'yelling pack' (a likely echo of the hostile mob that turned on Maud after her separation from MacBride), and, finally, the death of the pursued animal. 'The Death of the Hare,' looking back to Maud as 'mountain hare' in 'Memory,' anticipates the 'stricken rabbit' whose death cry 'distracts' Yeats's 'thought' in 'Man and the Echo.' It also anticipates the empathy with Maud in 'A Bronze Head' ('my child, my child'), as well as the female perspective expressed throughout 'A Woman Young and Old'—the sequence that ends *The Winding Stair*, just as the 'Man' sequence ends *The Tower*.

The poems that follow in the Man sequence emphasize the ecstasy and tragedy at the heart of the Yeats–Gonne relationship, especially in Poem VI, 'His Memories,' and VIII, 'Summer and Spring.' In the former, in the guise of an anonymous old man, his body 'broken,' Yeats claims, even more graphically than in the poem addressed to Maud's daughter, 'To a Young Girl,' that the relationship with his Helen, the 'first of all the tribe,' was sexually, and triumphantly, consummated. His 'arms' may be 'like twisted thorn/ And yet there beauty lay,'

And did such pleasure take—
She who had brought great Hector down
And put all Troy to wreck—
That she cried into this ear,
'Strike me if I shriek.'

Two decades later, that night in December 1908, no matter how fleeting, remains paramount among the 'memories' of Yeats's 'Man Old.' Since Maud was, ultimately, 'not kindred of his soul,' Yeats sought complete union, if only in memory, in poetry, and, specifically, masked as 'A Man Young and Old.' In 'Summer and Spring,' poem VIII of the sequence, two lovers grown old reminisce 'under an old thorn-tree.' Talking of growing up, they 'Knew that we'd halved a soul/ And fell the one in 'tother's arms/ That we might make it whole.' We recall, as we are meant to, 'Among School Children,' written in the same year. In that great poem, transitioning from the first to the second stanza, we shift abruptly from Yeats's persona as senator and school inspector, 'a sixty-year-old smiling public man,' to the private, inner man: the poet himself reporting an incident Maud, that 'daughter of the swan' and of Leda, once related from her childhood:

I dream of a Ledaean body, bent
Above a sinking fire, a tale that she
Told of a harsh reproof, or trivial event
That changed some childish day to tragedy—
Told, and it seemed that our two natures blent
Into a sphere from youthful sympathy,
Or else, to alter Plato's parable,
Into the yolk and white of the one shell.

The blending is poignant, but the tragedy lies in the need 'to alter Plato's parable,' since the merging here is empathetic and partial (there remains a separation between yolk and white even within the unity of the 'one shell') rather than the full sexual-emotional union of Aristophanes' haunting fable in Plato's *Symposium*. It is a 'whole' union the old man claims in 'His Memories' and in 'Summer and Spring,' which concludes with a sexual variation on the unity of being symbolized in 'Among School Children' by the dancer and 'great rooted blossomer': 'O what a bursting out there was,/ And what a blossoming,/ When we had all the summer-time/ And she had all the spring!'

Even here, however fecund the bursting out and blossoming, it is all memory and heartache. As in most of the Maud poems, 'Love,' mingling strength and sweetness, is at once vulnerable—that 'bitter sweetness,/ Inhabitant of the soft cheek of a girl'—and immensely powerful. I am quoting 'From the *Antigone*,' the finale of 'A Woman Young and Old,' the concluding poem of *The Winding Stair*. Adapting Sophocles' fourth choral ode (the Eros chorus and its anapestic coda) and expanding on 'No Second Troy,' where Maud would have 'hurled the little streets upon the great,' Yeats, mingling Sappho with Sophocles, calls on Love, 'O bitter sweetness' (Sappho's famous oxymoron), to 'Overcome the Empyrean; hurl/ Heaven and Earth out of their places,' that in 'the Same calamity,' brothers, friends, and families, even 'City and city may contend,/ By that great glory driven wild.'[4]

In 'No Second Troy,' Yeats tells us that Maud could not have 'done' otherwise, '*being* what she *is*.' That is her quintessence, as political firebrand and as Muse. And, from 'No Second Troy' to 'A Bronze Head,' what she *is*, under all her myriad 'forms,' is a Helen reborn. As Yeats reminds us in 'The Tower,' II (where he also alludes to Maud as 'a woman lost' and the 'great labyrinth' from which he admits he 'turned aside'), the 'tragedy began/ With Homer that was a blind man,/ And Helen has all living hearts betrayed.' That establishes the pattern for both Maud *and* Yeats, whose Self in 'Dialogue' is 'a blind man,' plunging into 'a blind man's ditch,' especially 'that most fecund ditch of all,' the folly one does or 'must suffer' if one falls hopelessly in love with a woman fated to re-enact the role of Homer's Helen. 'No Second Troy' and, even more, 'From the *Antigone*' (altered with the help of his friend Ezra Pound) suggest that, like Pound in Canto II, Yeats was aware of the punning epithets on her 'fatal' name in the choral ode in Aeschylus' *Agamemnon* where she is called (line 689) *helénaus, hélandros, heléptolis*: deadly destroyer of ships, of men, of cities. Mythologized by Yeats as a reincarnation of the Greek Helen, Maud Gonne is not only the paragon of beauty, but of a terrible beauty at once inspiring and, inevitably, *destructive*. Yet she is also 'a most gentle woman,' vulnerable and evoking protective feelings even in 'A Bronze Head' and, in displaced form, in 'The Death of the Hare.' At the end of this chapter, I will suggest

---

4   Poet-scholar Anne Carson's now classic 1986 book *Eros the Bittersweet* has enhanced the fame of Sappho's Fragment 130: 'Once again limb-loosening love makes me spin, the bittersweet [*glukupikron*], irresistible creature.'

a connection with Maud Gonne even in 'Man and the Echo,' which ends with the stricken cry of a rabbit.

§

In another late, great summing-up poem, 'The Circus Animals' Desertion' (1938), Maud emerges once again as the poet's inspiring Muse, the source of his painful but creative heartbreak. 'The Circus Animals' Desertion,' in three parts and five *ottava rima* stanzas, begins with the poet-playwright, like Coleridge in the 'Dejection' ode, at the end of his imaginative tether: 'I sought a theme and sought for it in vain.' Forced to 'enumerate old themes,' the aged poet-playwright admits that his formative dramatic works, though they eventually 'took all' his 'love,' were sublimations: 'emblems of' the 'Heart mysteries' associated with his unrequited love for Maud Gonne, a painful but productive obsession.

He omits the play actually featuring Maud in the title role, *Cathleen ni Houlihan* (which he had addressed in the immediately preceding poem, 'Man and the Echo'), to focus on still earlier and less overt dramatic works. Even the epic *The Wanderings of Oisin*, his first major work and the poem that brought him to Maud's attention, anticipates her coming into his life. The poem's hero, Oisin, is a 'sea-rider [...] led by the nose' by the goddess Niamh, who—as Hazard Adams points out, breaking his own anti-biographical critical creed—'exceeds her false world' of Fairyland, 'and threatens already (though we can't know this quite yet) to break into real life as the beloved of the later poems, finally named Maud Gonne.'[5] In 'The Circus Animals' Desertion,' Yeats asks and answers his own question: 'But what cared I that set him on to ride,/ I, starved for the bosom of his fairy bride?'

That epic's 'counter-truth,' his play *The Countess Cathleen*, dealt with physical starvation. The mythical Countess's benignly Faustian sacrifice of her own soul to save her starving people (a theme defended by young James Joyce alone among scandalized University College Dublin students) reflected the actual efforts of Maud, originally scheduled to play the title role, to feed the populace in famine-struck Donegal. But, intensifying Maud Gonne's bartering of the Horn of Plenty for an 'old bellows full of angry wind' (in 'A Prayer for my Daughter'), Yeats cries

---

5   Hazard Adams, *The Book of Yeats's Poems*, 37.

out: 'I thought my dear must her own soul destroy/ So did fanaticism and hate enslave it.' These 'Heart mysteries' were transformed into 'masterful' images, 'complete' because they 'grew in pure mind but out of what began?'

Having deconstructed his early work, including the first of his Cuchulain plays, to reveal its partial genesis in the unrequited love of Maud Gonne, Yeats audaciously gives us, as his mature genetic material, the lowest, most profanely debased matrix-forms of the central icons of his greatest poetry: the 'moonlit or starlit' dome of Byzantium generated out of, or reduced to, a squalid 'mound of refuse or the sweepings of a street,' lines echoing the 'Sweepings from Butcher's Stalls, Dung, Guts, and Blood' of Jonathan Swift's 'A Description of a City Shower,' precisely the sort of 'clutter' in which Richard Ellmann says Joyce 'revels,' but by which 'Yeats, conceiving of art as purgation, was repelled.'[6] Similarly, the ancestral sword of his canon- and life-defining poem, 'A Dialogue of Self and Soul,' that Japanese sword whose scabbard is bound and wound in 'flowering, silken, old embroidery,/Torn from some court lady's dress,' embroidery of 'Heart's purple,' which Yeats, fusing sword and silk, sets up as his life-affirming 'emblems of the day against the tower/ Emblematical of the night,' is reduced to a junkyard's 'old iron [...] old rags.' The Muse herself, tallying up the loss and gain in the transformation of pain into poetry, is degraded, beneath the old Paudeen who 'fumbles in a greasy till' in 'September 1913,' lower down in the social register: 'that raving slut/ Who keeps the till' in a transactional enterprise Yeats literally labelled (in an early draft of 'The Circus Animals' Desertion') 'Heart and Company.'

Though the drafts of the poem reveal that all references to the 'heart' were added late in the process of composition,[7] the Maud-inspired creativity that rose from Yeats's 'heart's root' and 'aching heart' was always already implicit. (In another belated addition, to 'Two Songs

---

6   *Eminent Domain*, 55. Seamus Heaney, though he described the 'carrying power' and 'music' of the Byzantium poems as 'phenomenal,' relocated Yeats's Byzantium to his own more Patrick Kavanagh-like roots in a Derry farmhouse: 'my starlight came in over the half-door of a house with a clay floor, not over the dome of a Byzantine palace; and in a hollowed-out part of the floor, there was a cat licking up the starlit milk.' Dennis O'Driscoll, *Stepping Stones: Interviews with Seamus Heaney* (New York: Farrar, Straus and Giroux, 2008), 318.

7   A point made by the same scholar who had discovered the handwritten note indicating Yeats's desired ordering of his final volume. See Curtis Bradford, 'The Order of *Yeats's Last Poems*', 515–16; and his *Yeats at Work*, 164.

from a Play,' the play being *The Resurrection*, we are told that 'Whatever flames upon the night/ Man's own resinous heart has fed.'[8]) The silk-wound sword of 'A Dialogue of Self and Soul,' and of 'Meditations in Time of Civil War,' III, though 'Curved like new moon,' is itself 'changeless'; yet, 'if no change appears/ No moon; only an aching heart/ Conceives a changeless work of art.'

Fulfilling his opening premonition that, 'Maybe at last being but a broken man/ I must be satisfied with my heart,' a submissive yet triumphant Yeats—now that his Platonic 'ladder's gone,' and acknowledging (like Crazy Jane) that 'fair and foul are near of kin,/ And fair needs foul'—concludes that the *source* of his 'masterful images,' which 'grew in pure mind,' is to be found at the corrupt but creatively fecund 'lower-most step' (as Pietro Bembo called it in *The Courtier*) of the Platonic *scala coeli*; 'I must lie down where all the ladders start/ In the foul rag and bone shop of the heart.'

In the end, the old man, deprived of his means of ascent—seemingly imaginative, perhaps phallic—must return to the foul but fertile place of origin at the foot of the ladder, where he 'must lie down.' The auxiliary verb 'must,' intentionally Janus-faced, implies less a final act of abasement, a defeat, and a passive acceptance of Fate than a chosen Destiny, a paradoxically necessary yet courageously autonomous imperative, even something of a triumph. Many of the Maud Gonne poems seem acts of abasement, and, in actual life, may have been 'the way to lose a woman'—as he said of the famous poem in which, being 'poor' and unable to afford 'the heaven's embroidered cloths,' he had spread his dreams 'under your feet;/ Tread softly because you tread on my dreams.' Whether or not they were the way to lose a woman, and Maud was never, really, a woman to be won, the poems themselves were triumphant.

Only an aching heart 'conceives' a 'changeless work of art,' and, as Maud herself claimed, the poems they birthed together would outlive them. Those changeless poems were conceived in the heart—not in what Alexander Pope, describing the Sylph-taught 'varying vanities' of his inconstant society coquettes, called, 'the moving Toyshop of their heart,' but in that grounded 'foul rag and bone shop of the heart,' the matrix of a far more profound suffering and creativity. Though, as Maud said, the

---

8   The rest of the two-part, four-stanza poem, songs to open and close the curtain of the play *The Resurrection*, was written in 1926; this final stanza was added in 1931.

poems written for her sake 'had wings,' their heart-mysteries were far removed from Pope's flighty Sylphs who 'sport and flutter in the Fields of Air.'[9]

The play omitted in 'The Circus Animals' Desertion,' *Cathleen ni Houlihan*, features in the confessional masterpiece written thirty-six years later, 'Man and the Echo,' which borrows the self-questioning (and the tetrameters) of Coleridge's confessional, 'The Pains of Sleep.' In 'Man and the Echo,' a Man (nameless but manifestly Yeats) halted in a rock cleft on the side of Knocknarea, 'shouts a secret to the stone,' a confession that 'All seems evil until I/ Sleepless would lie down and die.' He is in the same sleepless perplexity and anguish as Coleridge: 'All confused I could not know/ Whether I suffered or I did:/ For all seemed guilt, remorse or woe.' Whatever demons, some of them laudanum-induced, kept Coleridge awake at night, the cause of Yeats's guilt and remorse is made clear at the outset, in paradoxically shouting his 'secret' to the echoing stone:

> All that I have said and done,
> Now that I am old and ill,
> Turns into a question till
> I lie awake night after night
> And never get the answers right.
> Did that play of mine send out
> Certain men the English shot?

Two other queries follow (in which Yeats wonders if 'words of mine' could have helped 'save' Lady Gregory's Coole Park or Margot Ruddock's crazed mind), but the primary question, about 'that play of mine,' refers to *Cathleen ni Houlihan*, that ostensible celebration of blood-sacrifice written for and starring Maud Gonne as Ireland herself. Considered a 'sacrament' by nationalists like Con Markiewicz, the play *did* send out men that were shot in the Easter Rising; in fact, the first to die was an actor cast in a revival of the play. The 'terrible beauty' born that Easter had many causes, but Yeats, fingering the chain of responsibility, wondered 'if any link' was forged 'in my workshop.' Along with pride at its popular success, he felt guilt in having produced a patriotic but propagandistic play that was, at heart, a love-offering to his own terrible beauty, Maud Gone, and a betrayal of his own better judgment.

---

9   Pope, *The Rape of the Lock*, Canto I: 65–66, 99–100.

This would be an even weightier consideration if there is truth in the persistent rumor that Arthur Griffith—smitten with and politically allied with Maud Gonne (who funded his newspaper *The United Irishman*, and to whom he sometimes referred as 'my Queen')—may have contributed to the final electrifying image in which the Old Woman, Ireland herself, is transformed into 'a young girl with the walk of a queen.' We may never know for sure; but we *do* know that Maud introduced Yeats to Griffith in the hope that the Sinn Fein leader might help to induce Yeats to turn the Irish literary movement and the Abbey Theatre in a more politically nationalist direction. In 1914, Griffith wrote that Yeats 'added the present ending' of his 'very beautiful little allegory' at the 'suggestion of the present writer to emphasize its propaganda,' a claim he repeated to his fellow internee, Robert Brennan, in the immediate aftermath of the Easter Rising.[10]

Though we cannot simply dismiss the recklessness and penchant for violence in some of the late poems and in the rantings of his pamphlet *On the Boiler*, at his double-minded best, Yeats was as opposed as Joyce to the blinkered, rabid nationalism most memorably embodied in the crude and violent Citizen in the Cyclops episode of *Ulysses*. A reincarnation of Homer's Polyphemus, the one-eyed Citizen may also be a male equivalent of Ireland's one-eyed Morrigu, the sinister aspect of Cathleen ni Houlihan. I suspect Yeats thought 'that play of mine' not really *his* (quite aside from the mystery about the famous curtain line, most of the dialogue was written by Lady Gregory), and that, when he wasn't basking in what Lady Gregory couldn't help noting was 'his one real popular success,' regretted his submission to the blood-sacrifice mythology and politics of Maud Gonne. In 'Man and the Echo,' his responsibility for its lethal impact is the first 'question' that keeps him 'awake night after night.' In retrospect, Yeats may have wished that, on this occasion, he *had* 'turned aside' from the labyrinthine activist Maud.

There may be a hint of melodrama in the question Yeats asked himself: 'Did that play of mine send out/ Certain men the English shot?' No, it didn't, according to the irreverent Paul Muldoon, who has W. H. Auden

---

10   Unfairly depicted in 'The Municipal Gallery Revisited' as 'staring in hysterical pride,' Griffith, who (with Michael Collins) negotiated the Anglo-Irish Treaty, was not a man given to braggadocio. Brennan (who believed him) later became Ireland's ambassador to Washington, then Director of Broadcasting at Radio Éireann. See Colum Kenny, 'Friend or Foe?: How W. B. Yeats Damaged the Legacy of Arthur Griffith,' *Irish Times* (26 January 2021).

respond (in the 'Wystan' section of '7, Middagh Street'): 'Certainly not./ If Yeats had saved his pencil-lead/ would certain men have stayed in bed?' The point, placed in the mouth of Auden (who had declared in his elegy for Yeats that 'poetry makes nothing happen'), is that *history* is the 'twisted root,' and *poetry*, or 'art,' its 'small, translucent fruit/ and never the other way round.'[11] Muldoon is not alone in thinking that Yeats was over-dramatizing. Perhaps he was; but, on balance, I think the question Yeats posed to himself in 'Man and the Echo' was sincere.

Significantly, in one of the great moments in Yeats, 'Man and the Echo' ends with a violent intervention from the mountainside. Though his central hero is the Celtic Achilles, Cuchulain, 'that clean hawk out of the air,' Yeats's timid heart in hiding, though it 'ruffled in a manly pose' ('Coole Park, 1929'), here goes out, not to owl or 'heroic' hawk, but to its victim: 'A stricken rabbit is crying out/ And its cry distracts my thought.' The immediacy is vivid and deeply moving; but unless we imagine Yeats, 'old and ill,' actually composing in a rocky cleft on a mountainside, the scene is imaginary. Just as he was earlier thinking of men shot by the British, some of them victims impelled to action and to their deaths by 'that play of mine,' here he empathizes with the rabbit struck down by a violent predator, perhaps echoing Blake's couplet: 'Each outcry of the hunted Hare/ A fibre from the Brain does tear' ('Auguries of Innocence,' lines 13–14).

Both pouncing hawk and stricken rabbit have Yeatsian contexts. In the next and final chapter, I follow Yeats in associating the rabbit with Maud Gonne. But, given my emphasis throughout on Yeats's celebration of the intuitive and instinctive and his dread of abstract thought (mechanistic rather than organic), as well as his condemnation of political hatred, it is worth mentioning here that the hawk, despite its association with Cuchulain, is, in Yeats's symbology, emblematic of both abstract intellect and political hatred, making Maud symbolic hawk as well as rabbit— just to add to the menagerie of 'forms' she assumes in 'A Bronze Head.'

There is a cryptic poem titled 'The Hawk,' incongruously roosting amid a cluster of Maud Gonne poems in *The Wild Swans at Coole.* Its reference to

---

11   This long poem concludes Muldoon's 1987 collection, *Meeting the British*. The townhouse at 7 Middagh Street in Brooklyn Heights was, in 1940–41, the rotating home of artists and writers, including Carson McCullers, Paul Bowles, composer Benjamin Britten, Gypsy Rose Lee, and (as Muldoon reminds us) W. H. Auden.

the 'yellow-eyed *hawk of the mind*' is clarified by another poem from that volume, 'Tom O'Roughley,' in which the hawk is specifically identified with 'logic-choppers' and abstract intellect. Tom, a wise fool for whom 'An aimless joy is a pure joy,' has a mantra: 'Wisdom is a butterfly/ And not a gloomy bird of prey,' a contrast reflecting the symbolism on the ring Yeats had commissioned from Edmund Dulac, and which had arrived the very month, February 1918, Yeats wrote the poem. As he explained ten years later, glossing the 'brazen hawks' of abstract 'hatred' without 'pity' in the final movement of 'Meditations in Time of Civil War,' he had 'a ring with a hawk and a butterfly upon it, to symbolize the straight road of logic, and so of mechanism, and the crooked road of intuition: "For wisdom is a butterfly and not a gloomy bird of prey."' (VP, 827).[12]

In 'Man and the Echo,' the death-cry of the owl- or hawk- stricken rabbit 'distracts' the thoughts of the Yeatsian Man contemplating his own life, imminent death, and what may follow. In 'Politics,' intended as his final word, Yeats is again distracted, this time from discussion of the titular subject, 'war and war's alarms,' by 'that girl standing there.' My proposal in the next and concluding chapter, the boldest I advance in this book, is that 'that girl' is yet another 'form' of Maud Gonne, making her final appearance in the little poem Yeats wanted to be received as his poetic farewell. That argument may require an initial Coleridgean 'momentary suspension of disbelief.' But I hope to show that it is a plausible speculation. And not only is 'Politics' Maud-related, I suggest; it is also an affirmation of life related to the similar affirmation to be found, as Seamus Heaney has rightly insisted, in the seemingly grim and death-haunted 'Man and the Echo.'

---

12   Yeats, who often inscribed the butterfly portion of the aphorism in book dedications, elaborated on the full symbolism in a September 1934 letter to William Force Stead, an Oxford friend. 'The Butterfly' was the 'main symbol' on the ring 'I always wear': 'the other symbol is the hawk. The hawk is the straight road of logic, the butterfly the crooked road of intuition—the hawk pounces, the butterfly flutters.' (Robert Graves also identified, in his poem, 'Flying Crooked,' with the aerobatics of the butterfly.) Yeats *did* 'always' wear the ring, removed by George 'upon Yeats's death in 1939.' For this detail, and the letter to Stead, see Hassett, *Yeats Now: Echoing into Life*, 107–8.

15. Thought Distracted: 'Man and the Echo,' 'Politics,' and Conclusion

We know, from a handwritten note discovered sixty years ago, the poem Yeats wanted to appear as his last word, the final poem in his canon.[1] It was not, despite decades of editions, 'Under Ben Bulben,' an uneven (at its worst, obnoxious) poem saved by its resonant and influential final section enshrining Yeats's haunting epitaph: *'Cast a cold eye/ On life, on death./ Horseman, pass by!'* That epitaph—by the poet's command, 'no conventional phrase'—is less enigmatic read as a heroic reversal of all those pious inscriptions admonishing grave visitors to 'stop' and brood, succumbing to the morbid thought that as the corpse below is, so shall we be. Instead, we are to look on life and death with equanimity, then 'pass by,' getting on with our own lives. That is an affirmation of life, even in death.

The same is true of the three final poems in the canon, 'Man and the Echo,' 'The Circus Animals' Desertion,' and, last and seemingly least, 'Politics.' Though all three return us to the creative imagination and the human heart, they may seem anything *but* affirmative. They were printed together in a January 1938 issue of *The Atlantic*. In 2014, marking the seventy-fifth anniversary of Yeats's death, an *Atlantic* writer reproduced the poems as they had first appeared, characterized as 'three of his most brutal,' 'bitter,' and 'deeply unsettling,' pieces in which we find the poet relentlessly 'shedding the last vestiges of his

---

1   See Curtis Bradford, "The Order of Yeats's *Last Poems*.' The *Variorum* (pre-Bradford) ends with 'Under Ben Bulben.' But all three of the major modern editions, Finneran's (1983), followed by Jeffares' (1989), and Albright's (1990, 1992), print 'Politics' as Yeats's final poem.

   https://doi.org/10.11647/OBP.0275.16

pride and dignity.'[2] As Gloucester says in *King Lear*, 'and that's true, too.' But, as in Shakespeare's deepest tragedy, there is also a final, cathartic affirmation that rises out of undeniable darkness.

In the preceding chapter, I discussed 'The Circus Animals' Desertion,' and will return to it in my conclusion. I also discussed 'Man and the Echo,' and revisit it at this point in order to prepare for the affirmation to be found in the final poem, 'Politics.'

In the most memorable lecture in the superb series given during his tenure as Oxford Professor of Poetry, Seamus Heaney—expanding on remarks by Polish American Nobel laureate, Czeslaw Milocz—contrasted Philip Larkin's unflinching but hopeless death-poem, 'Aubade,' to 'Man and the Echo,' another confrontation of death by an aging poet lying awake at night. Though he admired 'Aubade,' Milocz protested its adoption of a purely rational-scientific assessment of death. Heaney cites with approval Milocz's assertion that 'poetry by its very essence has always been on the side of life,' expressing a 'faith' that is 'larger and deeper than religious or philosophic creeds,' which are 'only one' of faith's many 'forms.' Both Larkin and Yeats face death; but whereas 'Aubade' is, despite its wit, almost unrelievedly bleak, 'Man and the Echo' manages, despite its own opening bleakness, to endorse precisely what Larkin's brilliant but defeatist and wholly negative poem 'reneges on'—what Yeats calls, in resisting the temptation to 'lie down and die,' the 'spiritual intellect's great work.' Above all, Heaney notes, 'Man and the Echo' demonstrates that 'the consciousness of the poet is in full possession of both its creative impulse and its limiting knowledge,' limits rebelled against by the vitality of fully achieved poetry, able to partially 'redress' the harsh necessities of life.

The Yeatsian Man has two final questions: 'O rocky voice/ Shall we in that great night rejoice?/ What do we know but that we face/ One another in this place?' Though part of the interrogation, the option to 'rejoice' resonates, recalling the 'tragic joy' of 'The Gyres' (1936/37), where 'out of Cavern comes a voice,/ And all it knows is that one word "Rejoice".' But in the later poem both the Self and its cavernous Echo are told to 'hush.' Confronting his own death and possible afterlife, the poet has 'lost the theme,/ Its joy or night seem but a dream' because of a sudden, violent intervention from the natural world:

---

2   Gritz, 'The Deathbed Confession of William Butler Yeats.'

> Up there some hawk or owl has struck
> Dropping out of sky or rock,
> A stricken rabbit is crying out
> And its cry distracts my thought.

Heaney ended his Oxford lecture by focusing on Yeats's final couplet, noting that the yoking of 'crying out' and 'thought' is not a perfect rhyme; 'nor should it be,' for there is 'no perfect fit between the project of civilization represented by thought and the facts of pain and death' represented by the rabbit's 'crying out.' What 'holds the crying out and the thought together is a consciousness which persists in trying to make sense of a world where suffering and violence are more evidently set to prevail than the virtue of being "kind".'[3] The final rhyme, and the poem in general, Heaney concludes

> not only tell of that which the spirit must endure; they also show *how* [Heaney's italics] it must endure, by pitting human resource against the recalcitrant and the inhuman, by pitting the positive effort of mind against the desolations of natural and historical violence [...] Where Larkin's 'Aubade' ended in entrapment, 'Man and the Echo' has preserved a freedom, and manages to pronounce a final *Yes*. And the *Yes* is valuable, [possessing] a weight and significance because it overpowers and contains a *No*.

As Heaney observes, much more could be said about this deeply moving poem; but his focus on the final couplet, his concluding reflection, and his emphasizing, as Auden had before him, of Yeats's verb 'rejoice,' help us see that, for all its incertitude, 'Man and the Echo' is to be read as an affirmation of life. In that emphasis, Heaney is doubtless recalling one of the quatrains in what he called 'the best-known section of Auden's elegy for Yeats,' written in the trochaic tetrameters Auden borrowed from the sixth and final movement of 'Under Ben Bulben,' the funereal drumbeat section that constitutes Yeats's elegy for himself, including his epitaph. Auden invokes Yeats's ghost:

---

3   'Joy or Night,' in *The Redress of Poetry*, 162–63. One recalls the unexpectedly gentle reverence for life recorded by Yeats in 'Reveries over Childhood and Youth.' As a boy, he tells us, he fished and 'shot at birds with a muzzle-loading pistol until somebody shot a rabbit and I heard it squeal. From then on I would kill nothing but the dumb fish (*Au*, 55). We find the same 'kindness' in that iconic moment in January, 1889, when Nietzsche, spurner of 'pity,' famously collapsed in tears in Turin, embracing a carthorse being brutally flogged, a manic but revealing breakdown from which he never recovered.

Follow, poet, follow right
To the bottom of the night,
With your unconstraining voice
Still persuade us to rejoice.[4]

Here we have another valuable yes containing and overpowering the no. Though in the final paragraph of his Oxford lecture, Heaney cited Karl Barth on the 'enormous *Yes* [Heaney's italics] at the centre of Mozart's music,' he might have quoted the opening of Wallace Stevens's 'The Well Dressed Man with a Beard': 'After the final no there comes a yes/ And on that yes the future world depends./ No was the night. Yes is this present sun.' In 'Man and the Echo,' which begins with the Man descending to 'the bottom of a pit/ That broad noon has never lit,' the final affirmation, rising above that darkness and its necessarily tragic context, surmounts inevitable suffering, violence, and death itself—everything great and small, from the hatreds bred by politics and the desolations of history to the pitiable, compassion-inducing death cry of a rabbit struck down by a predatory bird.

We have discussed the hawk as symbol, Yeats's 'gloomy bird of prey' as emblematic of abstract thought and intellectual hatred. The hawk's prey in 'Man and the Echo' is a rabbit, an animal that, as we've seen, appears in two Maud-associated poems. In the first, the titular memory of his elusive Muse was impressed in crushed grass, a hollow left by the now fled 'mountain hare.' In the other, 'The Death of the Hare,' the Man's empathetic 'heart is wrung' by the thought of 'wildness lost' in the hunting down of a rabbit pursued to the death by a 'yelling pack': a displaced image of Maud set upon by the mob, identified by Yeats in 'The People' as those ingrates she had helped but who turned on her after her separation from John MacBride. But the cruelty of the hunt is *directly* connected to Maud in a striking remark Yeats confided in his unpublished memoir. By 1891, he imagined that Maud had come to 'have need of me,' a fact that evolved into wishful, then aggressive thinking: 'I had no doubt that need would become love [...] I had even as I watched her a sense of cruelty, as though I were a hunter taking

---

4   'In Memory of W. B. Yeats,' lines 66–69. The same meter was employed by Joseph Brodsky in his elegy for T. S. Eliot, and by Heaney himself in his elegy for his friend Brodsky: 'Joseph, yes, you know the beat,/ Wystan Auden's metric feet/ Marched to it, unstressed and stressed,/ Laying William Yeats to rest.' As Heaney reminds us, Brodsky died in 1996 on the same day, January 28, as Yeats had in 1939.

captive some beautiful wild creature,' and he deleted, even from papers meant to be private, the uncharacteristically forceful assertion: 'I wished now to make her my lover' (Mem, 49).[5]

These Maud-related images of the cruelty of the hunt return us to 'Man and the Echo,' to the poignant death cry of the rabbit, which confirms the radical finitude shared by man and beast, and simultaneously 'distracts' Yeats for the moment from thoughts about his own death. We cannot prevent or alleviate such suffering—the suffering, to a remarkable degree in poetry, of animals and even, in Wordsworth and Emily Dickinson, of flowers.[6] But we can register it in poetry evoking 'heart'-felt 'Thoughts that do often lie too deep for tears.' These final words of the 'Intimations' ode, like the final reverence for all living things expressed by Coleridge's repentant Mariner, seem immediately pertinent to the conclusion of 'Man and the Echo.' Wordsworth's deeply

---

5   Here, with Yeats at his most cruelly if secretly aggressive, Maud at her most unknowingly vulnerable, we may be reminded of an instant of Nabokov's equally obsessed Humbert Humbert and of Lolita, specifically of them together, Lolita on his lap, on the davenport in the Haze home. In this, the most explicit sexual scene in the novel, Humbert 'watched her, rosy, gold-dusted, beyond the veil of my controlled delight, unaware of it, alien to it [...] In my self-made seraglio, I was a radiant and robust Turk, postponing the moment of actually enjoying the youngest and frailest of his slaves.' (The Annotated Lolita, 60). However 'cruel' and lascivious Yeats might appear in this private fantasy, he is not, of course, to be compared with the morally grotesque Humbert. Yet this pedophile is also an artistic celebrant of his Muse and Beloved. In his prison cell with death imminent, Humbert affirms that, in his fleeting time and through the power of his language, he has made Lolita—as Yeats has made Maud Gonne—'live in the minds of later generations.' The novel ends as it had begun, with the word, 'Lolita,' and with a final rhetorical flourish, beneath the opulence of which we find both genuine feeling and a celebration of perdurable art, from cave paintings, through Medieval and Renaissance religious art, to 'sonnets,' Petrarchan and Shakespearean. 'I am thinking,' says Humbert, his theme perhaps merging with Nabokov's, 'of aurochs and angels, the secrets of durable pigments, prophetic sonnets, the refuge of art. And this is the only immortality you and I may share, my Lolita' (309). Maud said much the same of Yeats's poems for her.

6   I am about to cite Wordsworth's empathetic response to the 'meanest flower that blows.' Though examples are legion in Dickinson, consider no more than the 'happy flower' struck down by the 'blonde Assassin,' Frost, in her 1884 poem, 'Apparently with no surprise.' A striking example of non-human pain, a half-century later, is Samuel Beckett's moving 'Dante and the Lobster.' Assured that boiled lobsters feel no pain, the narrator, Belacqua, concludes otherwise: from 'the depths of the sea it had crept into the cruel pot [...] going alive into scalding water. It had to. Take into the air my quiet breath.' As in 'Man and the Echo,' abstract questions are made explicit in the suffering of the seemingly least human of creatures (as in David Foster Wallace's brilliant 2004 article, 'Consider the Lobster'), justifying Beckett's allusion to Keats's musing on his own death in the 'Ode to a Nightingale.'

felt response, 'thanks to the human heart by which we live,' to even 'the meanest [or, as he first wrote, 'humblest'] flower that blows,' was test run in the moral imperative of divinized Nature at the end of 'Hart-Leap Well,' his 1800 take on the killing of the albatross in his friend's *Rime*: 'Never to blend our pleasure or our pride/ With sorrow of the meanest thing that feels' (II.179–80). Wordsworth's two-part tale tells of a cruel hunter who takes sadistic joy in the death of a pursued hart who made a fatal leap from a cliff in a desperate attempt to return to the well it was born near. The eventual ruin of the pleasure-house the arrogant hunter built on the site illustrates the poem's 'hart'-felt moral.

Adapting that imperative and the moral of the chastened Mariner regarding 'all things both great and small,' Yeats's Man experiences a pang of empathy at the death of the rabbit. In a final parallel with Wordsworth, Yeats's thought-distracting response to the stricken creature's anguished cry from the mountainside—'But hush, for I have lost the theme'—resembles the moment in *The Excursion* (IV. 402–5), when the Wanderer's intellectual discourse is interrupted by a monitory 'voice' (anticipating the 'rocky voice' of 'Man and the Echo') emanating from Nature: 'List! I heard,/ From yon huge breast of rock, a voice sent forth/ As if the visible mountain made the cry.'

§

In 'Man and the Echo,' the pathos of mutability in the death cry of a stricken rabbit 'distracts' Yeats's thought. There is a similar distraction in the short lyric with which Yeats intended to end his *Collected Poems*. He might have concluded with, say, 'Cuchulain Comforted,' but Yeats chose to end, though it took editors almost a half-century to comply, on a still affirmative but lighter, ostensibly minor note. Casual, even unseemly on its surface, the little poem 'Politics' (May 1938) was written in response to its epigraph, a comment by Thomas Mann made during the Spanish Civil War and, as with Yeats's poem, with World War II looming on the horizon: 'In our time,' Mann insisted, 'the destiny of man presents its meanings in political terms.' Yeats's response is an imaginative cry to make love not war:

> How can I, that girl standing there,
> My attention fix

> On Roman or on Russian
> Or on Spanish politics,
> Yet here's a traveled man that knows
> What he talks about,
> And there's a politician
> That has both read and thought,
> And maybe what they say is true
> Of war and war's alarms,
> But O that I were young again
> And held her in my arms.

Why would Yeats, with other major candidates for the honor at hand, choose to end his canon with a *seemingly* slight, even ribald little poem, which rejects its titular subject in the opening lines? In part, I think, for that very reason, and because, under its colloquial surface, 'Politics' resonates with poetic tradition. Even in the midst of political turmoil and impending war, Yeats is affirming the primary theme of lyric poetry, epitomized in the anonymous medieval *cri de coeur* petitioning the 'Western Wind' to blow so that separated lovers might reunite: 'Christ, that my love were in my arms/ And I in my bed again!' Yeats concedes that traveled pundits and politicians have 'read and thought,' and 'maybe what they say is true/ Of war and war's alarms,/ But O that I were young again/ And held her in my arms.' In 'Politics,' selected by Yeats as his final word, the poet, dismissing war actual and potential, embraces the immemorial theme of lyric poetry—the longings of the heart, which have no enemy but time.

In doing so, Yeats almost replicates a move he had made when, in the midst of the *First* World War, he had disappointed two ardent American expatriate supporters of the Allies, Edith Wharton and Henry James, and angered a third, his friend John Quinn, by refusing to contribute a poem to the cause. Writing to Yeats in the very month of the 'Guns of August,' Maud Gonne, relieved that he 'seemed to have escaped the obsession of this war,' described the conflict as 'an inconceivable madness that has taken hold of Europe' (G-YL, 347–48). Precisely a year later, in August 1915, Yeats responded to a request from Henry James, Wharton's emissary, for a poetic contribution. Referring to the war as this 'bloody frivolity' (L, 600), and reducing requested support to intrusive 'meddling' in other people's business, Yeats had only this to offer 'On Being asked for a War Poem':

> I think it better that in times like these
> A poet's mouth be silent, for in truth
> We have no gift to set a statesman right;
> He has had enough of meddling who can please
> A young girl in the indolence of her youth,
> Or an old man upon a winter's night.[7]

In maintaining a Cistercian silence on the war as a 'subject,' Yeats, while seeming to fiddle while Europe burned, was casting a wide *human* net—addressing as audience female and male, the young and the old. In asserting that the poet's function is to 'please,' Yeats was also obeying the Horatian dictum that poetry must not only instruct, but 'delight,' intensified by Wordsworth in the Preface to *Lyrical Ballads* ('The Poet writes under one restriction only, namely, that of the necessity of giving immediate pleasure') and by Wallace Stevens as the climactic requirement of poetry in his 'Notes Toward a Supreme Fiction': 'IT MUST GIVE PLEASURE.' In both 1915 and 1938, Yeats was positioning himself against what we have come to call in our own hyper-polarized world 'interventionism' and the 'politicization' of art. Leon Wieseltier has recently launched some blunt Nietzsche-like aphorisms in favor of the first and against the second. In a 2021 essay, he poses a rhetorical question: 'Who ever did the right thing without intervening? Ethical action is always an intrusion,' especially when 'doing nothing' is to 'stand idly' by when the 'blood of others' is being spilled. He goes on, in effect, to turn Yeats's own word, 'meddling,' against him: 'Morality is a theory of meddling.'

But that is not the only table-turning. Toward the end of the essay, targeting today's activist artists, including, by name, the acclaimed creator of the hit musical, *Hamilton*, Wieseltier retrospectively attacks the position once espoused by Maud Gonne and Arthur Griffith when it came to the Abbey Theatre; even perhaps the position of James and Wharton in pressing Yeats to write a poem cheering on the Allies. Though supportive of moral interventionism, Wieseltier insists that,

---

7   The poem was published, retitled 'A Reason for Keeping Silent,' in *The Book of the Homeless* (1916), a volume to benefit war refugees organized and edited by Wharton. Of the many distinguished contributors, as Hermione Lee reports in *Edith Wharton*, Yeats alone 'refused the conventions of war writing.' Though she felt she had to include the poem, Yeats's decision to keep 'silent' was, as Lee adds, obviously 'not Wharton's view' (497). I am indebted here to my colleague, Wharton expert Julie Olin-Ammentorp.

when we politicize art, the 'first casualty' is 'our culture, just about all of it. Art is now politics by other means [...] "All art is political," says Lin Manuel-Miranda. Bullshit.'[8]

Yet one understands the distress of John Quinn, another ardent supporter of the Allies, who, in a letter to Yeats, pronounced the lines in which the Irish poet refused to contribute a war poem to the Allied cause 'unworthy of you and the occasion,' adding 'I do not believe in divorce between letters and life or art and war.'[9]

In 'Politics,' Yeats makes that 'divorce' his theme. Four years later, in a note appended to *Parts of a World*, a volume published in 1942, in the midst of the war that had been on the horizon when Yeats wrote 'Politics.' Wallace Stevens (once again surprisingly relevant) insisted that 'The immense poetry of war and a poetry of the work of imagination are two different things.' That volume includes a poem, 'Contrary Theses (I)' the title of which, as has been recently noted, 'invokes Yeatsian antinomies,' while the 'scenario of the poem itself—the intrusion of the soldier upon the poet's domain—restages, in abbreviated form' Yeats's 'The Road at My Door,' Poem V of 'Meditations in Time of Civil War.'[10] Stevens's soldier who walks or stalks 'before, before, before my door,' certainly resembles the soldiers on both sides of the Irish Civil War who, at different times, 'stand at my door' in Yeats's poetic sequence.

Stevens was probably unaware of the little poem 'Politics,' but his 'Contrary Theses' are at work there as well. From the outset, we have another contrast between public and private, between the 'immense' but still extraneous 'political' and the life-affirming human and erotic, with, given Yeats's penchant for embodiment, vital life taking the form of an imagined young woman instead of Stevens's sensuous but sublimated 'grapes plush upon the vine' and 'hives heavy' with honey. That last image suggests another Stevensian recollection of 'Meditations in Time of Civil War,' this time of the next and most moving poem in the sequence, 'The Stare's Nest by my Window,' quoted in full by Seamus Heaney

---

8   Wieseltier, 'Some Possible Grounds for Hope,' 364, 378.
9   *The Letters of John Quinn to William Butler Yeats*, ed. Himber, 192. Having nursed for two years in a French military hospital, Maud wrote to Quinn: 'You, I believe, still see beauty in war, I did once but hospital and broken hearts & the devastation & destruction of all art and beauty have changed me and I bow to any peace advocate.' *Too Long a Sacrifice: The Letters of Maud Gone and John Quinn*, ed. Janis and Richard Londraville, 206.
10   Lee M. Jenkins, 'Atlantic Triangle,' 17–30.

in his 1995 Nobel Prize acceptance speech, linking the Irish Civil War with the Troubles in the North a half-century later. Yeats's poem about honeybees building in crevices of the Tower walls, now emptied of the starlings who had housed there, ends with a no absorbed by a final yes, a dark lament regarding destructive internecine hatred followed by a life-affirming invocation of constructive, re-creative sweetness and light:

> We had fed the heart on fantasies,
> The heart's grown brutal from the fare;
> More substance in our enmities
> Than in our love; O honey-bees,
> Come build in the empty house of the stare.

'Politics,' which ends with another heart-felt and life-affirming 'O,' began with a question: 'How can I, that girl standing there,/ My attention fix/ On Roman or on Russian/ Or on Spanish politics?' Beneath its jauntiness, this echoes and refutes (for readers recalling their great 'Dialogue') Soul's demand that the erotically distracted Self '*fix*' his thoughts on what supposedly matters most, there the spiritual realm, here the political. For readers attuned to canonical reverberations, the seemingly minor 'Politics' echoes, verbally and thematically, that major poem at the center of Yeats's canon, 'A Dialogue of Self and Soul.'

In their debate, Soul had commanded Self to 'Fix every wandering thought upon' the spiritual; to keep the mind, which should be focused on the One, from 'wandering/ To this and that and t'other thing'—especially (in the case of 'a man/ Long past his prime,' who should 'scorn the earth') to things emblematical 'of love.' As earlier discussed, his unpublished notes to the poem reveal that Yeats was echoing Cicero's *Somnium Scipionis*, the dream of Scipio, whose ghostly grandfather had asked rhetorically, 'Why not *fix your attention* upon the heavens and condemn what is mortal?' But young Scipio 'kept turning my eyes back to earth,' just as the Yeatsian Self turns his eyes down to the blade 'upon my knees' wound in female embroidery, choosing, not to be delivered from 'the crime of death and birth,' but to plunge into life's ditch, especially 'that most fecund ditch of all,/ The folly that man does/ Or must suffer if he woos/ A proud woman not kindred of his soul.' Which is to say: Maud Gonne.

In 'Politics,' in a variation on Soul's imperious command that Self 'Fix every wandering thought' on the One rather than wander to the

Many, the restrictive one ('politics') is actually many (Roman, Russian, Spanish),[11] while the One is *that girl* upon whom the aged, lovelorn poet—'distracted' from supposedly more momentous but still merely topical issues—cannot help but 'fix' his 'attention.'

The old man may seem to be cavalierly abdicating his responsibilities in a world of war and war's alarms, but his instinctual and poignant cry from the heart is a hard-to-resist affirmation of life and an acknowledgement that Eros can still spur him into song. For Yeats, as for the enthralled warrior in *Antony and Cleopatra* and Thomas Hardy in 'In Time of "The Breaking of Nations",' star-crossed romantic love is simply a more profound poetic theme than 'war's annals' and politics: a theme that had haunted him from *The Wanderings of Oisin* on, certainly as meditated on in retrospect. And, whether or not we see the last line of 'Politics' as looking back to *The Wanderings of Oisin* and so 'giving' (as Warwick Gould once surmised) 'a circular, reincarnative shape to the "book" of Yeats's poems,'[12] the opening and closing lines of 'Politics' may bring us, in Yeats's version of Joyce's inevitable vicus of recirculation, back to Maud Gonne, who always tends to make Yeats end where he began.

For even here one wonders if 'that *girl standing there*' is not one more 'form' of Maud ('Which of her forms has shown her substance right?' he had asked in 'A Bronze Head'). In 'Among School Children,' having just recorded that 'tale' his 'Ledaean' Maud 'Told of a harsh reproof or trivial event/ That changed some childish day to tragedy,' the poet and senatorial school inspector looks out at the Many, one child or the other in the classroom, wondering 'if *she stood* so at that age—/ For

---

11   'Roman [...] Russian [...] Spanish.' Did *German* politics (even responding to Thomas Mann, a prominent opponent of Nazism) play no part in Yeats's 1938 thoughts about impending war? In a draft-version, he wondered 'if war must come/ From Moscow, *from Berlin*, or Rome?' Two years earlier, having declined to nominate for the Nobel Prize in Literature an anti-Nazi German writer, Yeats explained to Ethel Mannin why, despite her urging, the prize should not be politicized. He cited 'The Second Coming,' which 'foretold what is happening' now, in the late 'thirties, as evidence that 'he has not been silent,' and that he is not now 'callous'; that 'every nerve trembles with horror at what is happening in Europe, "the ceremony of innocence is drowned".' (L, 851)

12   Suggested by Gould in his appendix to *Yeats's Poems*, ed. Jeffares, 749n76. It may be 'too neat,' as Gould suspects; but, as evidenced by the rondural design of *The Winding Stair* and the chiastic-concentric structure of 'A Woman Young and Old,' Yeats was fascinated by such rondural circularity.

even daughters of the swan can share/ Something of every paddler's heritage'; and 'thereupon my heart is driven wild:/ She *stands before me as a living child.'*

It was Dorothy Wellesley who brought to Yeats's attention the Thomas Mann quote, embedded in a 1938 *Yale Review* essay by Archibald MacLeish titled 'Public Speech and Private Speech in Poetry.' Yeats was pleased by the praise of his work; and the immediate stimulus of his poem 'Politics' was MacLeish's remark that because of his age and relation to Ireland, Yeats was unable to use 'public' language on what was 'obviously considered' the right public material, 'politics.' I'm suggesting that Yeats's 'private' speech reverted to Maud. As it happens, it was to Dorothy that Yeats confided that the poem's subject matter—the distraction from discussion of potential war caused by 'that girl standing there'—was 'not a real incident, but a moment of meditation' (LDW, 163). Who better to meditate on than *'that* one'? If 'that girl standing there' in 'Politics' is in any way a 'form' of Maud—who had told Yeats long ago that while she was 'born to be in the midst of a crowd,' he had 'higher work to do' and should not involve himself 'in the *outer* side of politics' (G-YL, 72)—it would clarify both the old man's distraction from war and war's alarms, and the climactic placement of the anti-political 'Politics' as Yeats's poetic farewell: a final endorsement of the universal theme of love and of its particular incarnation in the woman and Muse who inspired virtually all of Yeats's love poetry.

In this reading, Yeats's intended 'last words' are neither 'tawdry' nor 'disgraceful' (as poet Don Share charged in an online *jeu d'esprit* of February 2013), but a final registration and rejection of the titular 'politics' that had been his 'one visible rival' (Mem, 63) in his obsessive love for Maud Gonne: his ultimate affirmation, even if he can no longer hold a young woman in his arms, of the overflowing cornucopia of life Maud had bartered away for that old bellows full of angry wind. Citing a travelled man that 'knows,' and a politician that has 'read and thought,' Yeats, once again pitting the wisdom of the body and of the heart against thought, book-knowledge, and politics, acknowledges and spurns their worldly expertise. The disdainful dismissal of the world of intellection and politics is arch and impertinent, yet vital and instinctual. As he insisted in this same letter to Dorothy Wellesley, 'No artesian well of the intellect can find the poetic theme,' the source of which, by implication, is deeper than mere intellect: a *natural* spring, even if, in this late case, it is less passionately asserted than poignantly reaffirmed.

When, in the 1983 Finneran edition of the *Poems*, 'Under Ben Bulben' was replaced by 'Politics' as the final poem, the command from beyond the grave—'Cast a cold eye, on life, on death'—yielded to something still elegiac but no longer oracular, moving rather than marmoreal: 'But O that I were young again/ And held her in my arms.' Commenting on Finneran's edition in a review titled 'A New and Surprising Yeats,' Seamus Heaney noted the dramatic change:

> A far cry from 'Cast a cold eye/ On life, on death'; equally histrionic, but implying a radically different stance in the face of death. It is as if we were to learn that Sir Walter Raleigh's last words had not been his famous shout to the reluctant executioner—'What dost thou fear? Strike, man!'—but that instead he had repeated the name of the maid of honor he was rumored to have seduced in the grounds of Hampton Court Palace years before.

Absolutely right about 'Man and the Echo,' Seamus Heaney seems to me at least partially wrong about 'Politics.' His witty Raleigh analogy registers the cavalier aspect of the poem, and mirrors what he and Milocz had to say in contrasting negative Philip Larkin, in 'Aubade,' to an affirming Yeats's 'radically different stance in the face of death' in the case of *both* 'Man and the Echo' and 'Politics.' But Heaney misses, I think, the full poignancy of that sincere rather than 'histrionic' cry from the heart in Yeats's final poem. To my ear, that 'O' conveys, as in the wartime invocation to the 'honey-bees' and to 'love,' an emotion deeper than casual lust, and implies a considerably longer stretch than a rumored seduction mere 'years before.'

To me, at least, it suggests a memory of Maud, and therefore memory stretching back a half-century. To be young again and imagining holding *her* in his arms combines two of Yeats's most fervent desires. Taken together, they would account for Yeats's otherwise inexplicable choice of 'Politics,' this almost flippant dismissal of war, to be his final poetic statement, a last farewell to his lifelong Muse and Beloved. In the 'gay goodnight' that ends 'A Man Young and Old,' Yeats 'celebrates,' with the chorus from Sophocles' *Oedipus at Colonus*, 'the silent kiss that ends short life or long.' Shortly before his own death, combining spiritual renunciation with sublimated eroticism, Yeats announced: 'the last kiss is given to the void' (LTSM, 154).

James Joyce would have approved of the old man's arch disdain for war and war's alarms, a dismissal of 'politics' he rightly thought had infected *Cathleen ni Houlihan,* and he would of course have agreed with Yeats's choice to end his canon by affirming human love, *Ulysses'* 'word known to all men.' For Yeats to end on that note, and perhaps imagining himself 'young again,' and holding a fantasized Maud Gonne 'in my arms,' would have seemed not only right but inevitable to the lover of Nora who gave Molly Bloom the final word and 'affirmation of life' shared by Yeats and Joyce. In the final passage of *Ulysses,* Molly and Leopold, sixteen years younger, are 'lying among the rhododendrons on Howth head,' a place loved by Yeats and Maud, and where he first proposed marriage to her. In her famously unpunctuated reverie, Molly first drifts back to her days in Gibraltar, when she wore flowers in her hair and was herself 'a flower of the mountain,' and remembers how she had been first kissed by a young man 'under the Moorish wall' (643:1604). And then we are back, in Molly's stream of consciousness, to that day when she was lying with Bloom among the flowers on Howth Head, where

> I got him to propose to me yes first I gave him the bit of seedcake out of my mouth and it was leapyear like now 16 years ago my God after that long kiss I near lost my breath yes he said I was a flower of the mountain yes so we are flowers all a womans body yes that was one true thing he said in his life and the sun shines for you today yes that was why I liked him because I saw he understood or felt what a woman is and I knew I could always get round him and I gave him all the pleasure I could leading him on till he asked me to say yes and I wouldnt answer first only looked out over the sea and the sky [...] and I thought well as well him as another and then I asked him with my eyes to ask again yes and then he asked me would I yes to say yes my mountain flower and first I put my arms around him and drew him down to me so he could feel my breasts all perfume yes and his heart was going like mad and yes I said yes I will Yes. (*Ulysses,* 643–44:1573–1609)

Though he is an execrable poet, Bloom does have, as one of the Dubliners rightly noted, 'a touch of the artist about him.' But even if, lying in bed with her, head to toe, Leopold was able to overhear Molly's erotic reverie, her memory of their first act of lovemaking, he could hardly find better words to capture his own elegiac feelings than those with which the aged Yeats, looking back, ended his Maud-evoking final poem: 'But O that I were young again,/ And held her in my arms.'

§

Yet, to draw to our own close, it must be said that the lovelorn heart, the 'rag and bone shop [...] where all the ladders start,' is not where they all *end*. For *in* the end, as Yeats also says in 'The Circus Animals' Desertion,' the poem immediately preceding 'Politics,' it was the playwriting and the poetry that 'took all my love,/ And not those things that they were emblems of,' those masks concealing yet revealing the 'Heart-mysteries' of his unrequited love for Maud Gonne. Even that was not the *whole* truth, and nothing but the truth. But it was in this sense, even more than in his marriage and intimate relationships with 'others,' that Yeats 'turned aside'—as he said in the lines from 'The Tower' cited in my epigraph—from the 'great labyrinth' of Maud Gonne. Fergus had falsely promised a forest haven where frustrated lovers would 'no more turn aside and brood/ Upon love's bitter mystery.' But Yeats could turn aside from Maud Gonne only, paradoxically, through the power of his own words written for her: not even *she* could triumph over the poetry she inspired and which then absorbed its biographical genesis.

Unsurprisingly, given that Yeats intensified polarities for dramatic effect, 'all' is by far the most frequent word in his vocabulary, appearing over a thousand times, doubling its nearest competitor, 'old.' 'All' is also the most frequent word in the vocabulary of Yeats's mentor, Blake, for whom 'without Contraries' there could be 'no progression.' I've noted the double extremity in 'The Cold Heaven': 'And I *took all* the blame out of *all* sense and reason.' (In fact, Yeats's double 'alls' are usually Maud-related; for example, 'Never give *all* the Heart' ends: "He that made this knows *all* the cost,/ For he gave *all* his heart and lost.') A year earlier, in 'Friends,' Yeats had asked, 'What of her that *took*/ All* till my youth was gone?' In old age he counters with another hyperbolic *more than* half-truth: the poems and plays *'took all my love,'* not those things that they were emblems of. These assertions embody the Blakean Contraries. Nietzsche—whose thought, Yeats believed, 'completes Blake and has the same roots' (L, 379)—insisted that 'oppositions' need not be 'arguments against existence,' but should be perceived instead as 'one more stimulus to life. Just such "contradictions" seduce us to existence.'[13] Such dialectical thinking illuminates the power-producing tension at the heart of Yeats's best poetry, most notably for our present purposes, 'A Dialogue of Self and Soul' and the Maud Gonne poems, tense with Contraries, yet riddled with the light of affirmation, tragic joy, and, ultimately, a secular beatitude incorporating and resolving all the antinomies, including 'love's bittersweet.' To quote the rhapsodic conclusion of the great poem acknowledging, absorbing, and incorporating 'the folly that man does/ Or must suffer' if he loves a woman like Maud Gonne:

> When such as I cast out remorse
> So great a sweetness flows into the breast
> We must laugh and we must sing,
> We are blest by everything,
> Everything we look upon is blest.

'I have,' says the Lord God (Deuteronomy 30:19), 'set before you life and death, blessing and cursing: therefore choose life, that both thou and thy seed may live.' As woman and Muse, Maud Gonne was both blessing and curse. But she and 'life' are affirmed when, with remorse cast out, sweetness flows into the breast, and we respond with joy, assured that we 'are blest by everything.' The 'seed' that lived, in lieu of their childless union, were the poems Maud inspired. In the same year (1911) that Yeats told us how, at the mere thought of Maud, 'so great a sweetness flows' from his 'heart's root,' his Muse (in that earlier-cited gender-reversing letter) wrote of their physically frustrating but imaginatively fruitful relationship: 'Our children were your poems, of which I was the Father sowing the unrest & storm which made them possible & you the mother who brought them forth in suffering & in the highest beauty & our children had wings—' (G-YL, 302).

Four years later, Maud wrote to Yeats, thanking him for sending her his just-written poem 'The People,' the very poem in which he most clearly distinguishes between them: she as the beautiful but terrible

---

13   *Genealogy of Morals*, III.2. Nietzsche's 'contradictions' and 'mask' tally with another
     Yeatsian mentor. In 'The Truth of Masks' (1885), Wilde tells us that 'A truth in
     art is that whose contradictory is also true.' *The Artist as Critic*, ed. Ellmann, 432.
     Nietzsche's theory of the 'mask' (described at length in *Beyond Good and Evil*,
     written in the same year as Wilde's 'The Truth of Masks'), added, for Yeats, heroic
     virility to the theatrical mask of Wilde.

embodiment of that 'purity of a natural force,' that unrest and storm, that impelled her fierce commitment to activist politics; he as a man and writer 'whose virtues are the definitions/ Of the analytic mind,' yet a proud mind so humbled by her loyalty to the people, even after they had turned on her, that he is abashed, 'because my heart leaped at her words.' In her 1915 letter Maud was also recalling his gallant if resisted attempt to protect her during that 1897 Dublin riot. 'I have never thanked you for the poem,' Maud ends her letter. 'To me you are too kind—You have often tried to defend & protect me *with your art*—& perhaps when we are dead I shall be known by those poems of yours—.' She had been even more candid five years earlier, with the *Green Helmet* poems, especially 'No Second Troy,' in mind: 'The demons of hate which possessed me are not eternal—what you have written for me will live' (G-YL, 356–57, 294).

Her heart leaping at *his* 'words,' she projects into the future, affirming his seemingly hopeless dream, as expressed in his poem 'Words,' of a Muse and beloved who at last 'understands it all,' and who would be, as they both expected, forever known to the world by 'those poems of yours.' Anyone reading, as we have, the best among Yeats's many poems to and about Maud Gonne—including 'No Second Troy,' 'Words' and 'The People,' the latter at once a 'debate-poem' and a 'magnificent instance of artistic self-transcendence'[14]—is bound to concur in her judgment: 'our children had wings—.'

---

14 'The People' as aptly described by M. L. Rosenthal, *Running to Paradise*, 17, 178.

Fig. 3 William Butler Yeats, photo by Pirie MacDonald (1932), https://commons.
wikimedia.org/wiki/File:W._B._Yeats,_1932._(7893552556).jpg.

Eulogy:
Harold Bloom (1930–2019)

On 14 October 2019, Harold Bloom died. He was 89, and had just taught two classes at Yale. Magisterial yet convivial, bigger than life yet almost comically elegiac, Bloom had been dying for decades. But to those who knew, admired, and loved this mixture of formidable colossus and warmhearted mensch, even for some who resented him, his death was *felt*. That inward impact was publicly registered. Almost every notable newspaper and magazine in the world carried his obituary, often (as in the case of the *New York Times*) on the front page: hardly par for a literary critic. Teacher, MacArthur Fellow, prolific author, holder of chairs at Harvard and NYU, Sterling Professor of Humanities at Yale, his home base, Harold Bloom, at the time of his death, was, and had been for many years, the most widely read and controversial literary critic in the world, both celebrated and reviled as the foremost champion of the Western canon.

Seeming to have read almost everything, within and beyond the Western classics, Bloom was famous for his agonistic theory of poetic influence, for his almost superhuman memory and for his astonishing reading speed. I once bumped into him in the Yale Co-Op. After greeting me with the usual, 'Hello, dear,' he asked if I'd come across anything interesting while browsing. I told him I'd just read the introductory chapter of a book arguing that the reason the Church resisted Galileo, and eventually put him under house arrest, had to do, not with astronomy, but with the challenge Galileo's science posed to the doctrine of transubstantiation. 'Really,' said Harold, 'Where's the book?' I took him to it. That introduction was twenty dense pages long and had taken me at least that many minutes to get through it. Harold, rapidly flipping pages, finished it in less than two, and then began to discuss it with me in detail.

	https://doi.org/10.11647/OBP.0275.17

Readers of the present volume may recall the story about a friend of Stephen MacKenna seeing Yeats in a London bookstore one morning. WBY was standing in an aisle reading the first volume of MacKenna's newly published translation of the *Enneads* of Plotinus. When the friend returned in the evening, there was Yeats, standing in the same place, and still reading, now about three-quarters through. MacKenna laughed and, after wondering aloud if Yeats ever bought the damned book (he did), added: 'You know, he has a really colossal brain.' Bloom's brain was, if anything, even more colossal. But, with a reading speed of some 8,000 words a minute, he might have finished the *Enneads* before MacKenna's friend *left* that bookstore. On the other hand, if it came to a choice, Harold would have traded his prodigious memory and reading speed for Yeats's poetic genius. One of the reasons he had such reverence for the world's great creative writers, Shakespeare above all, was that he knew that *that* miraculous gift had been denied him.

Bloom was an absorber of knowledge almost from birth. The son of a Jewish garment worker, he grew up in the Bronx, speaking Yiddish before he knew English. He was exposed to both Testaments of the Bible early on, though even then, he later said, he was skeptical about orthodox notions of spirituality. By the age of eleven, the precocious 'Childe Harold' was drawn to the sublime in secular literature as well. He was overwhelmed in particular by the Marlovian rhetoric of Hart Crane, a first love he always ranked second only to W. B. Yeats and Wallace Stevens among twentieth-century poets. Along with his Cornell mentor, M. H. Abrams, Bloom would later revive Romantic poetry, fallen into post-Eliotic academic disfavor, with Bloom tracing a lineage from Shakespeare, through Milton (he had much of *Paradise Lost* by heart) and the great British Romantics, then Emerson and Whitman and Dickinson, to their twentieth-century heirs: Crane, Yeats, Stevens, and others, many of them his friends, in a continuing Romantic tradition.

Bloom felt himself to be a man appointed to guard a position. The canon he felt obliged to defend was not only a victim of declining literacy, but under direct assault by academicians he described, in the spirit of Nietzsche, as 'the School of Resentment': those practitioners of postmodern critical approaches that subordinated aesthetic appreciation to external social and political considerations. No wonder he was resisted, even despised, by most Marxist, New

Historicist, Deconstructionist, and Feminist critics, all of whom he intemperately dismissed as 'a rabblement of lemmings.' One day when we were walking in Manhattan, Harold suddenly turned to me, 'You know why they hate me so, don't you, Pat?' His answer to his own question would have been a display of monstrous egotism if it weren't both self-consciously humorous and true: 'Because they know I know everything they know, and a lot more besides.'

Though John Keats recognized Wordsworth as the master poet of the age, and, along with Shakespeare and Milton, one of his own great precursors, he was hardly wrong to refer, famously, to the author of 'Tintern Abbey' and the 'Intimations of Immortality' Ode as the epitome of the 'egotistical sublime.' Both adjective and noun could be applied to Harold Bloom. But despite his arrogant dismissal of enemies and his polemical excesses, Bloom was in fact committed to aesthetic and spiritual enrichment extending far beyond the merely egoistic Self and an exclusively Western canon. 'Cultivating deep inwardness,' he insisted, 'depends upon the reading of the world's masterpieces of literary work and religious scriptures.' In a note thanking me for my letter of condolence, including an earlier version of these remarks, Harold's beloved wife, Jeanne, remarked that she especially liked my reference to Bloom feeling himself 'a man appointed to guard a position,' which caught, she thought, 'the fighting stance that motivated a part of his writing and teaching.' A 'part'—for that fighting stance could also reflect a generosity of spirit that made him, above all, a courageous guide to wisdom and consolation in distress—as I personally experienced at the time of my father's death.

Jeanne included in her note the following passage from Bloom, later inserted in the program for the 18 January 2020 Memorial Service at Yale's Battell Chapel, celebrating her husband's life and legacy, and still later as the final paragraph of Harold's 'Prelude' to his posthumously published final book, *Take Arms Against a Sea of Troubles: The Power of the Reader's Mind over a Universe of Death*: 'The great poems, plays, novels, stories teach us how to go on living, even submerged under forty fathoms of bother and distress. If you live ninety years you will be a battered survivor. Your own mistakes, accidents, failures and otherness beat you down. Rise up at dawn and read something that matters as soon as you can.'

The title of Bloom's *Possessed by Memory: The Inward Light of Criticism*, also published posthumously, emphasized his phenomenal powers of recall, summoning up and sharing with us all those literary masterpieces he had spent a lifetime absorbing and cherishing. The last time I got to spend time with Harold, we sat, along with Jeanne and my then student-assistant, Sean Abrams, at their kitchen table in the book-filled house on Linden Street in New Haven. He had recently been hospitalized with a broken hip, the result of only one of several falls he had taken in his final years. After we exhausted the possibilities of prose, we chanted poems back and forth from memory. I could have gone on for perhaps another hour; Harold would still be chanting. But the hour was growing late, and the old man's body was tiring, however willing his inexhaustible spirit.

In keeping with the quasi-spiritual 'deep inwardness' he urged us to cultivate, the more explicitly spiritual book Harold was planning at the time was to be an exploration of ideas of the afterlife in the Judeo-Christian, Greco-Roman, and Islamic traditions. Tentatively titled *Immortality, Resurrection, Redemption: A Study in Speculation*, the book, he confided, would play another variation on inwardness. Though he shared some form of 'spiritual hope,' Bloom, extrapolating from his own psychological and medical history—a battered survivor, enabled by love and literature to 'rise up at dawn'—speculated that his titular, ultimately redemptive triad occurs in *this life*. When the book appeared, fourteen months after his death, in the final month of the Year of the Plague, and retitled by Bloom *Take Arms Against a Sea of Troubles*, it was a literary rather than a normatively spiritual text, since, as he says in the Prelude, 'Now, for many of the most literate among us,' such figurations as immortality, resurrection, and redemption 'can only be tropes.'

Though he has departed this life, for those of us personally moved and intellectually influenced by him, Bloom will never be completely gone. He now survives, beyond that battered body, as a trope—for me, one of the similes of one of his favorite poets. In 'The Auroras of Autumn,' Wallace Stevens refers to stars putting on their 'glittering belts' and throwing around their shoulders cloaks 'that flash/ Like a great shadow's last embellishment.' Yet what seems like the last glimmer somehow perpetuates itself. So, for those possessed as he was by memory, will it be with the luminous shadow of Harold Bloom.

Select Bibliography

Adams, Hazard. *Blake and Yeats: The Contrary Vision*. New York: Russell & Russell, 1968 [1955].

___ *The Book of Yeats's Poems*. Tallahassee: The Florida State University Press, 1990.

___ *The Book of Yeats's Vision: Romantic Modernism and Antithetical Tradition*. Ann Arbor: University of Michigan Press, 1995.

Aeschylus. *Agamemnon*, trans. Richmond Lattimore. Vol. 1, *The Complete Greek Tragedies*, ed. David Grene and Richmond Lattimore. Chicago: University of Chicago Press, 1959.

Albright, Daniel. *The Myth Against Myth: A Study of Yeats's Imagination in Old Age*. London: Oxford University Press, 1972.

___ ed. 'Notes' in *W. B. Yeats: The Poems*. London: Dent, 1990; Everyman's Library, 1992.

Allt, Peter. 'W. B. Yeats,' *Theology* 42 (1941), 81–99.

Armstrong, Charles I. '"Born Again": W. B. Yeats's "Eastern" Turn in the 1930s,' in Gibson and Mann. 2016.

Arkins, Brian. *Builders of My Soul: Greek and Roman Themes in Yeats*. London: Rowman & Littlefield, 1990.

Auden, W. H. 'In Memory of W. B. Yeats,' *Collected Poetry of W. H. Auden*. New York: Random House, 1945.

___ 'Yeats as an Example,' *Kenyon Review* 10 (1948); reprinted in Hall and Steinmann, eds. 1961 [1950]. 344–51.

Augustine. *Augustine: Confessions,* ed. Sarah Ruden. New York: Modern Library (Penguin Random House), 2018.

Beckett, Samuel. 'Dante and the Lobster' in *I Can't Go On, I'll Go On: A Selection from Samuel Beckett's Work*, ed. Richard W. Seaver. New York: Grove Press, 1976.

Bendheim, Kim. *The Fascination of What's Difficult: A Life of Maud Gonne*. New York: OR Books, 2021.

Bhartrihari, *The Satakas or Wise Sayings of Bhartrihari*, trans. J. M. Kennedy. London: T. Werner Laurie, 1913.

Blackmur. R. P. 'The Later Poetry of W. B. Yeats,' in *Form and Value in Modern Poetry*. New York: Doubleday, 1957.

Blake, William. *The Four Zoas, Jerusalem, The Marriage of Heaven and Hell. The Poetry and Prose of William Blake*, ed. David V. Erdman, Commentary by Harold Bloom. Garden City: Doubleday, 1965.

___ *The Letters of William Blake*, ed. Geoffrey Keynes. Cambridge, Ma: Harvard University Press, 1970.

___ Robert Blair's *The Grave*, illustrated by William Blake. London: T. Bensley for R. H. Cromek, 1808.

Blavatsy, Helena Petrovna. *Isis Unveiled*, 2 vols. Wheaton, Il: The Theosophical Publishing House, Quest Edition, 1997 [1877].

___ *The Secret Doctrine*, 2 vols. Point Loma: The Aryan Theosophical Press, 1925 [1888].

Bloom, Harold. *Possessed by Memory: The Inward Light of Criticism*. New York: Alfred A. Knopf, 2019.

___ *Where Shall Wisdom Be Found?* New York: Riverhead Books, 2004.

___ *Yeats*. Oxford and New York: Oxford University Press, 1970.

___ 'Yeats, Gnosticism, and the Sacred Void,' in Bloom's *Poetry and Repression: Revisionism from Blake to Stevens*. New Haven and London: Yale University Press, 1976.

Bornstein, George. *Yeats and Shelley*. Chicago: University of Chicago Press, 1970.

Bornstein, George and Hugh Witemeyer, eds. Yeats, *Letters to the New Island. A New Edition*. London: Macmillan, 1990.

Bradford, Curtis. 'The Order of Yeats's *Last Poems*.' *Modern Language Notes* 76 (1961), 515–16.

___ *Yeats at Work*. Carbondale, Il: Southern Illinois University Press, 1965.

Brown, Terence. *The Life of W. B. Yeats: A Critical Biography*. Oxford: Blackwell, 1999.

Browning, Robert. 'Childe Roland to the Dark Tower Came,' in *Robert Browning's Poetry*, ed. James F. Loucks. New York and London: Norton, 1979.

Cardozo, Nancy. *Lucky Eyes and a High Heart: The Life of Maud Gonne*. Indianapolis and New York: Bobbs-Merrill, 1978.

Carson, Anne. *Eros the Bittersweet: An Essay*. Princeton: Princeton Legacy Library, 2014 [1986].

Castiglione, Baldesar. *The Book of the Courtier*, trans. Charles S. Singleton. New York and London: Doubleday Anchor, 1959 [1528].

Chapman, Wayne. '"Something Intended, Something Complete": Major Work on Yeats, Past, Present, and Yet to Come,' in Gibson and Mann. 2016.

Chatterjee, Mohini and Laura Holloway. *Man: Fragments of a Forgotten History*. London: Reeves and Turner, 1887.

Cicero, Marcus Tullius. *Somnium Scipionis*, from the sixth and final book of Cicero's *De re publica* [c. 51 BCE]; most of the text of Book 6 survives only because it was preserved in the *Commentary* of Macrobius.

Clarke, Susanna. *Jonathan Strange and Mr. Norell*, London: Bloomsbury, 2004.

Coleridge, Samuel Taylor. 'Kubla Khan,' 'Phantom,' in *Poetical Works*. ed. Ernest Hartley Coleridge. Oxford: Oxford University Press, 1967.

Cullingford, Elizabeth Butler. *Gender and History in Yeats's Love Poetry*. Cambridge: Cambridge University Press, 1993.

___ 'Yeats and Gender,' in Howes and Kelly, 167–84.

Daly, Dominic. *The Young Douglas Hyde*. Dublin: Irish University Press, 1974.

Dante, Alighieri. *La Vita Nuova*, [1294], in *Poems and Translations*. trans. Dante Gabriel Rossetti. Whitefish, Montana: Kessinger Legacy Reprints, 2010 [1841].

Dickinson, Emily. *The Letters of Emily Dickinson*, ed. Thomas H. Johnson and Theodora Ward, 3 vols. Cambridge, MA: Harvard University Press, 1958.

Diggory, Terence. *Yeats and American Poetry*. Princeton: Princeton University Press, 1983.

Dobrée, Bonamy. 'T. S. Eliot: A Personal Reminiscence,' in *T. S. Eliot: The Man and His Work*. ed. Allen Tate. New York: Delacorte, 1960.

Donne, John. *The Poems of John Donne*, 2 vols. ed. H. J. C. Grierson. London: Oxford University Press, 1912.

___ *John Donne: The Sermons*, 10 vols., eds. Evelyn M. Simpson and George R. Potter. Berkeley: University of California Press, 1953–62.

Donoghue, Denis. 'Reading "The Cold Heaven",' in *Yeats 150*. ed. Declan Foley. Dublin: The Lilliput Press, 2015.

___ 'Three Presences: Yeats, Pound, Eliot.' *Hudson Review* (Winter, 2010), 563–82.

Dryden, John. *A Discourse Concerning the Original and Progress of Satire*. Berkeley: University of California Press, 1974 [1693].

___ trans., *De rerum natura*. by Lucretius, in *The Poems of John Dryden*, ed. John Sargeaunt. Oxford: Oxford University Press, 1913.

Eliot, T. S. *After Savage Gods: A Primer of Modern Heresy*. London: Faber and Faber, 1934.

___ 'Shelley and Keats,' in T. S. Eliot, *The Use of Poetry and the Use of Criticism*. London: Faber & Faber, 1964 [1933]. The fifth of the Charles Eliot Norton Lectures, 1932–33.

___ 'Little Gidding,' in *T. S. Eliot: The Complete Poems and Plays, 1909–1950*. New York: Harcourt, Brace & Co, 1960.

___ 'The Poetry of W. B. Yeats,' First Annual Yeats Lecture, June 1940 in Hall and Steinmann, 331–43.

___ '*Ulysses*, Order and Myth,' in *The Dial* 1923; reprinted in *Selected Prose of T. S. Eliot*, ed. Frank Kermode. New York: Farrar, Straus and Giroux, 1975.

Ellmann, Richard. *Eminent Domain: Yeats Among Wilde, Joyce, Pound, Eliot, and Auden*. New York: Oxford University Press, 1967.

___ *The Identity of Yeats*. New York: Oxford University Press, 1964 [1954].

___ *The Second Puberty of W. B. Yeats*. Washington: Library of Congress, 1986.

___ *Yeats: The Man and the Masks*. 2nd edn. New York: Norton, 1978 [1948].

Emerson, Ralph Waldo. 'The Divinity School Address,' in *Emerson: Essays and Lectures*, ed. Joel Porte. New York: Library of America, 1983.

Ferguson, Trish. *Maud Gonne*. Dublin: UCD Press, 2019.

Filkins, Peter. 'A Reckoning,' *Salmagundi* (Spring–Summer 2021), 221–28.

Finneran, Richard, George Mills Harper, and William Murphy. eds. *Letters to W. B. Yeats*, 2 vols. London: New York: Columbia University Press, 1977.

___ *The Collected Poems of W. B. Yeats*. New York: Macmillan, 1983.

Flanagan, Thomas. 'A Terrible Beauty is Born.' *New York Times Book Review* (6 April 1997), 10–12.

Foster, R. F., *W. B. Yeats: A Life, I: The Apprentice Mage*. Oxford and New York: Oxford University Press, 1997.

___ *W. B. Yeats: A Life, II: The Arch-Poet*. Oxford and New York: Oxford University Press, 2003.

Frazier, Adrian. *The Adulterous Muse: Maud Gonne, Lucien Millevoye and W. B. Yeats*. Dublin: The Lilliput Press, 2016

Gardner, Helen. *The Composition of Four Quartets*. New York: Oxford University Press, 1978.

Gibson, Matthew and Neil Mann, eds. *Yeats, Philosophy, and the Occult*. Liverpool: Liverpool University Press, 2016.

Gonne, Maud. *An Autobiography of Maud Gonne: A Servant of the Queen*, eds. A. Norman Jeffares and Anna MacBride White. Gerrards Cross, Buckinghamshire: Colin Smythe, 1994 [1938].

Gould, Warwick. Note on 'Politics,' in his Appendix to *Yeats's Poems*, ed. Jeffares.

Graves, Robert. *The White Goddess*. New York: Farrar, Straus and Giroux, n.d. [1948].

Gregory, Lady August. *Lady Gregory's Diaries, 1892–1902*, ed. James Pethica. Gerrards Cross: Colin Smythe Ltd. 1996.

Gritz, Jennie Rothenberg. 'The Deathbed Confession of William Butler Yeats.' *The Atlantic* (28 January 2014).

Grossman, Allen. *Poetic Knowledge in the Early Yeats: A Study of* The Wind Among the Reeds. Charlottesville: University of Virginia Press, 1969.

Gwynn, Stephen. *Irish Literature and Drama*. New York: Thomas Nelson and Sons, 1936.

Hall, James and Martin Steinmann, eds. *The Permanence of Yeats*. New York: Collier Books, 1961 [1950].

Harper, George Mills. '"A Subject of Investigation": The Miracle at Mirebeau,' in *Yeats and the Occult*, ed. George Mills Harper. Toronto: Macmillan, 1975.

___ *The Making of Yeats's 'A Vision': A Study of the Automatic Script*. 2 vols. Basingstoke: Macmillan, 1987.

___ *Yeats's Golden Dawn: The Influence of the Hermetic Order of the Golden Dawn on the Life and Art of W. B. Yeats*. London: Macmillan, 1974.

Harper, Margaret Mills. *Wisdom of Two: The Spiritual and Literary Collaboration of George and W. B. Yeats*. Oxford: Oxford University Press, 2007.

___ and Robert Anthony Martinich. *Yeats's Vision Papers*. Vol 3. London: Macmillan, 1992.

___ 'Yeats and the Occult,' in Howes and Kelly, 144–66.

Hassett, Joseph M. *W. B. Yeats and the Muses*. Oxford: Oxford University Press, 2010.

___ *Yeats Now: Echoing Into Life*. Dublin: The Lilliput Press, 2020.

Heaney, Seamus. 'Joy or Night: Last Things in the Poetry of W. B. Yeats and Philip Larkin,' in Heaney's *The Redress of Poetry*. New York: Farrar, Straus and Giroux, 1995.

___ 'A New and Surprising Yeats' [review of Richard Finneran's edition of *The Collected Poems of W. B. Yeats*] *New York Times Book Review*, 18 March 1984.

___ 'William Butler Yeats,' in *The Field Day Anthology of Irish Writing*, vol. II gen. ed. Seamus Deane. Derry: Field Day Publications, 1991.

___ Remark on 'Cuchulain Comforted,' *The Irish Times*, 28 January 1989.

Heine, Elizabeth. 'Yeats and Maud Gonne: Marriage and the Astrological Record, 1908–09', *Yeats Annual* 13. London: Palgrave Macmillan, https://doi.org/10.1007/978-1-349-14614-7_1.

Himber, Alan, ed. *The Letters of John Quinn to William Butler Yeats*. Ann Arbor: University of Michigan Press, 1983, 2–33.

Hough, Graham. *The Mystery Religion of W. B. Yeats*. Brighton: Harvester Press; New Jersey: Barnes & Noble, 1984.

Howe, Ellic. *The Magicians of the Golden Dawn*. London: Routledge & Kegan Paul, 1972.

Howes, Marjorie and John Kelly, eds. *The Cambridge Companion to W. B. Yeats*. Cambridge: Cambridge University Press, 2007.

Jeffares A. Norman. *A New Commentary on the Poems of W. B. Yeats*. London: Macmillan; Stanford: Stanford University Press, 1984.

___ *W B. Yeats: Man and Poet*. London: Kyle Cathie, 1996 [1949].

___ *Yeats's Poems*, ed. and annotated by Jeffares, with appendix by Warwick Gould. London: Macmillan, 1989.

___ *W. B. Yeats: A New Biography*. London: Arena, 1990 [1949]

Jenkins, Lee M. 'Atlantic Triangle: Stevens, Yeats and Eliot in Time of War' in *The Wallace Stevens Journal*, 42 (2018), 17–30.

Joyce, James, *Ulysses*, the 'corrected text,' ed. Hans Walter Gabler, with Wolfhard Steppe and Claus Melchior. New York: Random House, 1986.

Kenny, Colum. 'Friend or Foe: How W. B. Yeats Damaged the Legacy of Arthur Griffith.' *Irish Times*, 26 January 2021.

Keane, Patrick J. 'Blake, Nietzsche, Wilde, and Yeats: Anti-Selves and the Truth of Masks,' *Numéro Cinq* 7 (February 2016), 1–23.

___ 'The Human Entrails and the Starry Heavens,' *Bulletin of Research in the Humanities* 84 (1981), 366–91.

___ *Terrible Beauty: Yeats, Joyce, Ireland and the Myth of the Devouring Female*. Columbia and London: University of Missouri Press, 1988.

___ *A Wild Civility: Interactions in the Poetry and Thought of Robert Graves*. Columbia and London: University of Missouri Press, 1980.

___ *Yeats's Interactions with Tradition*. Columbia and London: University of Missouri Press, 1987.

Keats, John. 'Ode to a Nightingale,' 'Ode on a Grecian Urn.' *The Poems of John Keats*, ed. Jack Stillinger. Cambridge: The Belknap Press of Harvard University Press, 1978.

Letters of John Keats, 2 vols., ed. Hyder Rollins. Cambridge: The Belknap Press of Harvard University Press, 1958).

Kiberd, Declan. 'W. B. Yeats: Building Amid Ruins,' in Declan Kiberd *Irish Classics*. Cambridge: Harvard University Press, 2001.

Lawrence, D. H. *Studies in Classic American Literature*. Cambridge: Cambridge University Press, 2003 [1923].

Lee, Hermione, *Edith Wharton*. New York: Knopf Doubleday, 2007.

Lewis, C. S. 'Dryden, Shelley, and Mr. Eliot,' in Lewis's *Rehabilitation and Other Essays*. Oxford: Oxford University Press, 1939.

Londraville, Janis and Richard, eds. *Too Long a Sacrifice: The Letters of Maud Gonne and John Quinn*. Selingrove: Susquehanna University Press, 1999.

Longenbach, James. *Stone Cottage: Pound, Yeats, and Modernism*. Oxford: Oxford University Press, 1988.

MacLeish, Archibald. 'Public Speech and Private Speech in Poetry.' *Yale Review* (Spring, 1938).

Mann, Neil. 'W. B. Yeats, Dream, Vision, and the Dead,' in Gibson and Mann.

Mannin, Ethel. *Privileged Spectator*. London: Jarrolds, 1939.

Macrobius, *Commentary on [Cicero's] the Dream of Scipio*, trans. W. H. Stahl. New York: Columbia University Press, 1952.

Mikhail, E. H. ed. *W. B. Yeats: Interviews and Recollections*, 2 vols. London: Macmillan, 1977.

Milton, John. 'On the Morning of Christ's Nativity,' in *The Portable Milton*, ed. Douglas Bush. New York: Viking Press, 1949.

___ *Paradise Lost*, ed. Gordon Teskey. New York: Norton, 2005.

Muldoon, Paul. *Meeting the British*. London: Faber, 1987.

Murphy, William. *Prodigal Father: The Life of John Butler Yeats, 1839–1922*. Ithaca: Cornell University Press, 1978.

Nabokov, Vladimir. *Lolita* (1955), cited from *The Annotated Lolita*, ed. Alfred Appel Jr., revised edition, New York: Vintage, 1991.

Nietzsche, Friedrich. *Beyond Good and Evil*, trans. Walter Kaufmann. New York: Vintage, 1966.

___ *Daybreak*, trans. R. J. Hollingdale. Cambridge: Cambridge University Press, 1982.

___ *The Gay Science*, trans. Walter Kaufmann. New York: Vintage, 1974.

___ *On the Genealogy of Morals*, trans. Adrian Del Caro. Stanford: Stanford University Press, 2014.

___ *The Portable Nietzsche*, ed. and trans. Walter Kaufmann. New York: Penguin, 1976.

___ *Nietzsche as Critic, Philosopher, Poet and Prophet: Choice Selections from his Works*, ed. Thomas Common. London: Grant Richards, 1901. Yeats's annotated copy is housed in the Special Collections Department of the library at Northwestern University (item T.R. 193 N67n).

O'Driscoll, Dennis. *Stepping Stones: Interviews with Seamus Heaney*. New York: Farrar, Straus and Giroux, 2008.

O'Shea, Edward. *A Descriptive Catalog of W. B. Yeats's Library*. New York and London: Garland, 1985.

Pagels, Elaine. *Beyond Belief: The Gospel of Thomas*. New York: Random House, 2003.

Petrarca, Francesco. *The Poetry of Petrarch,* trans. David Young. New York: Farrar, Straus and Giroux, 2004.

___ *Petrarch, a Humanist Among Princes: An Anthology of Petrarch's Letters and of Selections from His Other Works,* ed. David Thompson. New York: Harper & Row, 1971.

Plato. *Ion* and *The Symposium,* in *The Dialogues of Plato,* 2 vols. trans. Benjamin Jowett. New York: Random House, 1937 [1892].

Plotinus, *Plotinus: The Enneads,* 6 vols. trans. Stephen MacKenna. London: P. L. Warner for the Medici Society, 1917–1930.

Pope, Alexander. 'Epitaph. Intended for Sir Isaac Newton, in Westminster Abbey,' *The Rape of the Lock. The Poems of Alexander Pope,* ed. John Butt. New Haven: Yale University Press, 1966 [1963].

Pound, Ezra. *The Cantos of Ezra Pound.* New York: New Directions, 1969.

___ 'The Later Yeats' *Poetry* 9 (December 1917).

Rosenthal, M. L. *Running to Paradise: Yeats's Poetic Art.* New York and Oxford: Oxford University Press, 1994.

Saddlemyer, Ann. *Becoming George: The Life of Mrs. W. B. Yeats.* Oxford: Oxford University Press, 2002.

Sappho. Fragment 105A, Fragment 130, in *Sweetbitter Love: Poems of Sappho,* trans. Willis Barnstone. Boston: Shambhala, 2006.

Shakespeare, *King Lear, The Merchant of Venice, A Midsummer Night's Dream. William Shakespeare: The Complete Works,* ed. Alfred Harbage. Baltimore: Penguin Books, 1969.

Shelley, Percy Bysshe. *Alastor* and *The Triumph of Life,* in *Shelley's Poetry and Prose,* ed. Donald H. Reiman and Neil Fraistat, 2nd ed. New York and London: Norton, 2002.

Sidney, Sir Philip. *Astrophil and Stella,* ed. Maz Putzel. Garden City: Doubleday Anchor, 1967.

Sinnett, A. P. *Esoteric Buddhism—1885 Annotated Edition.* Rookhope: Aziloth Books, 2012 [1883].

___ *The Occult World.* London: Trübner and Co., 1889 [1881].

Skelley, Steven J. Yeats, Bloom, and the Dialectics of Theory, Criticism and Poetry. Unpublished 1992 dissertation.

Stans, Adele M. 'Insurrectionist in Chief: How Steve Bannon Led the Vanguard of the Capitol Riots.' *The New Republic* (April 2021), 36–43.

Stevens, Wallace. 'Contraries (I),' 'Madame La Fleurie,' and 'Notes Toward a Supreme Fiction.' *Wallace Stevens: Collected Poems.* London: Faber and Faber, 2006 [1954].

Strauss, William and Neil Howe. *The Fourth Turning: What the Cycles of History Tell Us About America's Next Rendezvous with History*. New York: Crown, 2009 [1996].

Symonds, J. M. 'Lucretius,' in *The Cambridge Companion to Lucretius*, ed. Philip Hardie and Stuart Gillespie. Cambridge: Cambridge University Press, 2007.

Szymborska, Wislawa. 'The Poet and the World,' trans. Stanislaw Baranczak and Clare Cavanagh. https//nobelprize.org/prizes/literature/1996/szymborska/lecture.

Tennyson, Alfred, Lord. 'Locksley Hall,' 'Ulysses.' *Poems of Tennyson*, ed. Jerome H. Buckley, Boston: Houghton Mifflin, Riverside Edition, 1958.

Tindall, William. *W. B. Yeats*. New York: Columbia University Press, 1960.

Toomey, Deirdre. 'The Cold Heaven,' *Yeats Annual* 18. Cambridge: Open Book Publishers, 2013, https://doi.org/ 10.11647/OBP.0028.

___ 'Labyrinths: Yeats and Maud Gonne,' *Yeats Annual* 9, reprinted in *Yeats and Women*, ed. Deirdre Toomey. London: Palgrave Macmillan, 1997.

Valentinus, 'The Twelve Keys,' in A. E. Waite, ed. *The Hermetic Museum*, trans. from the 1678 Latin text. 2 vols. Newburyport, MA: Weiser Books, 1999 [1893]. I, 315–57.

___ 'The Gospel of Truth,' in *The Gnostic Bible*, trans. Willis Barnstone. New York: Gnostic Society, 2003.

Vendler, Helen. *Our Secret Discipline: Yeats and Lyric Form*. Cambridge: Harvard University Press, 2007.

___ 'Loosed Quotes' [on "The Second Coming"], *Liberties* 1 (Fall, 2020), 126–39.

___ *Yeats's Vision and the Later Plays*. Cambridge: Harvard University Press, 1963.

Vinci, Leonardo da. *The Notebooks of Leonardo da Vinci*, trans. Edward MacCurdy, vol. 1. London: Cape, 1938.

von Hügel, Baron Friedrich. *The Mystical Element of Religion* London: J. M. Dent, 1961 [1908].

Ward, Margaret. *Maud Gonne: A Biography*. London: Pandora, 1993 [1990].

Washington, Peter. *Madame Blavatsky's Baboon. New York:* Schocken, 1996 [1993].

Whitehead, Alfred North. *Science and the Modern World*. New York: Free Press, 1953 [1925].

Wilde, Oscar. 'The Truth of Masks' (1885), in *The Artist as Critic: Critical Writings of Oscar Wilde*, ed. Richard Ellmann. Chicago: University of Chicago Press, 1968.

Wieseltier, Leon. 'Some Grounds for Hope,' *Liberties* 2 (Winter 2021), 360–80.

Wilson, F. A. C. 'Yeats's "A Bronze Head": A Psychological Investigation,' *Literature and Psychology* 22 (1972), 5–12.

___ *Yeats's Iconography.* London: Victor Gollancz, 1970.

Winters, Yvor. *The Poetry of W. B. Yeats.* Denver: Allen Swallow, 1960.

Woolf, Virginia. *The Diary of Virginia Woolf.* vol.3, ed. Anne Olivier Bell. New York: Mariner Books, 1981.

___ *Mrs. Dalloway.* Toronto: University of Toronto Press, 2013.

Wordsworth, William. 'Hart-Leap Well,' 'Ode: Intimations of Immortality,' 'The Tables Turned,' and 'Tintern Abbey.' *William Wordsworth: The Poems.* 2 vols, ed. John O. Hayden. Vol. 1. London: Penguin, 1977.

Wyndham, Diana. 'Versemaking and Lovemaking—W. B. Yeats's "Strange Second Puberty": Norman Haire and the Steinach Rejuvenation Operation.' *Journal of Historical and Behavioral Science* 39 (2003), 25–50.

Yeats, W. B.[1] 'Friends of My Youth.' undelivered 1910 lecture, ed. Joseph Ronsley, in *Yeats and the Theatre*, ed. Robert O'Driscoll and Lorna Reynolds. Toronto: Macmillan, 1975.

___ *Is the Order of R. R & A. C. to remain a Magical Order?* Privately printed pamphlet, reprinted as an Appendix to George Mills Harper's *Yeats's Golden Dawn.*

___ 'Preface' to *The Works of William Blake: Poetic, Symbolic, and Critical.* 3 vols., ed. W. B. Yeats and Edwin J. Ellis. London: Bernard Quaritch, 1893.

___ *Uncollected Prose by W. B. Yeats.* 2 vols. ed. John P. Frayne. Vol. 1. New York: Columbia University Press, 1975.

___ 'Introduction' to *The Oxford Book of Modern Verse.* ed. W. B. Yeats. Oxford: Oxford University Press, 1936.

___ Cornell University Press Manuscript Materials, 1992–present. Under the editorship of over a dozen Yeats scholars, this series presents the manuscript materials for virtually all of Yeats's individual volumes of poetry.

Young, David. *Troubled Mirror: A Study of Yeats's* The Tower. Iowa City: University of Iowa Press, 1987.

---

1   The primary Yeats prose texts used are cited on the Abbreviations page.

Index

Poems: page numbers refer to the
Variorum Edition of the poems (VP)

Index of Names and Terms

About the Cover

The cover illustration reproduces William Blake's water-colored ink drawing, 'The Reunion of the Soul & the Body,' part of a set, published as engravings (not by Blake but by Luigi Schiavonetti) illustrating Robert Blair's book-length poem, *The Grave* (1808). Departing from Blair's conventional ideas, Blake's series (long lost, but rediscovered in 2001), traces a progression from the initial descent into the Vale of Death to the admission into life eternal. But Blake not only emphasizes immortality over physical death; he depicts in this particular illustration the (male) body and (female) soul rushing passionately into 'each other's arms on the last day.' The flames suggest that Blake's reunion of soul and body incorporates Swedenborg's vision of lovers, frustrated on earth, meeting in eternity in incandescent angelic intercourse.

   This particular image and the Swedenborgian vision meant a great deal to Yeats. He used the engraved version of Blake's illustration as the cover design for all three volumes of his (and Edwin Ellis's) 1893 edition of Blake. Maud Gonne cited the *Grave* illustrations in a 1908 letter describing an astral projection in which she saw herself and Yeats spiritually entwined between heaven and earth. On the basis of his star-crossed love of Maud Gonne, Yeats came to believe, with Lucretius, that 'the tragedy of sexual intercourse is the perpetual virginity of the soul.' Two decades after Maud told him of her astral projection, Yeats echoed and altered her purely spiritual concept in 'A Last Confession,' the ninth poem in his sequence *A Woman Young and Old*. In the two final stanzas the woman presents us with a characteristically Yeatsian vision of eroticized spirituality:

> I gave what other women gave
> That stepped out of their clothes,
> But when this soul, its body off,
> Naked to naked goes,
> He it has found shall find therein
> What none other knows,

And give his own and take his own
And rule in his own right;
And though it loved in misery
Close and cling so tight,
There's not a bird of day that dare
Extinguish that delight.

Unsurprisingly, Yeats never forgot Blake's 'Reunion of the Soul & the Body.' Four months before he died—in a letter written to one of his Muses, Ethel Mannin, but with Maud Gonne as ever hovering in the background—Yeats described Blake's illustration of 'the soul and body embracing' as his own 'idea of death.'

About the Author

Patrick J. Keane, former Francis Fallon Chair, is Professor Emeritus of Le Moyne College, where a medal in his name is annually awarded to graduating seniors in the Arts and Sciences who have 'achieved excellence in the field of literary studies and who have demonstrated great scholarly promise.' Though he has written on a wide range of topics, his areas of special interest are 19th and 20th-century poetry in the Romantic tradition; Irish literature and history; the interactions of literature with philosophic, religious, and political thought; the impact of Nietzsche on 20th century literature; and transatlantic studies, exploring the influence of German Idealist philosophy and British Romanticism on American writers.

He has written several dozen articles (the most recent of which have appeared in *Salmagundi*, *The Mark Twain Annual*, and the *Yeats Annual*) and seven books: *William Butler Yeats: Contemporary Studies in Literature* (1973), *A Wild Civility: Interactions in the Poetry and Thought of Robert Graves* (1980), *Yeats's Interactions with Tradition* (1987), *Terrible Beauty: Yeats, Joyce, Ireland and the Myth of the Devouring Female* (1988), *Coleridge's Submerged Politics* (1994), *Emerson, Romanticism, and Intuitive Reason: The Transatlantic 'Light of All Our Day'* (2005), and *Emily Dickinson's Approving God: Divine Design and the Problem of Suffering* (2008). He lives in De Witt, in upstate New York.

About the Team

Alessandra Tosi was the managing editor for this book.

Alison Gray performed the proofreading.

Melissa Purkiss performed the typesetting and indexing.

Anna Gatti designed the cover. The cover was produced in InDesign using the Fontin font.

Luca Baffa produced the paperback and hardback editions. The text font is Tex Gyre Pagella; the heading font is Californian FB. Luca produced the EPUB, MOBI, PDF, HTML, and XML editions — the conversion is performed with open source software freely available on our GitHub page (https://github.com/OpenBookPublishers).

This book need not end here...

Share

All our books — including the one you have just read — are free to access online so that students, researchers and members of the public who can't afford a printed edition will have access to the same ideas. This title will be accessed online by hundreds of readers each month across the globe: why not share the link so that someone you know is one of them?

This book and additional content is available at:

https://doi.org/10.11647/OBP.0275

Customise

Personalise your copy of this book or design new books using OBP and third-party material. Take chapters or whole books from our published list and make a special edition, a new anthology or an illuminating coursepack. Each customised edition will be produced as a paperback and a downloadable PDF.

Find out more at:

https://www.openbookpublishers.com/section/59/1

You may also be interested in:

Romanticism and Time
Literary Temporalities
Sophie Laniel-Musitelli and Céline Sabiron (eds)

https://doi.org/10.11647/OBP.0232

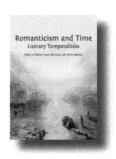

Tennyson's Poems
New Textual Parallels
R. H. Winnick

https://doi.org/10.11647/OBP.0161

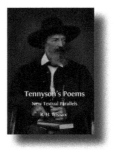

Yeats's Legacies
Yeats Annual No. 21
Warwick Gould (ed.)

https://doi.org/10.11647/OBP.0135

CPSIA information can be obtained
at www.ICGtesting.com
Printed in the USA
BVHW022237030122
625366BV00017B/988